A Nation in Medieval Ireland? Perspectives on Gaelic National Identity in the Middle Ages

Thomas Finan

BAR British Series 367
2004

Published in 2016 by
BAR Publishing, Oxford

BAR British Series 367

A Nation in Medieval Ireland? Perspectives on Gaelic National Identity in the Middle Ages

ISBN 978 1 84171 600 8

BAR Publishing is the trading name of British Archaeological Reports (Oxford) Ltd.
British Archaeological Reports was first incorporated in 1974 to publish the BAR
Series, International and British. In 1992 Hadrian Books Ltd became part of the BAR
group. This volume was originally published by Archaeopress in conjunction with
British Archaeological Reports (Oxford) Ltd / Hadrian Books Ltd, the Series principal
publisher, in 2004. This present volume is published by BAR Publishing, 2016.

Printed in England

BAR
PUBLISHING

BAR titles are available from:

BAR Publishing
122 Banbury Rd, Oxford, OX2 7BP, UK
EMAIL   info@barpublishing.com
PHONE   +44 (0)1865 310431
FAX   +44 (0)1865 316916
www.barpublishing.com

Preface

This book began as a doctoral dissertation defended in the Department of History at the Catholic University of America in 2001. Over the course of the next three years the dissertation evolved into this final production. I am grateful to David Davison, for his help in the final production of the monograph.

I would also like to thank all the librarians and libraries of the various universities and learned societies to which I have gained access: the libraries of The Catholic University of America, The University of Chicago, Webster University, Maynooth College, and Trinity College, Dublin; the libraries and archives of *Duchas* (formerly the Office of Public Works, Republic of Ireland, although by the time this reaches press that name will be changed yet again), The Royal Irish Academy, and The Discovery Program, Dublin; and especially the library of the Dublin Institute for Advanced Studies. Scholars can not give enough credit to librarians for their assistance. I will be eternally grateful to the Director of the Dublin Institute for Advanced Studies, Prof. Fergus Kelly, for office space, research facilities and camaraderie during the year 1999-2000. I was funded that year by a fellowship from the Rotary Foundation, and was sponsored by the Rotary Club of St. Louis, MO, and the Rotary Club of Bray, Co. Wicklow, Ireland.

Members of the Department of Medieval History at Trinity College, Dublin, were very welcoming to me both before I had formally met any of them and while I was resident in the College in 1999-2000. Profs. Terry Barry and Sean Duffy offered sound advice on a regular basis that year and in the time since. In particular, Prof. Katharine Simms worked as my formal advisor and mentor. She could not have been any more helpful, and certainly went beyond the title of "advisor," sharing ideas and thoughts throughout the year that were both challenging and enlightening. Dr. Helen Perros read drafts of the text at the dissertation stage and saved me from making glaring errors in the final production of the manuscript. And, finally, Prof. L.R. Poos, my advisor for over seven years, guided me through the maze of completing a doctoral dissertation, and ultimately in the final production of this monograph. He believed in this project and in my work from the outset of my start in the Department of History at the Catholic University of America in 1993, and I will always owe him a debt of gratitude. I don't think anyone could match the effort that he gave in the final push to complete this dissertation. Prof. Kieran O Conor of University College-Galway advised me as a friend and colleague during my year at Trinity College, and his insightful opinions and comments throughout the year allowed me to see the light at the end of the tunnel. I also wish to thank R. Mark Scowcroft, Niall Brady, Damian McManus, Aidan O'Sullivan, and Colman Etchingham for guidance, advice, and conversation over the years. I also wish to thank J. Kurt von Finck for his continued technical assistance over the years. My brother, Anthony Finan, read the final proofs of the text, and helped to clarify several points.

All of these people contributed positively to the production of this book over the years in one way or another; of course, any errors (obvious or otherwise) are mine alone.

Finally, I must thank my wife, Marti. She read read and helped me rewrite the entire manuscript, patiently traveled with me to conferences and to castles, and, more importantly, left her job, family, and Fish in 1999-2000 so that I could work on the dissertation full time while resident at Trinity College. I could not be more fortunate to have found her, nor could I have been more fortunate to find her when I did. When all is said and done, she was the one.

Thomas Finan, PhD.

St. Louis University

Table of Contents

List of Figures and Tables

Chapter One:
Nationalism and Medieval Irish History

This study investigates the nation and nationalism, national ideology, and national identity in Ireland during the thirteenth and fourteenth centuries. The study aims to explore whether such terms as "nation" or "nationalism" may be applied to medieval Ireland. While many historians and sociologists argue that the nation may exist only in the modern world with the advent of the nation-state, others have shown that, at least, ethnic groups which appear to be nations existed in medieval Europe, possibly in antiquity. In Ireland, historiographical issues related to the creation of the modern Irish state in the early twentieth century have always guided the study of the nation and nationalism.

The central questions addressed include whether there are observable manifestations of a nation, national identity, and ethnically-based ideology in Gaelic Ireland in the years 1200-1400, and the extent to which those manifestations may accurately be described in national terms. In this study, the nation shall be defined as a population sharing an ethnic history, tradition, language, and/or religion, and this population's connection with a particular, definable geographic region. In addition, this identity will be shown as often conflicting with the self-ascribed identity of another population sharing the same or neighboring geographic space. Hence, examples of a nation found in medieval Ireland will embody the double characteristics of being a means of self-identity for the Irish and of self-distinction from the Anglo-Normans.

The Modern Debate over Nationalism

The nation as subject matter has been a focus of historical and sociological inquiry since the early twentieth century, no doubt resulting from the rise during the late nineteenth and early twentieth century of "new" nations in western Europe (Germany, Italy, Ireland) and the construction of nations in third world regions by European colonial powers (such as the Belgian Congo and Iraq). The two are connected: for the greater part of the nineteenth century European countries and the United States were seen as the norms in terms of what a country *should* be (that is, an industrialized country with a centralized government). As a result, those first world regions regarded the ideal of country-as-nation as the logical goal for their colonies.

In one sense the two World Wars of the twentieth century prevented the nation from occupying the forefront of academic study because those events forced nationalism to be equated with extreme manifestations of nationalism, such as the ultra-right political movements of national socialism and fascism and the ultra-left movements of totalitarian communism. Billig maintains that this view of nationalism as a form of extremist politics allowed governments to define their respective state's ideology as simple patriotism (with its positive connotations of heroism, self-lessness, and the homeland as a gendered parent, ie., the Fatherland or Motherland), while the ideology of "other" countries could be presented as nationalistic (with its negative implications of irrationality, foreignness, emotionalism, and danger).[1]

By the mid twentieth century, though, sociologists and historians, particularly at the London School of Economics, began to investigate the complexities of the nation's origins, historicity, and function and to question the traditional, simplistic categorization of nations as either the "proper" form of government for civilized groups of humans or the "improper" form of government and group ideology espoused by misguided humans.

Özkirimli was one of the first theoreticians of the nation to adequately summarize the contemporary theories of the nation.[2] Put succinctly, he sees the field divided between two distinct groups; the primordialists and the mordernists. A third category, the ethno-symbolists, evolved during the last decade as a mediation between the primordialist and modernist positions.

The primordialist view states that nations have existed since time immemorial, and that the nation is a social grouping as natural as the social groupings of family and kin relations. Because the eighteenth, nineteenth, and early twentieth century Western minds assumed that the divisions between nations and countries were coterminous with ethnic and cultural boundaries, this idea of social grouping, or nation, was widely adopted as the basis for government and political and ethnic identity. The argument, in most cases, was a circular argument presented by the countries making claims to nationhood: the nation exists because a people with a supposed common historical and cultural origin inhabit a particular geographical space that had been occupied by the people's ancestors. For the modernist, as we shall see, these illusional sentiments are the precise problem in early twentieth century history, in that the self-justified attrocities of fascist Germany, Soviet

Russia, and Imperial Japan stem from this exclusionary ideology.

The modernist view of nations explains them as inherently a function of modernity, in which certain political and economic factors, such as capitalism, industrialism, urbanization, and secularism, contributed to the rise of nations and the assumption that, in the modern world, the nation-state is the base form of government. From the modernist perspective the primordialist view is deluded by the notion that a connection exists between past ethnic groups and present political situations. A group may claim nationhood since time immemorial, when in fact it is simply a form of using historical justification for a contemporary (and possible groundless) political claim. Aside from the basic assumption that the nation is a modern phenomena, however, those that hold the modernist position rarely share core ideas concerning the formation and growth of nations. Tom Nairn has proposed a neo-Marxist theory stating that the uneven development of economies in the world since the eighteenth century fostered resentment on the part of subject peoples. According to Nairn, though, their drive to form nations should be understood as misplaced class conflict.

The recent work concerning the nation by Anthony Smith mediates between these two extremes.[3] Smith and other ethno-symbolists argue that the primordialist view of the nation is incorrect in its assumption that the nation of the past is inherently connected to the nation of the present; on the other hand, they also argue that the modernist view is incorrect in its insistence that the nation is a totally new phenomena, since past ethnic groupings that can approximate a nation served as the base for future developments of nations. The past and the present are not the same; but certainly conditions in past societies contributed to the structures found in the present societies.

The ethno-symbolist also recognizes the value of analyzing myths, symbols, and other cultural artifacts in an attempt to describe what people of the past and present perceive to be true distinctions between vairous social groupings. These assumptions, while in some cases irrational and impossible to substantiate using any sort of quantitative or scientific method, continue to influence the ways in which people act in relation to "the other". We have no reason to suppose that people in the past acted any differently.

Nationalism and Medieval Irish Historiography

The main problem with the study of nationalism in *any* period of Irish history is the link between the modern practice of history in Ireland and the aspiration for the establishment of the Irish state.[4] The particular *kind* of Irish state that was established in the early twentieth century was defined as "not English" but instead "purely Irish."[5] The possibility of maintaining a union with Great Britain was extinguished with the Easter Rising of 1916, which was led by Sinn Fein, a political part that had emerged from the Gaelic revival of the nineteenth century. The national ideology espoused by the leaders of both the Gaelic revival[6] and Sinn Fein was centered on the supposed purity and superiority of a Celtic Irish society in opposition to the foreign and corrupt English culture.[7]

The study of medieval Ireland as a modern historical subject began with the publication of two works by Goddard Orpen and Eoin MacNeill in the early part of the twentieth century.[8] Orpen, a staunch unionist, and MacNeill, an equally staunch nationalist, could not have differed more in their approaches to analyzing medieval Ireland. Orpen chose to accentuate the beneficial aspects of Anglo-Norman settlement upon what he considered a chaotic and anarchic Irish civilization. For Orpen, the arrival of English common law and Anglo-Norman government civilized Ireland. MacNeill, however, envisioned a medieval Ireland in which the native Irish, noble and oppressed, continually struggled as a people to overcome the foreign domination of an imperialist Angevin kingdom. The Republican revolutionaries of the Easter Rising in 1916, seen especially in the writings of Patrick Pearce[9] and James Connolly, shared MacNeill's view of the Irish shared past.[10] It is still invoked today by modern Irish Republicans and nationalists, despite wide disagreement between the strands of Republicanism in the Republic of Ireland and those in Northern Ireland.[11]

A recent article by Stephen Harrison summarizes and clarifies the dialogue between Orpen and MacNeill.[12] Several points regarding Orpen and MacNeill's approaches to the past and their approaches to historical method are worthy of repetition. Clearly, Orpen and MacNeill approached the past from different perspectives, perspectives that were, as Harrison suggests, at least partially related to their contemporary political views. Harrison's article centers around the different interpretations of the Battle of Down in 1260, at which several Irish kings united under the leadership of Brian Ó Néill in a failed attempt to raise Ó Néill as the High King of Ireland and to counter Anglo-Norman control over Ireland. For MacNeill, the Battle of Down was a "lost opportunity following a selfless and patriotic act on the part of [the Gaelic] aristocracy."[13] While he viewed the Battle of Down as a real and credible threat to Anglo-Norman rule in Ireland, Orpen was far more skeptical of MacNeill's interpretation of the extent to which Ó Néill's power base existed in Ulster and beyond.[14] Orpen pointed out that the supporters of Ó Néill were often the younger sons of other kings in Ireland (such as Áed Ó Conchobhair and Tadhg Ó Briain), and that Ó Néill never garnered the widespread support of other kings in Ireland, despite the claims in the Irish annals.

Harrison's most cogent point in this debate is that MacNeill, in his approach to prove a continuity for an Irish historical tradition, identified a nation with an accompanying state system, while Orpen defined a state that was in need of a nation.[15] Both MacNeill and Orpen believed that to describe a nation was to describe a state, and to describe a state was to describe a nation. MacNeill defined the cultural manifestations of a nation then sought to define a political state from those cultural manifestations; in short, he could not find a coherent political entity within the Gaelic culture he observed. Orpen, though, could define an Anglo-Norman state in Ireland based upon the extension of an independent Anglo-Norman government brought to Ireland from England, but the distinct cultural trappings of that political nation were lacking. The colony in Ireland, for Orpen, was essentially a duplicate of government in England, but without the cultural trappings of English society. While they approached the past from different perspectives, MacNeill and Orpen were both products of the early twentieth century view of history as progression toward the modern world. The two also shaped the way in which history would be discussed for the rest of the century.[16] From the outset, then, medieval Irish history separates itself into two groups which are mirrored by modern nationalist and unionist political parties, and divided along the same lines. The preconceived notions of what *should* be found in the historical record clouded the judgements of scholars like Orpen and MacNeill. For Orpen, medieval Ireland was clearly divided between chaotic Irish and civilized Anglo-Norman, and the evidence he used supported this view.[17] MacNeill, though, used different evidence to show the Anglo-Normans as treacherous and impossible to deal with, while at the same time depicting the Irish as a noble savage fighting oppressive outsiders.[18]

In the last few decades the greater amount of work on the issue of medieval nationalism has focused on the later middle ages and early modern period(1400-1600) and explored whether Gaelic poetry accurately represents a Gaelic mentality during the sixteenth and seventeenth centuries. The debate is primarily found in journal articles; no monograph length study of the topic of nationalism in medieval Ireland exists.[19]

In his 1978 article, Brendan Bradshaw attempted to prove that that a collection of poetry in a *duanaire* (or poem book) for the Ó Broin reflected a new political consciousness, a consciousness derived from Gaelic history and culture and based upon, as he suggests, an "ideology of rebellion" against the oppressor.[20] Bradshaw also concluded that the body of poetry reflected a concerted national response to colonialism in the late sixteenth and early seventeenth century. Bradshaw suggested that the Gaelic poets of the Ó Broin created an identity for themselves using the remnants of their past found in earlier bardic poems and historical tracts.

Dunne challenged Bradshaw's argument by analyzing the same collection of poetry, and concluding that no sense of

Gaelic nationalism was found in the poetry.[21] He stated that the Gaelic response to external threat in the sixteenth century was more local than national, more pragmatic than idealistic, and more escapist than political. Dunne further stated that the final evidence proving a national identity did not exist is that no central state ever formed in Gaelic Ireland.[22] There was no political unity on the part of Gaelic lords, hence there is no possibility of declaring the existence of a nation. Dunne's definition of nationalism stems from a more traditional view which directly relates it to the "nation-state," such that it is impossible to conceive of a nation before the eighteenth century. Dunne's antiquated view simply re-iterates the early twentieth century view of the nation-state described by Orpen and MacNeill.

In 1986, Steven Ellis entered the debate with an article in *Irish Historical Studies* in which he argued that the problem with Irish history, and particularly Irish medieval history, is the whiggish perspective from which it was written, such that the medieval history composed in post-1922 Ireland attempted to create a history for the new state.[23] The new Free State as a political entity needed a history which would give it legitimacy. Ellis believed that this self-fulfilling prophecy, so to speak, created a nation of Ireland in the past, although the island was essentially a border region within a wider British realm. This border region was not an entity unto itself, but was part of a wider Gaelic region that included Scotland and the Isles. Any concepts of national identity that Bradshaw saw, for Ellis, were merely either propagandistic references to an Ireland that never was or a creation of political parties during the nineteenth and twentieth centuries. Furthermore, any references to a process of Gaelicization on the part of the individuals of Anglo-Norman descent living in Ireland in the later middle ages is a modern attempt to create a process of development leading to the contemporary Irish state.[24]

Bradshaw countered with an article published in 1989 in which he shifted the focus of the debate to the question of revisionism in Irish history.[25] The revisionist seeks to de-mythologize the past as a response to modern nationalist ideological history, and in the process rejects the possibility of any sort of nationalist ideology occurring in the past. While some Irish historians responded to the tradition of nationalist history by turning to revisionism, others, such as A.J. Otway-Ruthven, moved to what has been termed "value-free" history, which centers on the historical record's content in and of itself without further explanation.

Bradshaw posited that the traditions of value-free history and revisionist history in Ireland had become the dominant approach to the past since the 1930's, to the detriment of Irish history. To Bradshaw, value-free history cannot account for the non-physical aspects or intellectual process of history, nor can it adequately deal with the catastrophic dimensions of Irish history, a theme that Bradshaw describes as a very underexplored aspect of Irish history in general.[26] Bradshaw concluded by stating that Irish history in in all periods needs to incorporate empathy and imaginative methods to its study of material in order to free itself from, as he puts it, the dry and boring histories of the mid twentieth century.[27] For Bradshaw, the dry and boring histories of the mid-twentieth century (ie., that of Otway-Ruthven) were a result of the scholar's inability to move beyond the more superficial textual analyses of historical source material. On the other hand, it should be noted that many of those histories were written using sources only recently edited; those histories were merely first attempts at creating syntheses, and perhaps the real problem lies with historical accounts of medieval Ireland written later in the twentieth century.

Ellis leveled one more shot at Bradshaw in *Irish Historical Studies* in 1991. He stated that the real issue behind the question of revisionism, as a valid school of Irish history, is whether it has enhanced or distorted our understanding of the past. Ellis reminds us that the process of writing history lies essentially in relating the past to the present while preserving the past on its own terms, and to place contemporary understandings of the present on the past simply distorts our understanding of the past.[28]

These articles by Bradshaw, Dunne, and Ellis represent the polar understandings of the Irish past that have permeated scholarship since the late nineteenth century, and the inability of the field to synthesise these two views of the past, particularly when the issue at hand is the relevance of the nation. For instance, James Lydon attempted to form just such a synthesis by performing accurate and meticulous studies of medieval sources showing that distinctions such as race and nation that the modern historian might use to describe the people of medieval Ireland were in fact distinctions that the people of medieval Ireland themselves used.[29] Yet, he, like most medieval Irish historians of the mid- to late twentieth century, takes the information provided by documentary evidence at face value without forwarding any deeper conclusions about the mental and intellectual preconditions for those distinctions seen in the evidence.[30] He provides no social analysis or critique or insight into the ideologies that must have existed in medieval Ireland, nor does he enter into any dialogue with other modern Irish medievalists in order to reach a new synthesis concerning the nation in medieval Ireland. Granted, Lydon has investigated the topic far more fruitfully than anyone else in the field, but he, like most other scholars of medieval Ireland, rarely (if ever) considers alternate historic methodological approaches that may provide alternate understandings of source material. Art Cosgrove took a similar approach in an attempt to resolve the polarities between scholars of Irish medieval history mentioned above.[31] But, like Lydon, Cosgrove does not explore the human aspects of his subject; rather, he emphasizes the ambiguous identity

of the descendants of the original Anglo-Norman settlers described as "middle nation," without defining what a nation is.[32] Despite this problem, he contributes to the effort by acknowledging the work accomplished in the area of Gaelic identity, most notably by Katharine Simms and Donnchadh Ó Corráin.[33] The valid issue that he raises is the modern historian's responsibility to acknowledge that historian's present condition and whether that present condition influences that historian's interpretation of the past. Perhaps Irish medievalists need to consider other periods of Irish history in order to look for persistent patterns in the record.[34]

One other interesting note in terms of Irish medieval historiography is the inability within the Irish medieval historic tradition to place itself within any wider historiographical traditions. For instance, upon closer examination, the dualistic stances between nationalist and Unionist historians mirrors the divides between the primordialist and modernist views of the nation—yet no medieval Irish historian has drawn attention to this link. The nationalist Irish historical tradition maintains that Ireland as a national entity has always existed, and that the struggle of that nation to exert its own identity over and against outside forces describes the history of Ireland over the last nine centuries. On the other hand, the Unionist position sees the rise of the Irish nation and state as an inherently modern phenomenon, and any cultural connection to past Irish civilization is merely a created history or mythology.

Perhaps, then, a third, more radical Irish historical position is needed in the same sense that the ethno-symbolist acts as a mediator between the primordialist and modernist views of the nations. What might characterize such a position?

Possibly this: that the nation does not come into existence at a particular point in time, but, rather, develops, disintegrates, regathers, and reconstitutes itself over long periods of time. To understand the nation in Ireland, then, it is necessary to understand the ways in which the idea of the nation in Ireland came into existence and changed over centuries. Ideally, over this long span, certain trends and prominent themes will stand out that allow the observer to declare the particular features of that nation in Ireland that distinguish it from other nations in time and space.

Also, a study of the nation as it has appeared in Irish history must remove the notions regarding the continuity of the primordialist/Irish nationalist and of the modernist/Unionist historian. The problem with both the primordialist position concerning and the Irish nationalist historian is their argument for an overly-strong sense of continuity between the nation of the past and the nation of the present; for the Irish nationalist historian the legitimacy of the twentieth century Irish nation is justified in the primordialism of the Irish nation. At the other extreme, both the modernist and Unionist historian deny any connection between past and present when it involves the possibility of accepting the existence of another nation within similar geographic boundaries.

The debate between the nationalist Irish historiographical tradition, the Unionist position, and even the revisionist Irish historian often focuses on the problem of the relationship between any notion of an Irish nation and the modern Irish state. However, the nation is not a manifestation of the state, but vice versa. The nation forms the basis by which the state can come into existence. The cultural and ethnic givens of the people that make up the nation allow political institutions to claim legitimacy, and while they inform each other, the political institutions are necessarily secondary in terms of temporal development. This point is of particular importance for the study of the nation in the middle ages.

The Medieval Idea of the Nation in Ireland

At the Council of Constance, in the early fifteenth century, English representatives argued their claim to equal national status on the grounds that their culture and land were distinct from others.[35] For those representatives at Constance the national status was related to culture and geographic space. But as Richard Hoffman suggests, when the Anglo-Normans arrived in Ireland, they understood the inhabitants of Ireland as "other" on the basis of a racial or ethnic identity.

The term *natio* in medieval Ireland was used in the older sense of *familia* or *gens*; in fact, chroniclers used the term *natio* in thirteenth century Ireland more often to describe the great families of Anglo-Normans such as the Earls of Louth and Kildare.[36] Even at the end of the fourteenth century the term *natio* was used to describe particular political factions in Ireland, such as the Anglo-Norman factions termed "*diverse nationes Anglice*" who revolted in Munster in the middle of the fourteenth century.[37] Later in the century other rebellious Anglo-Norman lords were termed *nationes*.

To confuse matters more, though, the term *natio* was also used to describe wider ethnic groups with shared identities. This use of *natio* is remarkably similar to the modern usage of the term "nation." In one example, the term *natio* is juxtaposed with the term *gentes*; the meaning of the phrase *gentes Hibernie nationis* clearly reflects a mental distinction between a family and a wider social grouping. In this case, that wider social grouping is *Hibernie nationis*.[38] The term was also used in an attempt to unite the lands of Ireland and Scotland in the fourteenth century. The *natio* of Ireland and Scotland, which shared a common language and custom, should have been restored to liberty, according to King Robert I of Scotland. From this perspective, *natio* could be defined as "common language and custom."[39]

From the Irish perspective the terms *gaill* and *gall* were used to describe "native" and "foreigner" respectively, since the ninth century at the latest. The terms, first used to distinguish native Irish from Scandinavian invaders, reflects geographic and ethnic identities used to divide and strengthen identities. The terms *gaill* and *gall* were reused throughout the middle ages to describe natives and foreigners; when the Anglo-Normans arrived in Ireland in the late twelfth century, they were termed *gall* since they were in fact foreigners. Also, in the Irish annals, the terms *saxoin* or *sagsan* were used to describe foreigners from England in particular. In the fourteenth century Irish edition of *Expugnatio Hibernica,* Gerald of Wales is translated as if he was making a distinction between those foreigners who lived in Ireland and those who came from England, but the distinction is not consistent.[40] The distinction is more clear throughout the fourteenth century, when the inhabitants of Ireland with Anglo-Norman origins termed themselves of *mediae nacionis,* or "middle nation," in recognition perhaps of their awkward status. In the fifteenth century they were often referred to as Irish by those living in England, yet to the native Irish they were still considered *gall*.[41]

There were no distinct or precise terms used in medieval Ireland to describe the various groups who lived side by side, unfortunately limiting our ability to grasp the concept of the nation in medieval Ireland. And the term *natio* was never used in a consistent manner, nor were Irish terms for the Anglo-Normans such as *gall* or *saxoin* consistently applied.

The imprecise vocabulary of the nation in medieval Ireland suggests that the people of medieval Ireland (and England for that matter) saw clear differences in terms of ethnicity, culture, and language, but those differences led to ambiguity more than clarity in definition. The use of the term *natio* as "family" or "nation" is the best example of that ambiguity. Did a family of one of the great earls of Anglo-Norman Ireland or a family of a Gaelic lordship constitute a *natio* as "family" or "nation?" Perhaps this distinction, in medieval Ireland at least, did not hold as well as it might in the modern use of the terms "family" or "nation." Yet, the clear examples of the use of *natio* to represent a form of "nation" close to the modern concept leads us to define an idea that was rarely defined firmly in medieval Ireland.[42]

The Nature of this Study

The individuals who collectively consider themselves a nation share a particular world view based upon a cultural tradition, ethnic identity, and a limited geographical perspective for the community. The individuals recognize either a proper sovereignty over its own group destiny, or recognize that the claims of a perceived foreign sovereignty do not have legitimacy over its group destiny. These qualities are probably the most difficult to define, and are mostly qualitative in nature.

Modern scholars of the nation recognize that defining an all-encompassing theory that incorporates the nation in all of its manifestations in time and space is a practice in futility. One paradigm cannot explain all of the intricacies of the nation in every instance, and certainly one paradigm of an Irish nation cannot come close to defining that nation throughout the history of Ireland.

This study, then, will focus on the manifestations of the medieval nation in Ireland as found in the historical and archaeological record, and will thereby describe what a nation was in medieval Ireland. The minds of the thirteenth and fourteenth century inhabitants of Ireland understood distinctions between groups of people along national lines. This understanding, and the assumptions that are found with it, led to further assumptions about group identities and influenced the actions of people in medieval Ireland. Uncovering the understandings, assumptions, and motivations for the actions that are found in the historical record allows us to create a more accurate and precise picture of medieval Ireland.

[1] M. Billig, *Banal Nationalism,* (London, Sage Press, 1995), 55.

[2] Umut Ozkirimli, *Theories of Nationalism: A Critical Introduction* (New York: MacMillan Palgrave, 2000).

[3] See especially Anthony D. Smith, *National Identity* (London: Penguin Books, 1991).

[4] Steven Ellis, "Nationalist Historiography and the English and Gaelic Worlds in the Late Middle Ages," *Irish Historical Studies* XXV 97 (1986): 1.

[5] D. George Boyce, *Nationalism in Ireland,* 3rd edition (London: Routledge, 1995), 295.

[6] One of the stranger aspects to the Easter Rising in 1916 is that the overwhelming majority of the participants were Catholic, yet the ideology that they followed, that is, of Gaelic Irish nationalism, had been formulated during the Gaelic revival in the previous century by Anglo-Irish Protestants. See Boyce, *Nationalism in Ireland,* 311.

[7] Boyce, *Nationalism in Ireland,* 296.

[8] G.H. Orpen, *Ireland Under the Normans, I-IV* (Oxford: Oxford University Press, 1911-20); Eoin MacNeill, *Phases of Irish History* (Dublin, 1919).

[9] G.F. Dalton, "The Tradition of the Blood-Sacrifice to the Goddess Éire," *Studies,* 63 (1974): 343-54.

[10] O. Dudley Edwards and B. Ransome, Ed., *James Connolly: Selected Political Writings* (London, 1973), 64.

[11] Boyce, *Nationalism in Ireland,* 427.

[12] Stephen Harrison, "Re-Fighting the Battle of Down: Orpen, MacNeill and the Irish Nation State," in *The Medieval World and the Medieval Mind,* ed. Michael Brown and Stephen Harrison (Dublin: Four Courts Press, Forthcoming 2001); I am indebted to Mr. Harrison for allowing me to read his article before actual publication.

[13] Harrison, "Re-Fighting the Battle of Down," 4.

[14] Harrison, "Re-Fighting the Battle of Down," 5.

[15] Harrison, "Re-Fighting the Battle of Down," 6-7.

[16] Harrison, "Re-Fighting the Battle of Down," 6-8.

[17] Orpen, *Ireland Under the Normans, iv,* 298.

[18] MacNeill, *Phases of Irish History,* 331.

[19] In some cases, a monograph-length study of nationalism in Ireland includes a cursory treatment of the middle ages as background to the main focus of nationalism in the nineteenth and twentieth centuries. See Boyce, *Nationalism in Ireland,* 25-45.

[20] Brendan Bradshaw, "Native Reaction to the Westward Enterprise: A Case Study in Gaelic Ideology," in *The Westward Enterprise: English Activities in Ireland, the Atlantic, and America, 1480-1650,* ed. K. Andrews, N. Canny, P. Hair (Liverpool: Liverpool University Press, 1978), 1.

[21] T.J. Dunne, "The Gaelic Response to Conquest and Colonization: The Evidence of the Poetry," *Studia Hibernica* XX (1980): 11.

[22] Dunne, "The Gaelic Response to Conquest," 11.

[23] Ellis, "Nationalist Historiography," 1.

[24] Ellis, "Nationalist Historiography," 3.

[25] Brendan Bradshaw, "Nationalism and Historical Scholarship in Modern Ireland," *Irish Historical Studies,* XXVI 104 (1989): 336.

[26] Bradshaw, "Nationalism and Historical Scholarship," 336.

[27] Bradshaw, "Nationalism and Historical Scholarship," 337.

[28] Steven Ellis, "Historiographical Debate: Representations of the Past in Ireland: Whose Past and Whose Present?" *Irish Historical Studies* XXVII 108 (1991), 289-90.

[29] James Lydon, "The Problem of the Frontier in Medieval Ireland," *Topic: A Journal of the Liberal Arts,* 13 (1967): 5-22; idem, "The Middle Nation;" idem, "Nation and Race in Medieval Ireland," in *Concepts of National Identity in the Middle Ages,* ed. Simon Forde, Lesley Johnson, and Alan V. Murray (Leeds: Leeds Texts and Monographs, 1995), 103-24.

[30] One need only consider the other works in the collection of articles in *Concepts of Nationality in the Middle Ages.* While scholars of the medieval nation in other parts of Europe employ different methods to explain the prevalence of the nation in medieval Europe, most Irish scholars, including Lydon, still prefer to write political history as history.

[31] Art Cosgrove, "The Writing of Irish Medieval History," *Irish Historical Studies,* XXVII (November, 1990): 97-111.

[32] Cosgrove, "Writing Irish Medieval History," 110-1.

[33] Cosgrove, "Writing Irish Medieval History, 101, 103.

[34] Cosgrove, "Writing Irish Medieval History," 110-1.

[35] Richard Hoffman, "Outsiders by Birth and Blood: Racist Ideologies and Realities around the Periphery of Medieval European Culture," in *Studies in Medieval and Renaissance History, IV,* ed. J.A.S. Evans and R.W. Unger (University of British Columbia, 1983), 3.

[36] Lydon, "The Middle Nation," 3; the following discussion depends heavily on Lydon's seminal article on the subject.

[37] Idem, "The Middle Nation," 3.

[38] J.A. Watt, "Negotiations between Edward II and John XXII Concerning Ireland," *Irish Historical Studies* X (1936), 16.

[39] Lydon, "The Middle Nation," 5.

[40] Whitley Stokes, "The Irish Abridgement of the *Expugnatio Hibernica," English Historical Review* XX (1905), 77-115.

[41] E. Curtis and R.B. McDowell, *Irish Historical Documents* (London: Methuen, 1943), 38.

[42] Lydon, "The Middle Nation," 5.

A Nation in Medieval Ireland?

Chapter 2:
Bardic Poetry and National Identity

Bardic poetry has been recognized as a valuable source material for the study of Gaelic Ireland for several decades.[1] Over the last two decades scholars have generally agreed that it serves as a quite useful tool to understand Gaelic culture, even if the exact interpretation of that understanding has been a source of considerable debate.[2] Most of the work in this field considers poetry from the sixteenth and seventeenth centuries, the period from which the largest number of texts survive.[3] Moreover it is clear that the largest numbers of extant bardic poems are those created for both Gaelic and Anglo-Norman lords in the later middle ages and the early modern period, as opposed to those still in existence from earlier centuries. Studies of this large body of literature used to examine the Gaelic and Old English response to the settlement of new English colonists in the sixteenth and seventeenth centuries yielded results which are far from conclusive.[4] However, there is a body of bardic poetry from the period 1200-1400 that exists but has not been considered by historians of that period.[5] During this period grammatic standardization of bardic poetry occurred and the major Gaelic dynasties patronized bards on a large scale.[6]

Bardic Poetry as Historic Source Material

Bardic poetry may be broadly defined as a class of compositions by Gaelic poets in Ireland and Scotland, dating from the pre-Norman era through the seventeenth century.[7] It is not, however, the sort of poetry that conveys the poet's sense of originality, creativity or inspiration.[8] Bardic poetry aimed to be informational and flattering to the patron. The style and grammar of the poetry was repetitive, and a good bardic poet familiarized himself with a limited variety of poems, meters and styles and copied from those freely.[9] While the poets themselves were bound by these rules, the scribes who later recorded the poems often did not know these rules. When confused by a passage, scribes would used a contemporary grammatical structure to "fix" the problem. But, because of the existence of the *Bardic Syntactical Tracts* and *Irish Grammatical Tracts*, the modern scholar can reconstruct the original poem as composed by the poet. *Bardic Syntactical Tracts* and *Irish Grammatical Tracts*, two manuscript compilations of grammatical usage, seem to have been used as student's handbooks in bardic schools. In these tracts, students read examples of both poor and proper grammatical usage in poems. Modern scholars benefit by discovering which particular poems were used in the tracts, therefore deducing which poems were more widely read and studied by the bardic poets.

The poetry is often composed using four lines per stanza, with as few as ten stanzas or as many as several hundred stanzas making a complete poem. Roughly ten popular meters existed, and among those were five favorite meters.[10] As for the content of the poems, Irish mythology and pseudo-history often supplied motifs, since the poet was considered part of the group of official historians in society.[11] A typical bardic poet likened his kings to historical figures like Brian Bóroimhe or to mythological figures like CuChulain or the Dagda, while their physical attributes were compared to warlike animals such as boars or stags. The metrical conventions often dictated how names and words for attributes were chosen from the pre-existing stock of motifs.[12]

The poets themselves belonged to hereditary learned families, much like the royal and religious families of medieval Ireland. At some point in prehistory, some correlation between poets and druidic priests may have existed. In the early Irish law tracts, dating from the eighth and ninth centuries, the poet is frequently credited with the power of prophecy, similar to that of druids.[13] For example, while considered slightly different from magical incantations or prophecy, a just and well-delivered poetic satire was believed to cause facial and skin irritations to the person satirized.[14] Worse than poetic satire, the poet's spell (*firt filed*) was believed to kill, as was rumored in the case of the Lord Lieutenant of Ireland, John Stanley, as recorded in the *Annals of Connacht* in 1414.[15] This ability to perform satire, along with the basic function of providing praise for the patron, were considered the primary roles of the poet.[16] The bards received training in special schools where they learned to compose various topics using the range of meters already discussed. Students composed in a darkened room from which they emerged with the poem committed to memory. They then submitted the composition for criticism from their instructors and perhaps their peers.[17] In practice, though, the bards were not expected to perform for their patrons; instead, other individuals were trained in the practice of recitation, while still others were trained in playing the harp or *tiompán* (an instrument similar to a zither plucked with a quill), which seems to have been the only instrumental accompaniment. In terms of their respective ranks in society, poets occupied a very high status (in some cases even as high as a petty king, although there were multiple grades based upon the level of professional training of the poet[18]), the musical accompaniment held a lower position, while the singers held a lower level still.[19] As well, unlike most members of society, the poet held rights outside his own *túath*,[20] perhaps because poets had to maintain contact with colleagues in other parts of the country, or because they had to travel to find their audiences at various feasts and fairs.[21]

To practice his trade after training, the poet looked for a patron of the ruling class in need of a court poet and possessed of sufficient resources to employ a poet. The bond between the poet and the king was often portrayed in rather intimate terms, since king and bard depended heavily upon each other. The bard provided crucial propaganda for the king and acted as a family historian for the ruling dynasty, while the king paid the bard with large gifts or sums of money for each poem and offered protection from rival kings or warlords.[22]

Truth, as in the accurate presentation of factual information, remained a secondary issue for the poet.[23] The bard was supposed to create poems that accentuated the truth, even if the truth was insignificant. For instance, bardic accounts might suggest that "never has Ireland seen a more noble king than x," when in fact the king in question controlled a plot of land no bigger than a few square miles. However, the bard also had to present some factual material and could not just make up battles, since everyone at the poem's presentation knew whether a battle had taken place or if a king had turned his back on battle.[24] Thus, the poet was expected to inflate the personality of his patron, but within the obvious limitations presented by current public knowledge and opinion.[25] Further, because a poet could theoretically compose a poem that exaggerated the

truth as a form of sarcasm, he was bound to walk a balance between praise and blind flattery if he wanted to maintain favor with his kings and other potential clients. On the other hand, because the poets often composed poems for several different and in some cases enemy lords, the poet would also compose poems that were extremely general so as not to fall into disfavor with another lord. The poet often found himself in a precarious position, as reflected in the well-known poem of Gofraidh Fionn Ó Dálaigh in which he describes the composition of poems for Gael and for Anglo-Normans[26]; poets composed poems to please audiences with very different political views.[27]

Katharine Simms argues that the bards developed as a class of learned scholars through a three stage process culminating with their independence as a distinct class of scholar in the thirteenth century.[28] First, with the spread of Christianity in the early church period in Ireland (sixth through eighth centuries), the poetic order split into learned literate *fili* and oral bards. Monastic communities began to record the histories, legends and mythology of the Irish royal dynasties. Since the written word commanded a greater prestige than oral literature, these oral bards may have slipped to a lower status in society. While the actual tradition did not change, the manner of transmission became an indicator of status. Second, preceeding the arrival of the Anglo-Normans in Ireland in the 1170s, the new continental monastic ideas of the Cistercians and Augustinians replaced the earlier pre-Norman monasteries. The Church introduced by these new orders was less supportive of the native cultural arts than its pre-Reform predecessors and was clearly not supportive of the more antiquated styles of Church organization that existed in Gaelic areas. Some bardic poets, who had meanwhile became more literate and thus merged with the learned *fili*, continued to record the literature of Irish culture. Finally, bardic patronage increased with a resurgence in Irish self-identity, often called "The Gaelic Resurgence," which then led to the creation of more bardic poems and of the fifteenth and sixteenth century books of the bardic families. While the fourteenth century *Book of Magauran* is the earliest example of a *duanaire*, or "poem book," most medieval poems that exist today in manuscript come from those manuscripts of the fifteenth and sixteenth centuries.[29] Some poems in these collections are nearly contemporary with their transcriptions, while others were composed centuries prior to the creation of the books in which they survive. This seems a credible chronology, but Simms also posits that with this re-awakening of the bardic class came a conflict with the church, its rival for the gift-giving of Irish nobles, which led to accusations of pagan tendencies among the learned class. The poets used motifs and symbols with origins in a non-Christian setting, and the kings returned to traditional inauguration rituals in the fourteenth century. This is not to say that they were any more pagan than anyone else in medieval Irish society. The poets themselves were just as likely to use biblical motifs as classical Irish motifs, and they often composed poems that were of a very Christian character.

Due to the destruction of a great deal of historical source material through the centuries and a decreased reliance on written records in Gaelic society, the historian of Gaelic Ireland lacks the type of documents comparable to other European regions in the middle ages (such as English chancery documents), which forces a reliance upon less precise sources, such as poetry, dynastic sagas, and politically motivated annals. Bardic poetry, however, occupies a unique status among these types of sources. First, it was composed for a patron during that patron's lifetime, or immediately following the patron's death in the case of a eulogy. Therefore, they are readily datable. Second, the poetry is virtually unforgeable, since a poet had to compose in such complex meters. Anyone without direct and explicit knowledge of proper bardic constructions would produce rather obvious metrical mistakes revealing the composition as non-professional in origin. If a scribe recorded a poem in a manuscript and wished to change the name of the person to whom the poem was dedicated, he would drastically ruin the meter and rhyme. Therefore, if a poem states that the patron of the poem was an individual who lived at the end of the fourteenth century we can safely deduce that it was composed for that patron even if the poem is found in a much later manuscript. Moreover, the prohibitive cost of manuscript production mitigated against the transcription of poetry with poor meter. There very well might have been poems composed at "cut-rate" prices by poorly trained poets that have not survived. Finally, while we may want to question bardic poetry in terms of the intention of its author, bardic poetry leads us not to one man's ideas, but to a group's ideals, because bards had to please nobles, patrons, and dynasties. To some degree, this removed personal bias while also giving a glimpse at the moving ideology of the ruling class of a society which did not readily create historic documents. To receive payment, the bard needed to produce literature pleasing to the patrons; the the bard was less able to critique the political establishment personally. We might also consider the large corpus of material with which to work as another

asset in the consideration of bardic poetry.[30]

The Selection of Relevant Bardic Poetry

Katharine Simms created a database of bardic poetry (*The Catalogue of Bardic Poetry*) in which she compiled the first lines of bardic poems from catalogues of manuscripts and libraries and from collections of bardic poetry in published format. The database itself was created using the database function of ClarisWorks. It contains fields for the poem's first line, the author, the patron, the meter, the approximate date of composition, place of publication and/or translation, as well as several fields for the entry of motifs. The motifs are numbered according to a motif index also constructed by Simms. It is possible to sort the poems in a variety of ways, and it is also possible to use logical operations. As of 1999, there were over 1,600 poems spanning the entire bardic period in the database; it is possible that the database could rise to as many as 2,000. Some data for some poems are lacking due to the fact that they have been entered in outline form only and have not yet been examined by the cataloguer.

Related to the *Catalogue of Bardic Poetry* is a project underway at Trinity College, Dublin, in the Department of Irish. Under Damian MacManus, a collection of texts containing all of the known examples of bardic poetry (in published or manuscript form) will be published in CD-ROM format. The collection will include material already published, and will allow the researcher to search the corpus for particular examples of vocabulary or grammatical usage contained within a vast amount of text. At present, the corpus measures over two thousand pages. Furthermore, a large amount of material that has not been edited or published and still needs to be transcribed awaits inclusion. The expected completion of the project is by the end of 2004.[31]

It should be stated from the outset that the selection of poems for analysis in this study, while representative of the poems created in thirteenth and fourteenth century Ireland, is not a statistical sampling of poems. In other words, it is not a random sampling of all poetry composed in the period. The group of poems considered here may be politically skewed because of such random factors as the survival of a group of poems in a single manuscript that happens to have escaped destruction, as in the case of the *Book of Magauran*.[32] The survival of poems in such manuscripts may have been influenced by the prominence of the family that owns the book (as with the *Book of the*

O Conor Don, which is held in the O Conor family library at Clonalis House in Co. Roscommon) or by plain chance (as with the *Book of Mac Cartaigh Riabhach,* otherwise known as the *Book of Lismore,* which was discovered at Lismore castle in 1814 during the course of building operations).[33]

In another sense, the survival of a bardic poem in its written form depends upon the quality of the poem in question. An intricate poem using complex meter successfully would more likely survive in manuscript form than a poem composed using fairly simple meter, or a poem that was simply poorly composed.[34] This could mean that a stratum of poetry might not have survived into transcription due to its poor quality. This stratum might represent an aspect of Gaelic society different from the dominant worldview of the most powerful families who patronized the best poets in Ireland. However, this is an argument *ex silentio* and is more a curious thought than provable thesis.

The first major criterion for the database search involved sorting the poems which were likely composed in the thirteenth and fourteenth centuries. The total number of poems after this first sort numbered 272. These 272 can then be subdivided based upon the probable geographic origin of each poem, the patron's dynastic family, time period, and the name and family of the poet (if known).

These subdivided categories give a general background of the poems' creation, but an even clearer view appears after sorting the poems based upon particular motifs that seem prominent in the set. Using the motif index created by Katharine Simms, the following motifs (including the numerical classifications that correspond to Simms' motif index) were used as search variables:

> 260   War with Foreigners--razing their castles, expelling them from the land
>
> 261   Foreign Conquest of Ireland--foreigners sharing out lands, physical appearance of Ireland changed as a result of conquest, paying tribute to foreigners
>
> 262   Ireland's present woes foretold in prophecy
> > 1.   Destruction of foreigners prophesied
> > 2.   Conquest the fruit of God's anger against the sins of Ireland

> 270   The possibility of cooperation between the native Irish and some Anglo-Irish
>
> 283   Territory as king's spouse, or diocese as bishop's spouse, *leannan, ceile,* king as bridegroom, sovereignty earned by kiss
>
> 284   Fertility in the reign of a just prince, fair weather, profitable ship-wrecks, milk-producing cows, heavy nut-crop
>
> 360   Prophecies of a ruler (by Colmcille, Mogh Ruith, Flann file, Fionn MaCumhaill)
>
> 361   Prophecies of Aodh Eangach
> 391   Comparison between home territory and high-kingship: possible prospect of high-kingship rejected in favour of delightful homeland or delightful homeland not to divert patron from high-kinship

The rationale behind choosing these motifs for particular analysis is the embodiment of each as an aspect of national identity according to the poets and the patrons. That identity was defined based upon two basic assumptions. First, there was a clear difference between the Anglo-Normans and the native Gaelic people. The two peoples came from different ethnic communities; one possessed an Anglo-Norman worldview and the other maintained a Gaelic worldview. The two groups entered into conflict over control of land, which exacerbated the ethnic differences between the two groups. Second, the learned poets often described their patrons as reborn Brians, or Conns, or other such figures representing Gaelic leaders who repelled foreign invaders. In addition, the poets cited prophecies that foretold the contemporary political situation and described the patron as a deliverer for the Irish people. This determinist way of viewing history, in which the contemporary world is foretold in the past, provides a meaningful way to analyze the poetry because it describes the kind of expectations held by the learned poets and their patrons. Prophecy, in this sense, is another form of political propaganda.

Figure 2.1 displays the geographic origins of the extant poems in the database. While this is not a statistical representation and should only be used for descriptive purposes, it does seem clear that throughout the period the majority of extant poems were created in Connacht, but

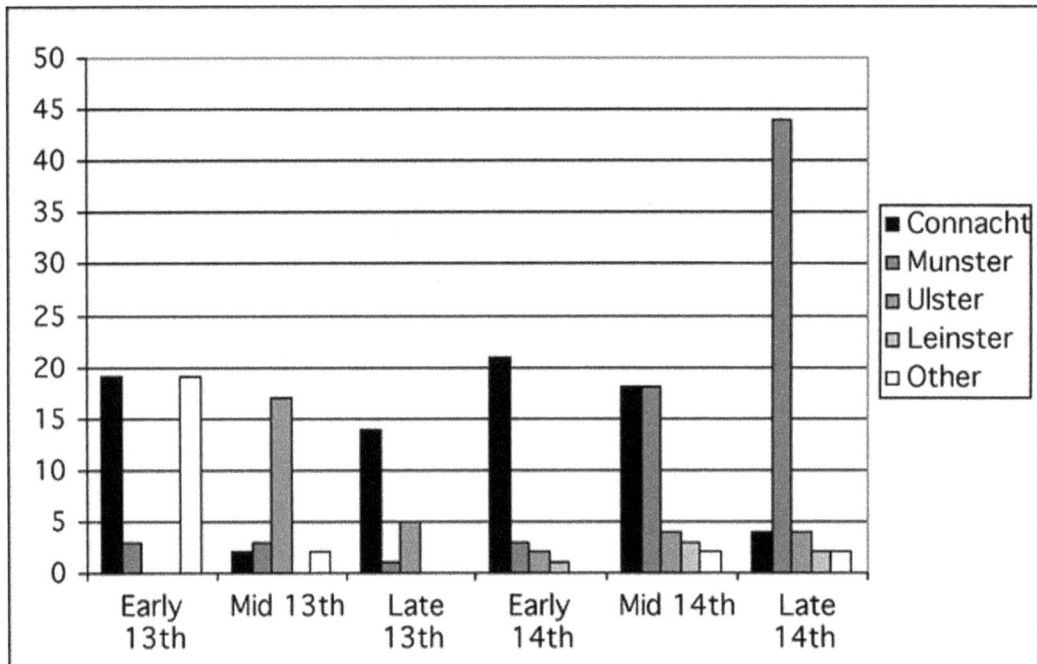

Figure 2.1: Geo-Temporal Distribution of Bardic Poetry

that in the late fourteenth century the number of surviving poems created in Munster dramatically increased. Later, this study will show that the reason for this preponderance of poetry in Connacht is the patronage of the bards by the Ó Conchobhair dynasty of Connacht. Aside from the slight spike in the mid- thirteenth century in Ulster, Ulster and Leinster do not seem to have been centers for the creation of poems.

Several groups of Gaelic and Anglo-Norman families exhibit more pronounced patronage of bardic poets than others this period (See Figure 2.2). Beginning with Cathal Croibderg, the Ó Conchobhair dynasty of Connacht acted as one of the greatest supporters of poetry, with a total of 31 poems represented in the sample. The Mac Gowran family are also represented by 30 poems, while poems composed for the Mac Carthaigh, Ó Domhnaill and Ó Briain kings numbered in the high teens. Eleven poems were composed for Anglo-Norman patrons during this period.

Several families of poets were responsible for this output of poems. The most prolific family of poets during this period was the Ó Dálaigh family, with a total of 43 poems attributed to them, while the O Higgin family produced just over 40 poems. These two families produced poems for most of the different Gaelic and Anglo-Norman lords

as shown in Figure 2.3.

The poems were composed at fairly regular intervals throughout the two hundred years of which this study is concerned. However, several spikes in the output of poetry exist that coincide with political events which occurred in Ireland during these two centuries. Figure 2.4 shows that from the beginning of this period, a high number of poems survive, but the number of surviving poems from the middle of the thirteenth century decreased. The high numbers early in the century are no doubt due to the number of poems composed for Ó Conchobhair kings in Connacht, particular for Cathal Crobdherg and his son Áed. The rise in the early fourteenth century, which continued throughout the century, coincides with the "Gaelic Resurgence," and reflects the growing tendency of Gaelic lords to commission bardic poems to show wealth and prestige and to assert authority. The decline in the late thirteenth century could reflect the declining fortunes in Ireland itself; lawlessness throughout the land was noted at the Parliament of 1297; however this lawlessness was also a persistent problem at the end of the thirteenth century.[35] As well, we should recall the turmoil in the colony resulting from the attempt to raise Ó Néill as High King by the princes of Ireland which led to Ó Néill's death at the Battle of Down in 1260. Although other factors, such as the varied survival rate of poems in later manuscripts,

14

Patrons of Bardic Poetry, 1200–1400

Family	Number of Poems
O Neill	8
Anglo-Norman Lords	11
Mac Carthaigh	14
O Briain	16
O Domhnaill	19
Mag Shamhradhain	30
O Conchobhair	31

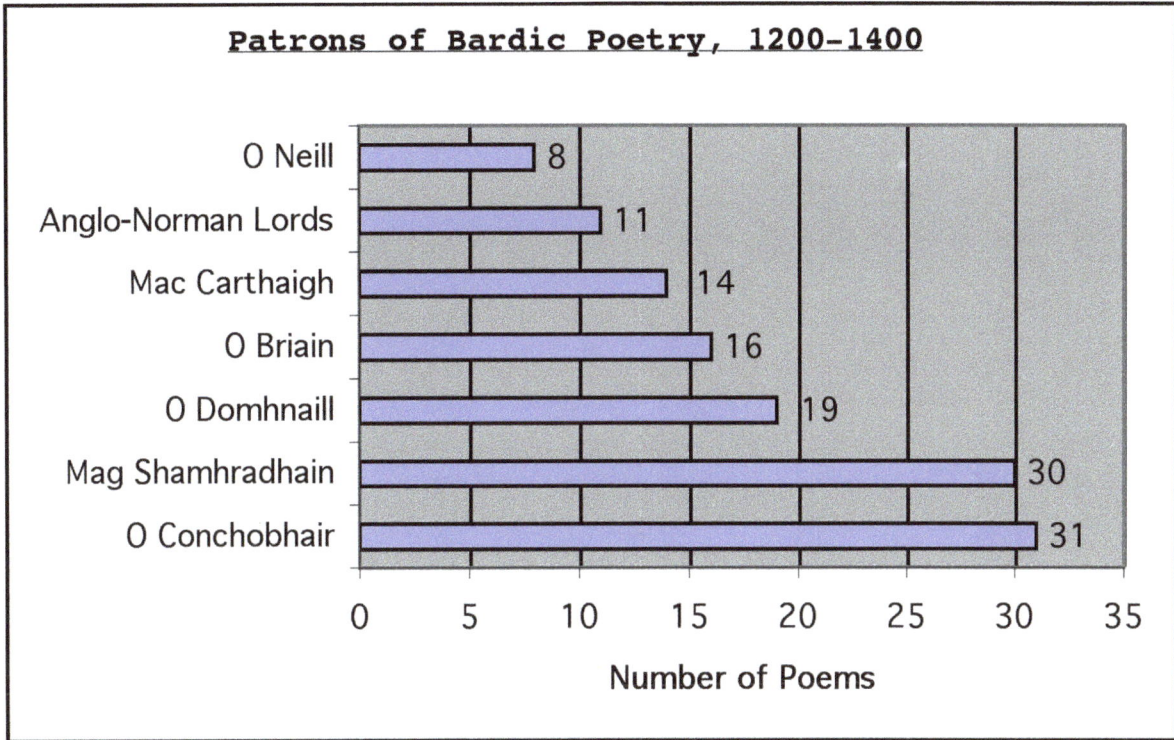

Figure 2.2: Families of Patrons of Bardic Poetry

play a role in ultimate temporal distribution of surviving poems, it does seem clear that the pattern observed in Figure 2.4 corresponds clearly to historic events.

Versions of poems in this selection are found in a collection containing 128 manuscripts. While just under 300 poems with which this study is concerned occur in the datables, those poems often exist in several different versions. As shown in Figure 2.5, of the 610 earliest versions, 112 refer to manuscripts in which fewer than ten other examples of poems from the selection are found.[36] In other words, over eighty percent of the transcribed versions of the poems exist in large collections of poems. The manuscripts which provided the greatest percentage of the 610 poems are the *Book of the O Conor Don* (68), the *Book of the Dean of Lismore* (37), the *Book of Fermoy* (37), the *O'Gara Manuscript* (32), and the *Book of Magauran* (33). Several other manuscripts contain between ten and thirty poems per manuscript.

In a review of Michelle O Riordan's book *The Gaelic Mind and the Collapse of the Gaelic World*, Marc Caball suggests that one of the main flaws with O Riordan's work is her failure to distinguish between the poems found in *dunaire*, or "poem-books," and those poems found individually in composite manuscripts (manuscripts that include other types of literature such as sagas or

hagiography).[37] He maintains that the assembly of poems into *duanairí* itself was functionally different from the recording of poems individually. The inclusion of poems in a duanaire represents a more "traditionalist" approach to preserving the poetry, while the individual poems found in composite manuscripts reflect a more innovative strand in the tradition since these poems were often stylistically and substantively innovative.[38] Ó Cuív discussed the role of the creation of bardic *duanaire*, and in his discussion posits the existence of a great deal of ambiguity in the process.[39] Indeed, the creation of a book such as the *Book of the O Conor Don* could have been based upon an earlier *duanaire* of the same type, or even from more than one such *duanaire*. An example of this would be the seventeenth century manuscript, RIA MS 1 (23 D 14), which Ó Cuív suggests is a clear derivative of National Library of Ireland MS G 992.[40]

Caball's point is valid. The creation of the great bardic poetry collections in itself represents a decision-making process on the patron's part similar to the creation process on the part of the original bardic poets. But it should be stated that we simply do not have enough evidence from the first few centuries of the bardic period to state whether the transmission of the poems from the earliest part of the period to the later was oral or written. Like the poets, the later scribes created collections for a particular patron.

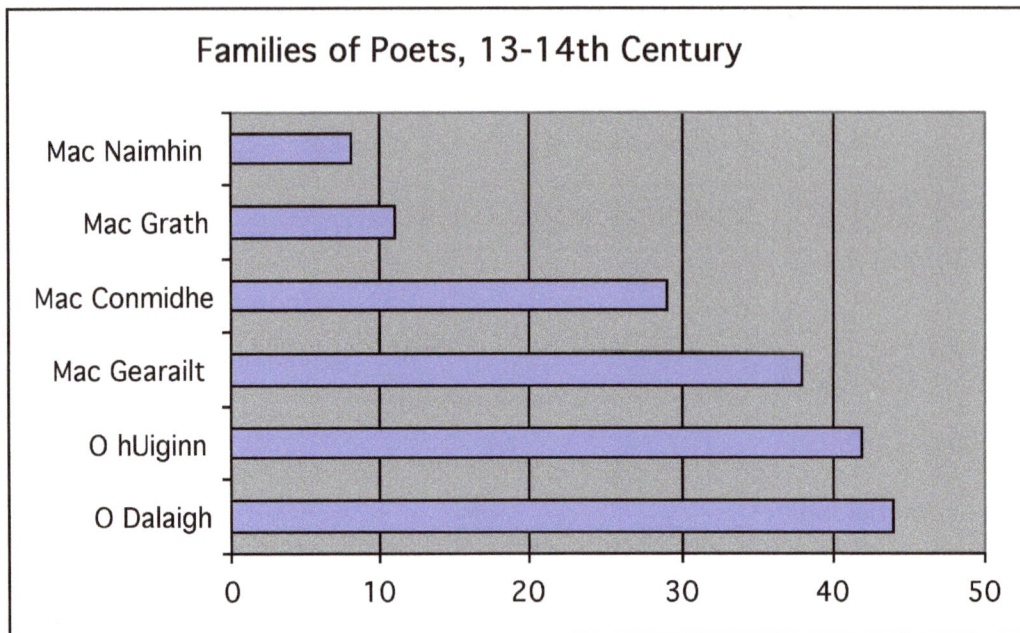

Figure 2.3: Families of Bardic Poets

Hence, the scribes may have limited their selections on that basis (patronage) more than just antiquarian interest. On the other hand, as shown in the graph in Figure 2.5, by using the *Catalogue of Bardic Poetry* as the basis for the search queries, this study can include as many poems from composite manuscripts or from scattered fragments as from the larger collections in the *Book of the O Conor Don, O Gara Manuscript, Book of the Dean of Lismore,* or the *Book of Magauran.*

While essentially valid, Ó Cuív's points about the transmission of the poems in manuscript need more elaboration because poems in this selection often appear in more than one manuscript. Of the over 270 poems in the selection, 154 are found in multiple manuscripts. For comparison purposes, nearly all of the 44 versions of poems from the *Book of the O Conor Don* that exist in other manuscripts are found in at least three different manuscripts. Some of these other versions are clearly copies of the *Book of the O Conor Don,* such as RIA 626 (3/C/13), which is O Curry's transcription of the *Book of the O Conor Don.* However there are poems with no clear connections, such as the relationship between the poems in TCD MS 1318 with the poems in the *Book of the O Conor Don.* The case may be that some of these poems served as exemplars for the scholars of the seventeenth century to record and transcribe. *Bardic Syntactical Tracts*

(the collection of syntactical teaching aids for the bardic schools) contains references to many of these poems, so it is clear that the scholars of the later middle ages, and possibly the scribes of the seventeenth century, were aware of the poems that collectively made up the corpus of exemplary bardic poetry.

Caball also bases his points regarding the composition of a *duanaire* upon the idea that bardic poetry was compiled to serve a political purpose in the seventeenth century.[41] While this is certainly true for that century, the fact remains that poetry recorded in the seventeenth century was originally performed in the thirteenth and fourteenth centuries, and there must of have been *duanairi* similar to the fourteenth century *Book of Magauran* from which the later scholars transcribed the poems. Nevertheless, for an understanding of the role that bardic poetry played in the thirteenth and fourteenth centuries, it is necessary to consider the poetry as orally presented and not textually composed.[42] The bards created the poems following the metrical and syntactical rules of their profession, and if there textual corruption exists, it is no doubt due to the transcription, not the poem or poet.[43] As Caball writes, individual poems cannot be read in isolation; but the *Catalogue of Bardic Poetry* allows the scholar to consider a wider cross section of poetry than before. The *Catalogue* makes possible for the first time the survey of the corpus of

16

Temporal Distribution of Poetry

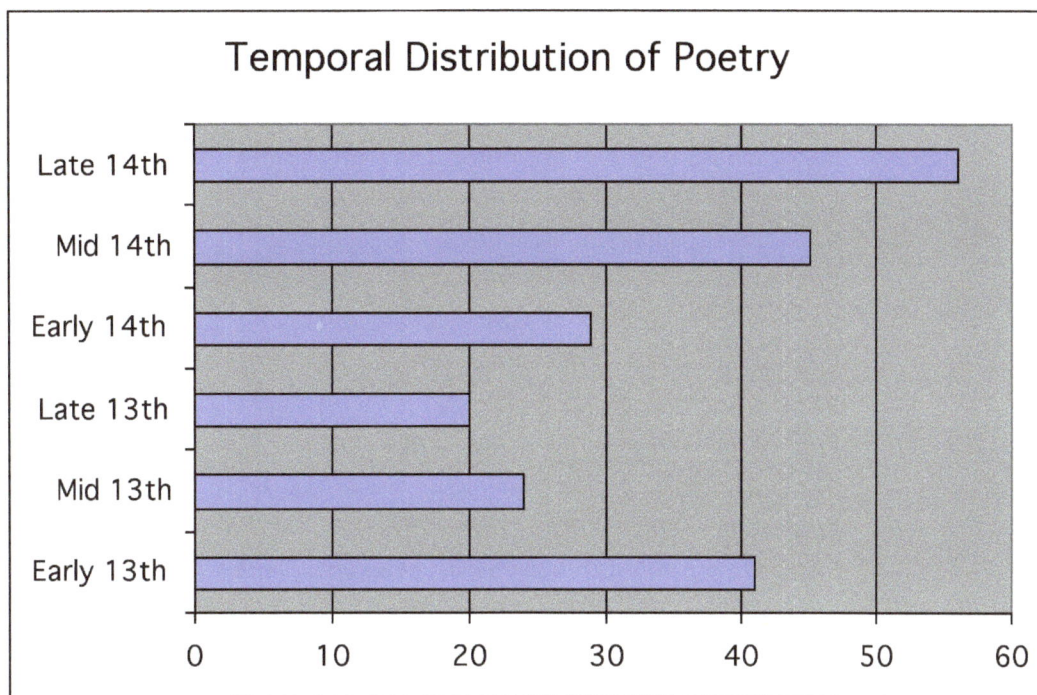

Figure 2.4: Temporal Distribution of Bardic Poetry

surviving poetry as a whole. The limitations of previous studies are overcome by comprehensively considering the poetry as a body of literature as opposed to randomly scattered pieces of that literature.

Analysis of the Resulting Motifs

One way for a poet to support the political claims and ambitions of his patron was through the use of references to prophetic literature to argue that the patron's kingship was foretold in the past. This tradition of using prophetic literature is stylistically similar to the device of comparing the patron to Lugh, Conn, or some other mythological figure. However, according to Breandan O Buachalla, a fundamental difference exists between suggesting that the patron is like a mythological figure and stating that the patron is, in fact, Aodh Eangach (the "long-awaited deliverer of Ireland" prophesied in Ireland's ancient past).[44] For the poet, O Buachalla suggests, the reference to a mythological character was meant to compare the patron with an historical figure from a previous age. By stating that the patron was the fulfillment of prophecy (and, more particularly, Aodh Eangach for O Buachalla), the poet offered not a comparison, but a statement of ontology concerning the patron.

The inhabitants of Ireland were noted for their belief in the future arrival of a deliverer. Giraldus Cambrensis stated that the Irish believed in several Irish prophet-saints, including Patrick, Columcille, and Bearchán. He also explicitly refers to the prophecy of Bearchán when he writes that the Irish believe that "...the English will be dislodged from Ireland by a king who will come from the lonely mountain of Patrick, and on the night of Our Lord's day will overrun a castle in the wooded region of Uí Fhaeláin."[45] *The Annals of Ulster* and *Annals of Loch Cé* refer to a "false Aodh" in 1214, perhaps alluding to the fact that this particular Aodh did not fulfill any sort of prophecy; no other record of this Aodh has survived.[46]

The poets of Ireland were not unique in their inclusion of prophetic material in their poetry. The use of prophetic literature in medieval Europe was very widespread, and was created in a wide variety of different cultural settings. J.R.S. Phillips pointed out that prophecy was used to bolster the troubled reign of King Edward II of England.[47] Contemporary English chronicles complained of his ineptitude, both in domestic and foreign policy. Propaganda poems that considered Edward a long-awaited king who would again unite all the peoples of the British Isles countered these negative claims. The original source of this prophecy is the *Prophetia Merlini,* made famous in the twelfth century by Geoffrey of Monmouth in his

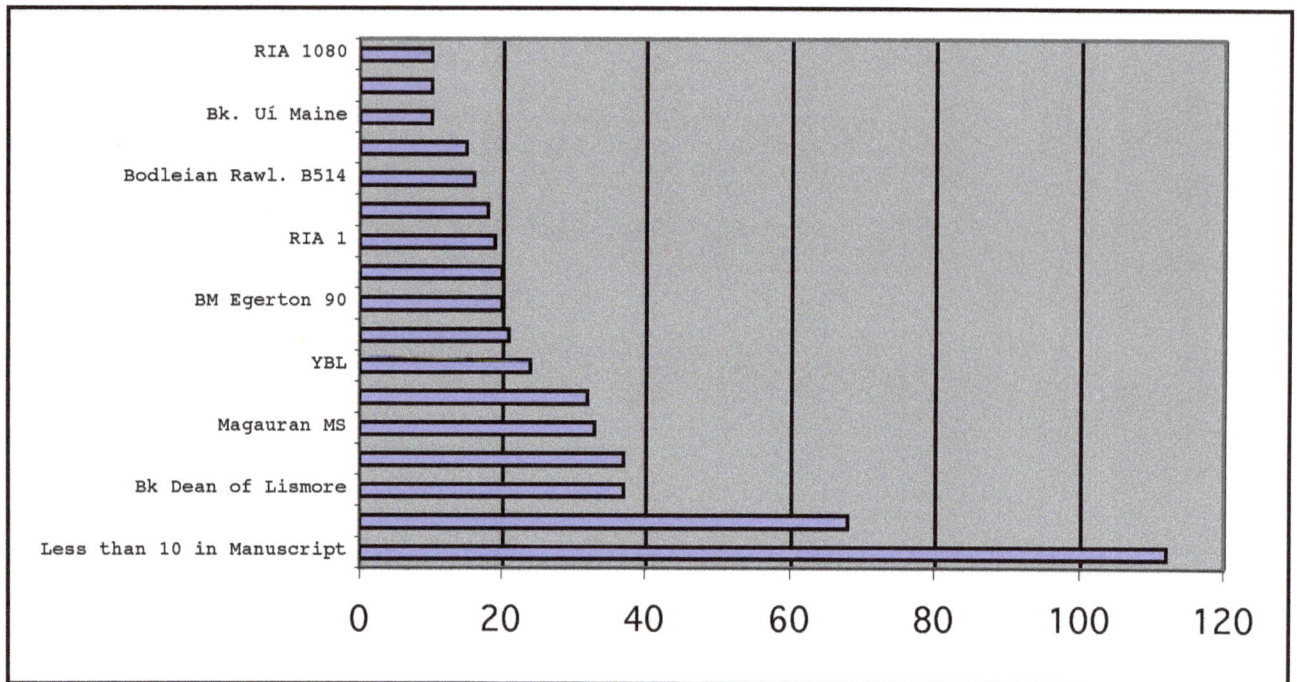

Figure 2.5: Manuscript Collections of Bardic Poetry

Historia Regum Britanniae. Edward, born at Caernarvon in Wales in 1284, was supposedly presented to the Welsh nobility and accepted by acclaim as king, in accordance with Merlin's prophecy.

We can observe a similar use of prophetic literature in fourteenth century Wales in the rebellion and reign of Owain Lawgoch. As Owain led the Welsh in a revolt against the English, his mandate with the Welsh nobility was a prophecy that an Owen known as Owen *Lawgoch*, Owen "Red Hand," would come and restore a Welsh kingdom and cast out the English. This Owain was seen as the fulfillment of this prophecy, and he garnered widespread support among his countrymen and with King Charles V of France.[48] With the help of the French he planned to invade Wales and re-establish Welsh independence, but was later murdered by an English assassin at the siege of Mortange-sur-mer in 1378.[49] Later, Owain Glyndwr formally cast himself as the fulfillment of prophecy and termed himself *mab darogan*, or "son of prophecy."[50] He wrote to King of Robert III of Scotland and, in a generic

manner, to the lords of Ireland in an attempt to garner support for a popular rising against the English people (*la lange Engloys*), and also to bring to fruition the prophecy of Merlin which stated that the English would be destroyed by a Scots-Welsh-Irish coalition.[51] By 1404-5 the revolt reached its apogee, and it seemed that Wales might actually enter a new Golden Age. Owain may have died in 1415 by which time the revolt fizzled; but his contemporaries had no conclusive proof that Glyndwr died, fostering the belief that he survived and may yet return.[52]

Outside observers thought the Irish expected a deliverer prophesied by past Christian saints. As noted, according to Giraldus Cambrensis the Irish believed in several Irish prophet-saints, including Moling, Patrick, Columcille, and Bearchán. Giraldus also states that the Anglo-Norman John de Courcy owned a manuscript in Irish containing several prophecies by Irish saints, notably the prophecy of Columcille. Presumably, de Courcy saw himself, or wanted to portray himself, as their fulfillment.[53]

18

The parallels between the Welsh and the Irish poetic traditions are striking, especially in their use of the prophecy theme and the expected deliverer. On one level, the social dynamics of prophecy itself account for the common features. The expectation of a deliverer for a people presupposes several social conditions. First, the motif must refer to a Golden Age clearly not part of the present condition. The deliverer in the prophecy will help society return to that Golden Age. Before the return to that Golden Age can be achieved, though, cataclysm and catastrophes will signal the arrival of that deliverer. Third, a group of oppressors prevent the society from returning to the Golden Age by conquering the people. The oppressors are cast as "foreigner" and oppress the people because of a perceived cultural superiority. Lastly, the deliverer arrives and leads his people in some sort of final victory over the group of oppressors. Without these social conditions, the motif of prophetic deliverer becomes not only meaningless, but farcical.

On another level, the similarity between Irish and Welsh prophetic literature is due to the the similar manner in which the literature was passed within the respective traditions. In Wales, heroes such as Cadwaladr, Cynan, and Owain exist in a sub-stratum of poetry that was thought from the sixth or seventh century.[54] The poetry is ascribed to sixth century authors such as Myrddin and Taliesin. The poems were apparently produced during the incursions of Anglo-Saxon kingdoms into the kingdoms of Wales. Later, these prophetic works were adopted by Geoffrey of Monmouth in his *Prophetia Merlini* found in the middle of his *Historia Regum Britanniae*, and in *Vita Merlini*. After approximately 1200, Owain, a minor figure in the earlier prophetic literature, came to the fore as the most frequently invoked deliverer.[55] The poets continued to attribute the prophecies to Myrddin and Taliesin, and continued to describe the enemy as Saxon, even though the contemporary enemy was the Anglo-Norman.[56]

In Ireland, a similar process seemingly took place. The original literature ascribed to Patrick, Colum Cille, and Bearchán was supposedly composed in the early stages of Ireland's conversion to Christianity, but was actually composed during the tenth and eleventh centuries to add political support to various kings.[57] The Scandinavian enemies in this literature were described as "foreigners," or *gall*, or as *saxoin*. Learned scholars of Ireland preserved this body of literature which became imbedded within the learned tradition of Ireland in a similar sense as the mythology of invasion imbedded in *Lebor Gabhala*.[58]

Like the motif of invasion so prominent in *Lebor Gabhalla*, the motif of prophesied deliverer was recast in the thirteenth century to describe the new relationship between Gaelic king and Anglo-Norman lord. Like the Welsh tradition, the Irish poets often used the same language to describe the "foreigner," referring to them as *saxoin* as well as *gall*.[59]

The first example of the prophetic deliverer theme to be examined is the motif that the "Ruler is Aodh Eangach." This theme has been examined by Brendan O Buachalla. The earliest source of the motif of Aodh Eangach is found in quatrain 62 of *Baile in Scáil*.[60] The story refers to the character Conn Ceddcathach, who steps on the *Lia Fal* ("The Stone of Destiny") on the Hill of Tara. *Lia Fal* shrieks, revealing the number of kings to succeed Conn. Accompanied by three druids and three *fili*, or poets, who were attempting to interpret the shriek of Fal, Conn is surrounded by a mist. A mounted warrior arrives and takes them to a fort. We later learn that this warrior is dead, but walking, and that his name is Lug mac Ethlend.[61] An otherworldly woman who lives in the fort offers wine to the warrior who then successively reveals the future kings of Ireland, one of whom is Aodh Eangach.[62]

Another Aodh, although not referred to as Aodh Eangach, appears in a prophecy attributed to St. Colum Cille as Aodh Cliabhglas, or "the gray bodied." He is a king who will assume the rule of Erinn and will be followed by seven other kings with reigns of twenty-seven years each. After the last king, a large Rowing Wheel (*Roth Ramhach*, perhaps something like a large mill wheel) will appear carrying one thousand beds with one thousand foreign men in each bed. Another fleet of ships containing more foreigners will arrive, and the forces of Ireland and these invaders will battle in a cataclysmic conflict at Tara which will destroy both armies.[63]

Berchán's prophecy is another source for the theme of Aodh Eangach. The earliest version of any part of this prophecy is found in the Book of Leinster copy of *Cogad Gáedel re Gallaib*, which includes three stanzas refering to the coming of the Vikings. The text describes Berchán as one of the great prophets of Ireland, along with Patrick and Colum Cille.[64] Later variants of the poem are found in several Royal Irish Academy manuscripts, but none possess the entire poem. The text used by A.O. Anderson in his 1930 edition is RIA MS 679 (23/G/4), written by Seán Ó Catháin, c. 1722-9),[65] while more recently Hudson used RIA MS 1225 (Stowe D.ii.1, the *Book of Uí Mhaine*, late fourteenth century) for the first 115 stanzas.[66] The distinction is important, because in stanza 72 Anderson reads his text as

"Nos geibh craobh dherg as Chrúachan,
an Éirinn na mbith n-úathmhar;
an t-Aódh éngach do leith Cuinn,
bhrisfes an cath ag Líath druim."[67]

Hudson, in his reading of the *Book of Uí Maine* version, reads the same stanza (which he numbers as 79) as

"Nos geib crobderg a Crúachain
in nÉirind n-anbthigh n-úathmáir
is é in tengrach do Leith Cuind
brisfes in cath ac Líathdruim."[68]

Hudson's use of the *Book of Ui Mhaine* for line c of this stanza is questionable; he himself states that, as it stands, the word *tengrach* does not make much sense, and that the version of Bearchán's prophecy in the *Book of Ui Mhaine* is not textually related to the other, later versions of the poem. Given the prophetic nature of the poem in general, Anderson's reading seems far more credible.

Taking Anderson's reading, then, we notice a correlation between "*craobh dherg as Crúachan*," "the red hand coming from Cruachan," and "*an t-Aodh éngach*," which Anderson translates as either "Aodh who leaves a trail of fire," or "Aodh the pennoned one." *The Dictionary of the Irish Language* suggests a translation of "noisy" for *éngach*, as in "causing clamor in battle."[69] This correlation between Aodh Eangach and "the red handed one" explains the first group of poems using the motif of Aodh Eangach.

In "Sil Neill's Era Has Come to an End," a poem composed for Cathal Crobderg in the early thirteenth century, Niall, one of the ancient kings of Tara, makes love to the sovereignty goddess, and in return she reveals future kings of Ireland through a vision of fish.[70] In the vision, a red-finned salmon appears, and attacks coarse fish[71] with ugly shapes that came to attack the other fish, which represent the Irish. The coarse fish represent the British (*Bretnaig*), the English (*Sacsain*), and the French (*Frangaig*), while the salmon with red fins is Cathal Crobderg himself. The fact that the prophecy identifies the coarse fish as British, English, and French might reveal the poets' awareness of ethnic differences even among the foreigners themselves, since the invaders were primarily of Welsh/British,

English and French extraction. Further, the passage shows that the poem and the prophecy itself were constructed after the arrival of the Anglo-Normans. The title of Cathal Ó Conchobhair as "*Crobhderg*" ("red handed") seems to stem from the fact that he actuall had a red birth mark on one or both of his hands according to one poet, but the term could just as easily refer to the red coming from the blood of battle.[72] The Ó Dálaigh poet of *Tairnic an sealsa ag Siol Neill* does not mention the prophecy of Berchán in this poem, and the allusion to the vision revealed to Neill is similar to the prophecy revealed to Conn in *Baile in Scáile*, although a direct parallel should be discouraged.

Another poem composed for Cathal Crohderg, "The Red Hand of Croghan has Come," states that "the Redhanded of Croghan has come, as Berchán foretold."[73] Another prophet, Marban, also foretold his arrival.[74] In this poem, the poet refers to both the prophecy of Berchán and the red hand of Cathal Crobderg, forming a link between the two. As the fulfillment of prophecy and as the proper mate for Ireland, the reign of Cathal brings prosperity to the land, signifying that the land of Ireland recognizes her true lover. The poet reveals that it is Cathal's left hand that is red, while his right hand is white. Given this detail, it may be the case that Cathal's hand was, in fact, red.[75]

In a poem to Cathal Crobderg's son, Áed (Aodh), "Keep Your Face in Front of Me, Aodh," the poet declares that Aodh is the deliverer also foretold by Berchán.[76] In this poem describing Aodh's physical appearance, ancient kings of Ireland are found around his flowing blond hair, symbolic of their familial link to him.[77] In a sense, it is as if the other kings are giving him support by appearing behind him. The poet emphasizes the link with past kings by the declaration that no Williams or Henrys exist in his ancestry, and that these new invaders of Ireland will be cast out by Aodh as Aodh Eangach, or "*Aodh don fáistine*," (Aodh of the prophecy).[78] In the final quatrain of the poem Aodh is declared "*A Aodh Cruachna*," or "Aodh of Cruachan (the ancient capital of Connacht)" and "*a mhic an Chroibhdherg cuilfhinn*," or "handsome son of the Red Handed one." This inauguration poem substantiated the legitimacy of Áed as king in several ways. First, Áed's physical appearance heralds the arrival of the prophesied deliverer Aodh Eangach. Second, the poet declares Áed part of a lineage which includes the ancient kings of Ireland, and draws a distinction between that lineage and a lineage including Anglo-Norman names. Finally, Áed is the son of Crobderg, who was himself prophesied in the same quatrain by Berchán.[79] Áed succeeded his father to the Kingship of Connacht in 1224, and immediately attempted to establish his just kingship by mutilating several criminals on the day of his inauguration.[80]

Áed never gained strong support from the people of Connacht, and revolts from other branches of the Ó Conchobhair dynasty troubled his reign. In 1215, Áed 's father attempted to gain a grant of all Connacht except for Athlone for himself and his heirs through good service to the Crown and to the King's representatives in Dublin; however, Richard de Burgh received the same grant on the same day.[81] After Cathal's death in 1224, the Dublin government pressured Áed to prove his fidelity and to pay the arrears of rent that had built up. After the Anglo-Norman lords proved that Áed did not show good service, then, the grant to de Burgh was activated. The *Annals of Loch Ce* state that by burning the castle at Athlone in 1226 Áed had responded to the treachery of the Anglo-Norman lords, particularly the justiciar Geoffrey de Marisco who attempted to entrap him. In 1228, Áed reached an agreement with Geoffrey de Marisco. Afterwards, while still in de Marisco's castle, Áed was axed by the jealous husband of a woman who shared in Áed's bath.

Another Áed of the Ó Conchobhair dynasty who received the title of Aodh Eangach, Áed Ó Conchobhair, died in 1309 while raiding in Breifne.[82] Two poems were composed in praise of his fortress at Cloonfree, Co. Roscommon.[83] In one, the poet provides great detail regarding the fortification, stating that unlike Tara, which has seven ramparts, the fortress of Aodh needs only one.[84] This fortress at Cloonfree was identified as the fortress of Aodh Eangach, and Áed Ó Conchobhair was declared the prophesied one, or *"tairrnhgeartaigh."*[85] The poet attributes the poem to a Flann File, or "Flann the Poet."[86] While this Flann is unidentified,[87] the poem states that the prophecy was made for the chief of Emain. Further, the Áed of the prophecy will be recognized by magician (*dráoithe*) and prophetess (*banfáidh*) alike, and no reference is found stating that the prophecy originated with a Christian prophecy, such as that of Berchán.[88]

Tainig tairngire na n-éarlamh contains one of the other examples of the Aodh Eangach motif and described Áed Ó Domhnaill[89] as the arrival of Aodh Eangach. The prophecy's source used by the poet, Gilla Brigte Mac Con Midhe, is also that of Berchán, although he does state that the prophecies of Columcille and Comhghall of Bangor also foretold his arrival.[90] He states that according to the prophecy of Berchán, a pillar would be built on the side of Tara, from which would come Aodh Eanghach.[91] Furthermore he declares that the source of the prophecy are the saints of the Irish past, and are of Christian origin,[92] perhaps for the same reasons that the poet of "Keep your face in front of me, Aodh" (*Congaibh róm t'aghaidh a Aodh*) made it clear that the source of his prophecy for Áed Ó Conchobhair had its origin in Christian prophecy, and not pagan prophecy.[93] The Aodh in question in this poem was the son of a member of the Ó Domhnaill, and, curious enough, his mother was Lasairfhíona, daughter of Cathal Crobderg. The poet suggests that the mixing of these two families compares to the mixing of wine, and the result is sweet to taste.[94] The association with Connacht is further emphasized several quatrains later, when Áed is named as a descendant of Conall from Carn Fraoich, the inauguration site of the Ó Conchobhair.[95] The foreigners throughout the poem are termed *"gall"*, and Mac Con Midhe states that they are in possession of Ireland (*Fódhla*).[96] Ultimately, Áed will deliver *Fódhla* from these enemies.

Poets in the thirteenth and fourteenth centuries used other prophecies as source material. Giraldus states that the Irish had four prophets in particular: Moling, Braccan [Berchán], Patrick, and Colum Cille. He also states that the Irish preserved books in their native tongue which include these prophecies. Again, the *Book of Leinster* incorporates several prophecies of Berchán and Colum Cille in the text of *Cogadh Gaedhel re Gallaibh.*[97]

The prophecy of Patrick alluded to in "What I have said of the evils" (*Beag nach lor a luaidhim dhe*) describes the future as revealed to Patrick in the form of a vision.[98] A tree appeared on a plain, full of fruit; other trees appeared and encircled it.[99] The poet then proposes that the tree is the patron (identified by MacKenna, the editor of the poem, as Tomas MacGowran, who died in 1361), and as the tree bears fruit, so did the patron of the poem cause trees to blossom and bear fruit in his land, which was then eaten by birds. The poet explains that the tree is the patron, and the birds are the poets that the patron supports.[100] However, this prophecy does not seem to correspond with known versions of the Patrick's prophecies, nor does it correspond with the prophecy *Bailé Chuinn*, which is, in part, found in the *Tripartite Life of St. Patrick.*[101]

Sean More Ó Clumáin composed a poem for Tadhg Ó Conchobhair c.1340 in which he states "Is this a proof that the Prophecy is coming to pass?" (*An deimhin a-nos teacht don tairrngire?*)[102] This Tadhg could only be chosen by divine inspiration, or *balg fis*, and the poet explicitly states that the prophecy that undergirds Tadhg's kingship comes from God, and not from pagan sources like *Lia Fáil*, or the "Stone of Destiny," said to shriek when the true king would pass by.[103] The poet states that Tadhg marched on Cruacha (perhaps with reference to marching west from Tara?), and will destroy the castles of the foreigners (*gall*).[104] The prophecy that Tadhg fulfills is not described, although the reference to *Lia Fáil* and marching westward could allude to the prophecy in *Baile in Scáil*.

Another poem composed for the Ó Conchobhair kings of Connacht in the early thirteenth century, "Oh Man, Do not Sit on the Fairy Mound," includes a prophecy attributed to a benevolent spirit, Áine.[105] Ó Cuív stated that this prophetess appeared to protect Cathal Ó Conchobhair from being misled by another spirit, Aíbenn. Apparently, these spiritual women personified sovereignty goddesses associated with Munster, and the Munster goddesses were adopted by the Ó Conchobhair dynasty as they exercised hegemony over parts of Munster in the late twelfth century. A further connection to Munster was Cathal Ó Conchobhair's marriage to Mor Ó Briainn.[106] The poet traces the descent of the Ó Conchobhair dynasty from Cathal (d. 1010) through Cathal Crobderg and Áed mac Cathal, but skips Ruaidrí Ó Conchobhair's reign as king of Connacht or of Ireland. Cathal Crobderg was said to emanate from Cruachan as the single root that would support the men of Ireland, while his son Áed was described as Áed Idan, or "pure." Áed was to win many battles, and he too would rule at Cruacha.

This poem, however, makes no allusion to the prophecies of Bearchán or Columcille, nor does it make any reference to Cathal Crobderg as "the red handed one," nor does it refer to Áed as "the prophesied one. What this seems to suggest is that in the thirteenth century another stream of prophetic literature unrelated to Christian prophecy was also being used by Ó Conchobhair poets.

Most of these poems that include the reign of the patron appearing in prophecy also include an element of the arrival of the foreigners and the woe they brought. The general origin of this motif stems from the prophetic Irish literature concerning the arrival of Scandinavians in the eighth and ninth centuries. The prophecies discussed concerning Berchán, Colum Cille, and Patrick provide clear examples of this sort of reference. In the *Prophecy of Colum Cille,* the foreigners arrived on Lough Ree and siezed over the churches of Ireland. The prophecy was used earlier to describe contemporary events, which, in turn,

were used later by poets of the thirteenth and fourteenth centuries since the motif describing the Scandinavians also conveniently described the Anglo-Normans.

In "*Ceidtreabh Erend Inis Saimher*," the poet, Gilla Brigte Mac Con Midhe, refers to a prophecy regarding a hazel tree on which acorns representing newly arrived foreigners are covered over by branches representing the brown-haired sons of Conn.[107] The poet refers to the foreigners as "*Danair*," or "Dane.[108]" Though not further defined in the text, the term itself refers to the prophecy's origin in the earlier Viking invasions. The source of the prophecy was not uncovered by the editor of the poem, Williams, nor could it be uncovered for this work.

A theme directly relating to the concept of nationalism in bardic poetry is that of conflict between the two different peoples in Anglo-Norman Ireland. Joep Leersen devoted considerable attention to the theme in *Mere Irish-Fior Gael*.[109] Leersen based his approach upon a view that culture and nationality are ideological constructs, and that those constructs are the products not of some social situation, but of an underlying mental world view which requires explanation in and of itself.[110] The methodology employed by Leersen in this study is one of imagology, following the work of German literary theorists at Aachen University in the 1960s and 1970s. Leersen defines imagology as "…the study of the discursive or literary expression of national attitudes."[111] Further, this expression of national attitudes governs the very fabric of discursive or literary activity of a given period. The writer composes within a specific national tradition, and the product of that author's labor is received (or not) by that national tradition.

This imagalogical view of literature is also rooted in the innate dichotomy between those who are part of the nation and subscribe to the tradition and those who are termed "foreigner" by the native tradition. Thus, the issue with national identity, according to Leersen, involves defining not only how the national tradition identifies itself, but also how it defines itself in opposition to another group.[112] The images used to define the two groups are often viewed as stereotypical views of the other, but Leersen suggests that to move beyond these stereotypes, the scholar must understand to whom exactly the term is applied.

Leersen, however, refuses to see any connection between "nation" and geographical space; hence, he can not appreciate the nature of national identity in the period with which this study is concerned.[113] He argues that the idea of a nation is not connected to the political state or geographical space, and that the simple act of saying "we are a nation" suffices to create a nation.[114] With this definition, Jews who subscribe to certain dietary practices can be called a nation, as can any demographic group that has a common, shared self-identity. This is an unacceptable definition, since it does not differentiate between national self-identification and any other group's self-identification.

Leersen is fundamentally correct in his statement that the act of self-identification is made in opposition to another group; that act of identification is also based upon the recognition that the other or foreign group is "from there," and not "from here." In fact, as G. Cubitt posits, these perceived distinctions (whether real or not) define the self-identification, and these perceived distinctions can have cultural, religious and geographic dimensions.[115]

In this sense, the traditional use of the term "nation" to define a group which regards itself a people with shared tradition, history, and culture and which associates itself with a particular geographic area is appropriate. The theme of conflict in the poetry, then, is of paramount importance, since it represents groups of people fighting each other and those groups either invading or defending geographic space.

The theme of invasion and resistance to invasion was a common motif in the literary tradition of Ireland, especially before the arrival of the Anglo-Normans. R. Mark Scowcroft, in his discussion of *Leabhar Gabhála*, defines a recurrent pattern which he calls "invasion-myth."[116] He uses the term "myth" to describe "a narrative archetype sufficiently autonomous and pervasive in tradition to affect its growth."[117] In his discussion, Scowcroft clearly demonstrates that this invasion-myth was re-used throughout the tradition of *Leabhar Gabhála*, and that the binary oppositions, as the basis for the invasion-myth, were combined to form new oppositions in later examples of the *Leabhar Gabhála* tradition.[118] The sort of synthesis that took place in the creation of *Leabhar Gabhála* was an effort to provide significant form to what Scowcroft terms the "accidents of experience;" in other words, the real experience of the compilers of the *Leabhar Gabhála* tradition was explained within the themes of the narrative.[119]

It may even be said that the myth of invasion and conflict

continued throughout the Scandinavian invasions for the same reason, and that it was instrumental in the creation of *Cogad Gaedhel re Gallaibh*, or *The Battle of the Irish and the Foreigners*. Ní Mhaonaigh showed that *Cogad* is a twelfth-century composition written at the behest of a direct descendant of Brian Bórama, and that it is an example of political propaganda for the Ó Briain dynasty in general.[120] Ní Mhaonaigh's concern in her article aimed to justify a particular date for the original composition of the text (which she attributes to the reign of Brian Bórama's great-grandson, Muirchertach, or in the very early twelfth century[121]). But the title of the work itself suggests a basic diadic conflict between *Gaedhel* and *Gall*, and this dichotomy falls into the same sort of paradigm expounded by Scowcroft for *Leabhar Gabhála*. The conflict in the text is defined in terms of natives and foreign invaders. The text was composed, however, at a time when the larger Scandinavian incursions into Ireland had subsided. Further, the text was created to glorify the reign of Muirchertach, whose actions served as archetypes for the creation of the textual character of Brian. However, the core issue that defined the actions of the character Brian was the defense of a homogenous entity, Ireland, from an invader. Whether or not that homogenous entity actually existed in a political or institutional sense is immaterial; the point to remember is that the mental concept of that homogeneity did exist, and that concept framed the world view of the learned class in medieval Ireland which produced the literature.

The theme of foreign invasion is also found in bardic poetry of the thirteenth and fourteenth century, and actually follows Scowcroft's pattern of an invasion motif. Thirteenth and fourteenth century poets followed the pattern because it was part of the learned tradition with which the poets were versed. As well, the application of the paradigm of foreign invader proved popular because contemporary events corresponded to that tradition maintained by the learned scholars. Just as the scholars who composed and transmitted *Cogad* reapplied the myth of invasion to satisfy contemporary issues, the poets of later medieval Ireland continued to draw upon the diadic structure of native-invader to define the relationship between Gael and Anglo-Norman.

The relationship between native and invader expressed in this example reflected a base ideological relationship, but in reality this relationship rarely existed, nor did the diadic division between native and foreigner as represented in *Cogad* reflect the complex relationship between "Irish and Viking" or "Irish and Irish" at the time of Brian or his great-grandson Muirchertach. The relationship as defined in the literature was a means of explaining the distinction between native and foreigner, and while Irish and Viking as well as Irish and Anglo-Norman often interacted at all levels of society, the base distinctions applied to the identities of Irish, Viking, and Anglo-Norman were clear to those who maintained the tradition.

Several poems already cited in this study embody this motif since it also corresponds with either the prophecy of the ruler or the prophecy of a deliverer. As mentioned, part of the basis for such a prophecy is the notion of a people in need of rescue or salvation, who require that rescue from a hostile and foreign invader. Gilla Brigte Mac Con Midhe composed a poem for Áed Ó Domhnaill in which he states that the foreigners (*gall*) are in possession of Ireland (*Fódhla*), and that the prophesied Aodh would deliver *Fódhla* according to Bearchán's prophecy.[122] In a poem to Tadhg Ó Conchobhair (d. 1374) the prophecy refers to the destruction of the castles of the foreigner (*gall*).[123] In the late fourteenth or early fifteenth century Tadhg Og Ó Higinn composed a poem for Toirdhealbhach Ó Domhnail in which he cites the prophecy of Flann which described how the foreigners (*goill*) would be banished after the prophesied king re-establishes the three assemblies of Ireland.[124]

More often than not, though, the poets used the motif to frame actual events. In a lament for Maoileachlainn Ó Domhnaill , the poet Gilla Brigte Mac Con Midhe cries out that the land itself turned against his patron, and that it is to be blamed for his death because, unlike Ó Domhnaill, the land did not repel the foreigners.[125] There is even a reference to the fact that in *Leabhar Gabhála*, the seas did not allow a foreigner to breathe upon the land of Partholán, one of the mythic inhabitants of early Ireland.[126] In this case, though, the land betrayed Ó Domhnaill. Just as a faithful king ensures a prosperous land and an unfaithful king causes the land to suffer, the unfaithful land causes misfortune to befall even the best king.[127]

Gilla Brigte Mac Con Midhe also composed a lamentation poem for Brian Ó Néill after Ó Néill's death at the battle of Downpatrick in 1260. Brian's head was cut off by the foreigners (*le Galloibh*) and brought eastward to London. The poet portrayed the conflict with the foreigners as a game of chess in which the king had already been check-mated; the line reads "*Cogadh Gaoidheal re Galluibh,*" and clearly refers to text already discussed concerning the war of a previous Brian against Viking foreigners.[128] The

foreigners in this poem are once referred to as English (*Sacsanaigh*), but are more often referred to as *Gaill*.[129] If one reads the poem without any other historical evidence, it would seem that Ó Néill enjoyed the support of most, if not all, of the other Irish kings. The *Annals of the Four Masters* confirm this view, but other sources, including *Annals of Innisfallen* and *Caithréim Thoirdelbaigh*, suggest that the alliance behind Ó Néill was not as strong as Mac Con Midhe suggests. Further, Áed Buide Ó Néill, who succeeded Brian as king of Tír Eoghain, was an ally of the Anglo-Normans and no doubt benefited from Brian's death.[130]

In yet another poem attributed to Mac Con Midhe, the fertility of the land is associated with the reign of the Ó Néill kings (likely Brian [d. 1260] and his brothers Ruaidrí and Conchobhar), but this fertility is also tied to the absolute absence of foreigners in the land.[131] In the same stanza this theme is linked with an absence of crime during the reigns of these kings. The next stanza states that all the Gaoidhil of Ireland exist under one ruler. This one ruler is probably Niall Ruadh, the father of Brian, Ruaidrí and Conchobhar, since later in the poem the three sons are referred to as future high kings of Ireland (*trí hadhbhair aird ríogh Éirionn*).[132]

A poem composed for Magnus Mac Gowran (d. 1303) by Raghnall O Higinn compares Magnus to Brian Bóroimhe , and attributes the peace of the land to his rule.[133] The way that Magnus wages battle is compared to that of the ancient Greeks, and the land is better for his rule. However, only one reference to the foreigners (*gall*) exists in the text.[134] The poet extended considerable praise to Mac Gowran's skill in battle, and the ways in which that skill extended to all other aspects of his reign. The foes referred to in the text are often generic foes, or enemies, or other chiefs.[135] In other words, the poem lacks the dichotomy between native and foreigner, even though the poet is clearly referring to conflict with the Anglo-Normans.

Another Mác Gowran poem composed for Tomás (d. 1343) describes the same pattern. The poet, Maol Pádraig Mac Naimhin, praises the patron for his ability in battle, maintaining that he is a match for twenty opposing foes. His true home is Tara (*Teamhair*), meaning that he should rule from the mythic capital of Ireland. The enemies Tomás defeats are again generic enemies and are not identified by any notion of a particular foreigner or group with which he is in conflict.[136]

Maol Pádraig Mac Naimhin composed a poem to the same Tomás upon the latters' release from prison. Mac Naihmin described Tomás as a good king, upon whose capture the land suffered. All ruin visited the land while foes raided at will. The only example of clear comparison between native and foreigner lies in a stanza suggesting that Tomás' capture by the English would have been preferable to his treacherous capture and incarceration in a "foreign-like" (*gallghlas*) prison by a Gael (*mór dhamhnas an bhreith do-bhir / a bheith I ngallghlas Ghaoidhil*).[137]

In yet another poem concerning Tomás' release from prison, the poet Aonghus Ó hEoghusa complains that the lack of mutual love among the *Gaodhil* causes their ruin since internal rivalry over land allows the foreigner (*Goill*) to attack at will. Instead of attacking each other, the poet maintains, the Irish should unite against the foreigners.[138] Ó hEoghusa suggests the forces that Tomás should muster and the best method of attack to gain profit and avoid suffering.[139]

The noted poet Gofraidh Fionn Ó Dálaigh composed a poem for Murchadh Ó Madadháin between 1341 and 1371 describing Murchadh as another king who leads his men into battle.[140] The poet compares him to Murchadh, son of the eleventh century Brian Bóroimhe at the Battle of Clontarf. The banner waving around the patron Murchadh signifies his strength, and the banner's being raised aloft announces the time to face the foreigners (*Do tógbadh meirge Murchaidh / Is trát aighthe ar allmhurchaibh*).[141] When the banner is raised, the Irish raise a shout to proclaim their battle fury (*Gáir Gaoidheal as an giolla / Ag maoidheamh a móir-ghriolla*).[142] The hosts surround Murchadh, though, and when the banner falls, the foreigners are able to rally (*D'Éir claonta meirge Murchaidh / Aonta feisge ag Allmhurchaibh*).[143]

Related to the motif of the war with the foreigner, another theme presents the idea that Ireland itself was conquered by those foreigners, and that the people of Ireland allowed this state of affairs. When using this motif, the poets usually mean to describe a contemporary state of affairs with the Anglo-Normans. As well, though, because negotiating with foreigners is unacceptable, the poets encourage their patrons to change the situation through force.

In a poem for Domhnall Mór Ó Domhnaill (d. 1241), Gilla Brigte Mac Con Midhe encouraged the members of the Ceinéal Eoghain and the Ceinéal Conaill to put their differences aside and fight against the common enemy, the foreigners, since they all share common ancestry through their mythological ancestor, Niall Naoigheallach.[144] These two houses must rule Ireland, from sea to sea, and together should be holding the fair of Tailtiu (the fair held by the high king of Ireland at Tara). Their potential rivals, the southern Ó Néill, are weakened by the presence of the foreigners around Tara; the time is therefore right to retake the high kingship.[145] But the poem itself does not suggest that that Ó Domhnaill should rise against the foreigners; the poet merely states the noble histories of both families, and their fair and just rulership.[146] Ó Domhnaill, according the Mac Con Midhe, was responsible for drawing a circle of defense around Ireland in order to acquire cohesion, but ultimately the reason for Ó Domhnaill success is the prophecy of Columcille.[147]

Two centuries later, Tadg Óg Ó Higinn encouraged Maolruanaidh Ó Cearbhaill (d. 1443) to unite with the other Gaelic lords and drive the foreigners out of Ireland.[148] He warns Ó Cearbhaill to be wary of the foreigners, since they have fixed chains on the peoples of Ireland (*Mumha*). The situation had grown so desperate that even if a Gaoidheal had the right to rule the fields of Ireland, the occupation of the foreigners make that impossible. The only solution to this predicament is if some additional help is forthcoming.[149] The foreigners are in control of the lowlands and subjecting the Irish to bondage. Ó Higinn mentions that past peoples of Ireland united at the battle of Magh Mucroimhe[150] which should be the model for contemporary cooperation against the foreigners. Hinting at the possibility of allying with the Anglo-Normans, Ó Higinn tells Ó Cearbhaill the advantage in sharing the land with the foreigners, but only until the Irish can make a sensible union among themselves. Then the foreigners should be driven back over the sea.[151]

The inauguration rites of the Irish kings incorporated elements which created a formal link between the reign of the king and the land ruled by the king. In some cases, the king symbolically married the land, such that the land was portrayed as a woman whom the king supported as a wife.[152] The *Annals of Connacht* describe a scene using this imagery in the inauguration of Fedlimid Ó Conchobhair in 1310. First, Fedlimid was declared king by public acclamation. Second, he married the province of Connacht, after which he was waited on by his foster-father, Mac Diarmata, who was responsible for Fedlimid's election. Finally, the annalist states that this entire ceremony was performed in such a manner as to be remembered by the old men and recorded in old books.[153]

The exact vocabulary used by the annalist suggests that the inauguration included a feast, but here the word *feis* is more likely "to spend the night with." Hence, the festival at a royal center such as Tara, known as *Feis Temro*, could be seen as the wedding night celebration of the king joined with the land.[154]

If the land proved fertile during the reign of the king, this meant that the king himself was good and just; if the land was laid waste or suffered famine or pestilence it meant that the king was to blame. Inattentiveness to the land that he ruled or perhaps unopposed raids by other kings may have jeopordized the land. In either case, it was the responsibility of the king to protect and nurture the land. Concerning the death of Cathal Croibdearg in 1224 the *Annals of Connacht* record that

> "A heavy and terrible rain fell in Connacht this year, which brought about disease and very great sickness among the cows and beasts of those regions after they had eaten the grass and leaves; and when men drank of the milk of these cattle and ate of their flesh, they suffered internal pains and various diseases. Nor was it strange that these portentous things should happen in Connacht, for another great affliction befell the country, that is the loss of Cathal Crobderg, son of Toirrdelbach Ó Conchobair, king of Connacht."[155]

Even in the thirteenth century, then, the concept of a relationship between the good king and the fertility of the land was recognized.

This motif in itself is not representative of any sort of national ideology in the thirteenth and fourteenth centuries, nor is it unique to Ireland.[156] In the later poems (from the late sixteenth century) bards personified Ireland as a woman in a manner that might be called nationalistic. The personification of Ireland as a woman, Cathleen Ní Houlihan, in need of a good king was very commonplace in seventeenth and eighteenth century poems, and was framed within the context of an Ireland which had essentially lost most qualities of Gaelic society.[157]

On the other hand, T.F. O'Rahilly recognized the relationship between the king and the sovereignty goddess -- a personification of either Ireland or the local territory ruled by the king.[158] *Baile in Scáil* refers to Ireland or *Ériu*

as a beautiful woman crowned with a gold crown and seated on a throne, serving draughts in a gold cup to each successive king of Ireland.[159]

Direct references to the land as a spouse of the king are fairly common in the thirteenth and fourteenth centuries. Indeed, this motif is common throughout the corpus of bardic poetry. In a poem for Niall Ó Gairmleadhaigh (d. 1261), Gilla Brigte Mac Con Midhe explains the genealogy of the Ó Ghairmleadhaigh with the statement that the seed of this family surpass in nobility the seeds of wheat.[160] Niall, as the lord of the territory, acquired the keys of kingship, likening the land to hosts of women who are without husbands until the rightful king gains the kingship *(treabha ban nach bí ag fearaibh / rí go ngabh Ó Gairmleadhaigh)*.[161]

An inaugural poem composed for Áed Ó Conchobhair more clearly refers to the relationship between the wedding of the goddess of sovereignty to the king and the wedding of the land to the king.[162] *Éire* drinks a draught, and shares it freely with Áed since he is her appropriate spouse.[163] Ireland *(Banbha)* awaits the reign of Áed with great anticipation, and dons her most beautiful garment for him *(Gabhais Banbha a brat torraidh / uimpe I gcoinne Í Chonchubhair)*.[164] She is a darling lover of the legendary high king Cormac mac Airt *(leannán caigealta Chormaic)*.[165] In addition to describing this loving relationship between Áed and *Éire*, the poet describes *Éire* as a woman in bondage *(tromdhámha in Éirinn dá hár / géibhinn congmhála Cruachan)*.[166] She is in bondage because of the actions of the foolish Diarmait Mac Murchadha and the other men of Leinster, who originally brought the foreigners to Ireland.[167] Áed accuses the foreigners of having taken his realm *(Goill do gabháil a domhain / agras Aodh Ó Conchubhair)*.[168] Despite Ireland's bondage, she will achieve freedom by making love with Áed (here referred to as the king of Port Partholáin, another reference to one of the mythological rulers of Ireland from *Leabhor Gabhala* [*Do léig d'Éirinn a hanáil / fes le rí Phuirt Phartholáin*]).[169] Since foreigners also oppress other kings of Ireland, the poet suggests that they accept Áed as their king.[170]

Rarely was the High Kingship of Ireland actually made manifest. In an ideal sense, the dynastic kings ruled the four provinces of Ireland, Leinster, Munster, Connacht, and Ulster. These provinces were subdivided into smaller *túatha*, each ruled by a king such that there were over one hundred "kings" in Ireland at the time of the arrival of the

Anglo-Normans. Several kings (Ruaidrí Ó Conchobhair, Toirrdelbach Ó Conchobhair, and Brian Bóroimhe), through success in battle, shrewd political relationships, and control of their own dynasties, succeeded in claiming kingship over all Ireland. However the annals refer to kings as "High King with opposition" or "High King without opposition" which suggests that a claim to be the ruler of all Ireland was often met with contention.

In some cases, the land that the king ruled was compared to the reign of the High Kingship of Ireland itself. The *túath*, land that the king ruled, might be considered "so very well ruled" that it would be obvious that the king possessed the potential to be High King. In other words, the poet made the claim that by ruling his land justly and faithfully, the king actually proved that he had the qualifications of a High King.

Oddly enough, one of the earlier poems using this motif was not even composed in Ireland, but on the Isle of Man, for Raghnall, King of Man, sometime between 1187 and 1208.[171] It is clearly one of the earliest surviving examples of bardic poetry from the thirteenth century. Raghnall was made king in 1187 after the death of his father Godred in 1187. According to Ó Cuív, the mere fact that the poet composed a poem for Ragnall suggests a strong connection between Man and other Gaelic realms.[172] Raghnall also claimed connection to the de Courcy family by marriage, and when Hugh de Lacy defeated de Courcy in Ulster in 1204, he went to Raghnall in search of an ally. Together de Courcy and Raghnall invaded Ulster with a large force in 1205 but were defeated by Walter de Lacy. Raghnall returned to Man, and for the next two decades competed with his brother Olaf for control of Man and the Isles. At the same time, Raghnall was at pains to convince Kings John and Henry III that he could be a faithful subject.

The poet declares that the land of Raghnall, *Eamhain Abhlach*,[173] is Man's version of Tara[174] (*Emain na n-aball cumra / Teamair Mhanann cin mhebla*), and by juxtaposing the two the poet declares that Raghnall has the makings of a High King. Perhaps this was not an imaginary concept for the poet or Raghnall; later in the poem the poet encourages Raghnall to plunder Dublin (*Airgfe Ath Cliath in chomlaind / 's do sciath ar scath do glanbhuinn*) conceivably alluding to the possibility that Raghnall might stage an invasion of Dublin, which, in the context of the first decade of the thirteenth century, may not have been an extreme idea.

The land of Tomás Mác Gowran (discussed previously) was compared to all of Ireland itself.[175] The poet reflects the reality that Tomás controls only one tuath among the many existing in Ireland. However this is no matter, since that land proves so exceptional that Tomás is content with that estate alone.[176]

The house of Diarmait Ó Briain was also compared to Tara in such a way as to describe potential aspirations for the High Kingship.[177] The poet of this poem, Gofraid Fionn Ó Dálaigh, cites an adage that one moves from a small house to a large house so that one's resources may also be enlarged; the house in which Diarmait resides is large, Ó Dálaigh says, but the one to which he aspires is much larger (*giodh mór an treabh (as a ró a ruaig) / mó an teach a ttéid*).[178] Several quatrains later, the poet clearly employs this adage when the two houses are plainly identified as the House of Tál and the House of Teamhair.[179] In a similar manner, the bard for Tomás Mág Gowran sidesteps the fact that Tomás only ruled a small tuath with the observation that ruling this marvelous tuath compared to ruling all Ireland. Ó Dálaigh mentions that the House of Tál holds far less fame than Tara. yet the latter does not bring more joy, love or fame.[180] Ó Dálaigh further juxtaposed the houses by linking each to one of the mythological sovereignty goddesses who represent the land. When *Banbha* (one of those names for Ireland) is given to a man, Tara becomes his castle (*an Bhanbha mar do-bhearair d'fhior / Teamhair a theagh*).[181] When *Mumha* (Munster, the southern province of Ireland) is given to a king, though, Tál becomes his castle (*Teach ríogh Mumhan ainm Tighe Táil / tugadh tuir Bhaoi*).[182] Ó Dálaigh implies that greater things are in store for Ó Briain and later warns Ó Briain that it would be grievous to leave his ancestors' land. To do so, in order to live in the Land of Midhe, however, confers no shame, since that land contains Tara of the kings and *Lia Fál* (the Stone of Destiny), not to mention the other ancient monuments of the Boyne Valley, including Aongus' fairy fort (Newgrange) and Uisneach, the mythological center of Ireland.[183] After recounting Ó Briain's pedigree at length,[184] Ó Dálaigh suggests the land is not protected by forbears; instead, it is protected by one with a strong hand and noble blood. Noble blood alone does not make the king, in other words, but the noble blood that is willing to be spilled will ultimately win the land of Ireland.[185] Ó Dálaigh elaborates by reflecting on the relationship between the king and the land; it is difficult for her to be without a ruler, and it is more difficult on her, indeed, when the hero given to her is driven to disaster.[186]

Áengus Ó Dálaigh describes the fortress of Áed Ó Conchobhair (d. 1309) at Cloonfree . Though not very large, the poet maintains that the fortress equals any other fortress in Ireland. While the fortress of Aodh Eangach includes but one rampart, around Tara there are seven (*Aonmhúr atá ag Áodh Eangach / seacht múir fá mhúr cláoin-Teamhrach*).[187] Though it only has one rampart, the fortress of Cloonfree is as secure as Tara because Áed (the prophesied one) owns this fortress. The fortress not only exceeds the glory of Tara, but it is actually likened to Troy (*Ráith Áodha 'na haimsir fein / créd acht Tráoi oile íséin?*).[188] Áed incurs no reproach to abandon Croghan (the ancient capital of Connacht), if he aims to take up residence at Cloonfree (*Tréigion mhúir Chruachna ar Chlúain Fráoich*).[189]

Conclusions

If we define a nation as an association between a particular group of people sharing a common history and tradition and a particular geographical space, then bardic poetry of the thirteenth and fourteenth centuries undoubtedly expresses that idea of a nation. This point is clear in light of the three criteria discussed in this chapter: prophecy, conflict, and the relationship between king and land.

A king could claim the right to kingship on the basis of descent from a primordial king, descent from a great historic king, or by a sort of acclamation by the nobles of a territory.[190] In a few cases, a king could even claim his legitimacy to rule based upon authority granted to him by the King of England. This was precisely the case with Cathal Croibderg or his son Áed Ó Conchobhair. By declaring that an ancient prophecy foretold a particular king's reign of Ireland, a patron's poet could create yet another form of legitimation for a king.

The first motif investigated, that of prophecy, yielded two basic ideas imbedded within the prophecies. First, the idea of a prophesied deliverer presupposes a coherent group in need of deliverance. Aodh Eangach was prophesied to deliver Ireland itself, not a smaller *túath*, nor one of the four provinces of Ireland, nor just one particular group of people or ruling dynasty. The poets may have used the motif for literary effect and emphasis; nevertheless, they would not likely employ a motif that was incomprehensible to the patron and an audience. We can thereby state that the poets, their patrons and their audiences maintained at the very least a mental representation or ideology of a unified self-image as Gael. The second idea discovered

in the prophecies reveals that references made to those in need of deliverance point to Ireland itself, not a sub-unit of Ireland. They do not say Connacht or Ulster need to be saved nor do they refer to a particular royal dynasty.

The second group of poetic motifs investigated in this chapter involves the concept of conflict. This motif, based upon a multi-layer tradition maintained by the learned class of Ireland, has its roots in *Lebor Gabála*. The basic diads established between native and foreigner and between this land and that land continued throughout the early medieval period in *Cogad*. By the thirteenth and fourteenth centuries, when the learned scholars of Ireland turned to the composition of bardic poetry, the theme of diadic conflict featured so strongly in the tradition that it proved impossible to compose poems without this theme. As well, the motif adapted as readily to the contemporary situation between native and Anglo-Norman in the thirteenth and fourteenth centuries as it had to the situations during the period of Viking invasions.

On most levels Gael and Anglo-Norman often cooperated for their own personal benefit, just as the Gael and the Viking raiders did before them. It is also true that the Gael never formed a cohesive, sustained front against the Anglo-Norman. These facts do not diminish the power of the motif as expressed in the poetry. Human beings always live within constructs of which contain conflicting mental frames. The medieval poets and their patrons required their situation to be placed within a traditional frame. Part of that frame included the casting of Anglo-Normans as foreigners, and the description of themselves as oppressed, noble warriors willing to defend their lands at all cost.

The final theme investigated pertains to the poet's description of various types of land in relation to the patron. In several cases, the poets personified the land of Ireland as a sovereignty goddess; again, the poets dipped into their bag of images to paint a positive image of their patrons. But, further, the personification was of Éire herself, and not a generic goddess. Although the patrons often ruled small territories, the poets cast them as the husband of Ireland and not of a mere local territory.

In several other examples, either the land ruled by the patron was compared to the high kingship of Ireland, or the capital of the land ruled by the patron was compared to Tara (which, by the thirteenth century, existed more as an idea rather than a real place, since Tara was located in lands controlled by the Anglo-Normans). Certainly the poet used this motif in order to extol the status of the patron; but we may again consider the possibility that the poets used motifs meaningful to the patron. In this sense we may conclude that the concept of an entity, Ireland, ruled by a single, centrally located king was not inconceivable but was both impractical and nearly impossible to attain.

[1] Brian Ó Cuív, "Literary Creation and Irish Historical Tradition," *Proceedings of the British Academy*, XLIX (1963): 233-62.

[2] Katharine Simms, *From Kings to Warlords* (Sussex, Boydell Press: 1987); Katharine Simms, "Bardic Poetry as a Historical Source," in *The Writer as Witness: Historical Studies XVI*, ed. T. Dunne (Cork: Cork University Press, 1987), 58-75; Kenneth Nicholls, *Gaelic and Gaelicised Ireland in the Middle Ages* (Dublin: Gill Publishing: 1972).

[3] Brendan Bradshaw, "Native Reaction;" T.J. Dunne, "The Gaelic Response to Conquest and Colonisation: The Evidence of the Poetry," *Studia Hibernica, XX* (1980): 7-30; Michelle O Riordan, *The Gaelic Mind and the Collapse of the Gaelic World* (Cork: Field Day Books, 1990); Leersen, *Mere Irish and Fíor-Ghael*; Ellis, "Nationalist Historiography."

[4] For instance, see Bradshaw, "Native Reaction," 65-66, and Dunne, "The Gaelic Response to Conquest and Colonisation," 11-13.

[5] The reasons for this gap are very complex. On one hand, the large amount of material dating from later periods seems to draw scholars more readily. The gap might also reflect divisions between the branches of medieval Irish studies. Linguists (such as Damian MacManus at Trinity College, Dublin) tend to be purely concerned with the literary and morphological aspects of the poetry while historians are generally not able to devote the effort necessary to comprehensively understand the linguistic complexity of the poetry. For example, it is curious to note that Katharine Simms, one of the contemporary scholars who has used bardic poetry as historical source material, has never published a critical edition of a poem. And, finally, there is a tendency in Irish medieval studies to focus on historical politics as opposed to literary history, the history of thought, or the history of ideology. Bardic poetry as a source can not be treated in the same way as government rolls or chancery documents because it is literature.

[6] Damien MacManus, "Classical Modern Irish," in *Progress in Medieval Irish Studies*, ed. Kim McCone and Katharine Simms (Maynooth: Department of Old Irish, St. Patrick's College, 1996), 165.

[7] Osborn Bergin, *Irish Bardic Poetry*, ed. David Greene and Fergus Kelly (Dublin: Dublin Institute for Advanced Studies, 1984), 3.

[8] Bergin, *Irish Bardic Poetry*, 4.

[9] The ability of the individual bardic poet to call upon the vast corpus of exemplars becomes clear when individual poems are compared with the *Bardic Syntactical Tracts* and *Irish Grammatical Tracts*. These are two collections of bardic teaching tools, with examples of both good and bad poetry. Because much of the poetry has been digitized by the Department of Irish at Trinity College, Dublin, it is possible to cross reference particular lines from a poem with the these grammatical reference books to show that grammarians were well aware of the tradition that preceded them (See below). See Lambert McKenna, *Bardic Syntactical Tracts* (Dublin: Dublin Institute for Advance Studies: 1944); Osborn Bergin, *Irish Gramatical Tracts I.* in *Eriu* 8 (1916); II. §1-11, *Eriu* 8 (1916); II. §12-87, *Eriu* 9 (1921-23); II. §88-207, *Eriu* 10 (1926-28); III, IV. *Eriu* 14 (1946); V. *Eriu* 7 (1955).

[10] Eleanor Knott, *Irish Syllabic Poetry, 2nd Edition* (Dublin: Dublin Institute for Advanced Studies, 1994), 13-20.

[11] Fergus Kelly, *A Guide to Early Irish Law*, (Dublin: Dublin Institute for Advanced Studies, 1988), 47n72.

[12] James Carney, "Literature in Irish, 1169-1534," in *A New History of Ireland, ii., Medieval*, ed. Art Cosgrove (Oxford: Clarendon Press, 1981), 694.

[13] Kelly, *A Guide to Early Irish Law*, 43.

[14] Bergin, *Irish Bardic Poetry*, 4; Kelly, *A Guide to Early Irish Law*, 43-44.

[15] *Annals of Connacht*, s.a. 1414.

[16] Kelly, *A Guide to Early Irish Law*, 43.

[17] Bergin cites an eighteenth century narrative that supposedly describes the training of bards at that time; the passage maintains that the method of training had not changed from the middle ages; Bergin, *Irish Bardic Poetry*, 5-8. However, several poems edited by Bergin allude to a mode of training that has similarities with the above quoted passage; Bergin, *Irish Bardic Poetry*, no.

27, 38, 42.

[18] Kelly, *A Guide to Early Irish Law*, 47.

[19] Bergin, *Irish Bardic Poetry*, 21; Kelly, A Guide to Early Irish Law, 43-49.

[20] The túath has two related meanings in medieval Ireland. In the first sense, it can mean the tribal grouping of people who are ruled by a king, and in the other sense it can mean the land that the people inhabit that is also ruled by the king; Dictionary of the Irish Language, s.v. túath.

[21] Kelly, *A Guide to Early Irish Law,* 46.

[22] Kelly, *A Guide to Early Irish Law*, 45.

[23] Simms, "Bardic Poetry as a Historical Source," 69.

[24] Carney, "Literature in Irish," 695.

[25] Simms, "Bardic Poetry as Historical Source," 60.

[26] "A Ghearóid déana mo dháil," ed. Lambert McKenna, *Irish Monthly* (Sept, 1919): 509-14.

[27] Carney, "Literature in Irish," 696.

[28] Katharine Simms, "Literacy and the Irish Bards," in *Literacy in Medieval Celtic Societies,* ed. Huw Pryce (Cambridge: Cambridge University Press, 1998), 238-9.

[29] See also Carney, "Literature in Irish," 690-1.

[30] Simms, "Bardic Poetry as Historical Source," 58-61.

[31] These two projects work together for the scholar. On one hand, the scholar can use the Catalogue to search for relevant material based upon poets, patrons, or motifs. On the other hand, the corpus created by MacManus allows the scholar to search a vast amount of text for particular vocabulary or phrases, and to isolate passages from poems that were used by the poets in *Bardic Syntactical Tracts* or *Irish Grammatical Tracts.*

[32] *The Book of Magauran: Leabhar Méig Shamhradháin,* ed. Lambert McKenna (Dublin: Institute for Advanced Studies, 1947). The manuscript from which the edition is taken is one of the earliest examples of a duanaire, or family book of poems that contains eulogies devoted to the family.

[33] Carney, "Literature in Irish," 692.

[34] Katharine Simms, "Irish Literature: Bardic Poetry," in *Dictionary of the Middle Ages*, ed. J.R. Strayer, Vol. 6 (1985), 535b.

[35] See the collection of essays in James Lydon, ed., *Law and Disorder in Thirteenth Century Ireland: The Dublin Parliament of 1297* (Dublin: Four Courts Press, 1997).

[36] It should also be noted that the Catalogue only has five fields for manuscripts, and that some of the poems exist in as many as fifty manuscripts. However, the Catalogue records the five earliest manuscript editions of each poem if there are more than five.

[37] Marc Caball, "The Gaelic Mind and the Collapse of the Gaelic World: An Appraisal," *Cambridge Medieval Celtic Studies*. 25 (Summer, 1993): 89.

[38] Caball, "The Gaelic Mind: An Appraisal," 90.

[39] Brian Ó Cuív, *The Irish Bardic Duanair or "Poem Book,"* (Dublin: National Library of Ireland, 1973), 11.

[40] Ó Cuív, *The Irish Bardic Duanair*, 11-12.

[41] Caball, "The Gaelic Mind: An Appraisal," 90-91.

[42] This has been a point debated by scholars, but the consensus at present is that the poems were produced primarily for oral recitation, and then later recorded in manuscript form. See MacManus, "Classical Modern Irish," 181.

[43] MacManus, "Classical Modern Irish," 165-87.

[44] O Buachalla, "Aodh Eangach and the Irish Hero-King," 202.

[45] *Topographia Hibernie*, III.26 ed. O'Meara: 95.

[46] *Annals of Ulster*, s.a. 1214; *Annals of Loch Ce*, s.a. 1214.

[47] Phillips, J.R.S. "Edward II and the Prophets," in *England and the Fourteenth Century: Proceedings of the 1985 Harlaxton Symposium,* ed. W.M. Ormond (London,

1986), 189-201.

[48] R.R. Davies, *The Revolt of Owain Glyndwr* (Oxford: Oxford University Press, 1995), 86-7.

[49] Elissa Henken, *National Redeemer: Owain Glyndwr in Welsh Tradition* (Cardiff: University of Wales Press, 1996), 48.

[50] Davies, *The Revolt of Owain Glyndwr,* 160-3.

[51] Walter of Bower, *Scotichronicon,* viii, ed. Watt, 110-11.

[52] A.D. Carr, *Medieval Wales* (London: St. Martin's Press, 1995), 115.

[53] *Expugnatio Hibernica,* 177.

[54] Henken, *National Redeemer,* 28.

[55] Henken, *National Redeemer,* 44.

[56] Henken, *National Redeemer,* 44.

[57] See, for instance, Benjamin Hudson, *The Prophecy of Berchán: Irish and Scottish High-Kingship in the Early Middle Ages* (London: Greenwood Press, 1996), 21.

[58] *Lebor Gabala,* or *The Book of Invasions,* is a composite text that incorporates several different mythological invasions of Ireland.

[59] Bergin, *Irish Bardic Poetry,* no. 43.

[60] Kuno Meyer, "Das ende von Baile in Scáil." *Zeitschrift fur Celtische Philologie.* XII (1918): 237; the text is extremely difficult and fragmentary, and there is the possibility that this particular passage does not really refer to an Aodh Eangach per se.

[61] Kuno Meyer, "Mitteilungen aus Irischen Handschriften," *Zeitschrift fur Celtische Philologie,* iii (1918): 460.

[62] Eugene O'Curry, *Lectures on the Manuscript Materials of Ancient Irish History* (Dublin: Four Courts Reprint of 1861 Edition, 1995), 388-9.

[63] O'Curry, *Lectures on Manuscript Materials,* 388.

[64] *Cogadh Gaedhel re Gallaibh, The War of the Gaedhil*

with the Gaell, ed. J.H. Todd (London: Rolls Series 48, 1867), 204.

[65] A. O. Anderson, "The Prophecy of Bearchán." *Zeitschrift Fur Celtische Philologie.* XVIII (1930): 1-54.

[66] Hudson, *Prophecy of Berchán,* 21.

[67] Anderson, "The Prophecy of Bearchán," 29.

[68] Hudson, *The Prophecy of Berchán,* 35.

[69] *Dictionary of the Irish Language,* s.v. *éngach.*

[70] Brian O Cuiv, "A Poem for Cathal Croibhdhearg O Conchubhair," *Eriu.* XXXIV (1983): 161-71.

[71] A coarse fish is a particular type of freshwater fish native to waters of the British Isles. The name "course" does not have anything to do with the actual features of the fish itself.

[72] Quiggin, "A Poem by Gilbride MacNamee," q. 7.

[73] E.C. Quiggin, "A Poem by Gilbride MacNamee in Praise of Cathal O Conor," *Miscellany Presented to Kuno Meyer* (Dublin, 1912), 172-4.

[74] Quiggin, "A Poem by Gilbride MacNamee," q. 10.

[75] Quiggin, "A Poem by Gilbride MacNamee," q. 7.

[76] "*Connuimh rom taighidh a Aodh*" (RIA MS 490, p. 162): q. 20.

[77] "*Connuimh rom taighidh a Aodh,*" q. 16.

[78] "*Connuimh rom taighidh a Aodh,*" q. 20-1.

[79] Anderson, "The Prophecy of Bearchán," q. 72.

[80] *Annals of Connacht,* s.a. 1224.

[81] *Calendar of Documents Related to Ireland,* no. 653.

[82] "*Beg nár bháith Áodh oighidh cuinn*" RIA MS. A/iv/3.

[83] Quiggin, "O'Conor's House at Cloonfree;" Thomas Finan and Kieran O Conor, "The Moated Site at Cloonfree," *Journal of the Galway Archaeological and*

Historical Society (July, 2002).

84 Quiggin, "O'Conor's House at Cloonfree," q. 14.

85 Quiggin, "O'Conor's House at Cloonfree," q. 2.

86 Quiggin, "O'Conor's House at Cloonfree," q. 37.

87 Simms, *From Kings to Warlords*, 27.

88 Quiggin, "O'Conor's House at Cloonfree," qq. 38-39.

89 The O'Donnel dynasty was located in north west Ulster and was often allied to the O'Connor dynasty of Connacht.

90 *"Tainig tairngire na n-earlamh." The Poems of Giolla Brighde Mac Con Midhe.* ed. and trans. N.J. Williams, (London: Irish Texts Society, 1980), no. vi.

91 *"Tainig tairngire na n-earlamh,"* q. 4.

92 *"Tainig tairngire na n-earlamh,"* qq. 5-7.

93 Simms, *From King to Warlord*, 27; *"Connuim rom taighidh a Aodh,"* qq. 20-1.

94 *"Tainig tairngire na n-éarlamh,"* qq. 10-13.

95 *"Tainig tairngire na n-éarlamh,"* q. 20.

96 *"Tainig tairngire na n-éarlamh,"* q. 3.

97 *Cogadh Gaedhel re Gallaibh*, 204.

98 *"Beag nach lor a luaidhim dh*e." *The Book of Magauran*, no. 21.

99 *"Beag nach lor a luaidhim dhe,"* qq. 19-26.

100 *"Beag nach lor a luaidhim dhe,"* qq. 24, 26.

101 O'Curry, *Lectures on Manuscript Materials*, 385

102 *"An deimhin anois teacht an Tairrngaire," Aithdioghluim Dána, A Mischellany of Irish Bardic Poetry, Historical and Religious, including the Historical Poems of the Duanaire in the Yellow Book of Lecan.* ed. and trans. Lambert McKenna (London: Irish Texts Society, 1939-40), no. 4, q. 2.

103 *"An deimhin anois teacht an Tairrngaire,"* q. 14.

104 *"An deimhin anois teacht an Tairrngaire,"* q. 3-4.

105 Brian Ó Cuív, "A Poem of Prophecy on Ua Conchobair Kings of Connacht," *Celtica*, 19 (1987): 31-54.

106 I am indebted to Prof. Helen Perros for pointing me to this connection.

107 "Ceidtreabh Erend Inis Saimher," *Poems of Giolla Brighde Mac Con Midhe.* ed. and trans. N.J. Williams (London: Irish Texts Society, 1980), no. 5, qq. 21-22.

108 *Dictionary of the Irish Language*, s.v. *danar*.

109 Leersen, *Mere Irish, Fíor Ghael*, 6-7.

110 Leersen, *Mere Irish, Fior-Ghael*, 2, 4.

111 Leersen, *Mere Irish, Fior-Ghael*, 7.

112 Leersen, *Mere Irish, Fior-Ghael*, 8-9.

113 Leersen, *Mere Irish, Fior-Ghael*, 15.

114 Leersen, *Mere Irish, Fior-Ghael*, 17.

115 G. Cubitt, "Introduction," *Imagining Nations.* ed. G. Cubitt (Manchester: Manchester University Press, 1998), 6.

116 *Leabhar Gabhála*, or *The Book of Invasions*, is a mythological text that was core to the learned tradition of Ireland. The text is mainly concerned with several successive invasions of Ireland in pre-history and culminates with the arrival of the present inhabitants of Ireland. While superficially the text seems to represent a an Irish "origin myth," Leabhar Gabhála also integrates the early history of Ireland with Biblical history by suggesting that some of the early individuals in Ireland were descendants of Noah.

117 R. Mark Scowcroft, "*Leabhar Gabhála*, Part II: the Growth of the Tradition," *Ériu* xxxix (1988): 33.

118 Scowcroft, "*Leabhar Gabhála*, Part II," 38.

119 Scowcroft, "*Leabhar Gabhála*, Part II," 45.

120 Máire Ní Mhaonaigh, "*Cogad Gáedel re Gallaib*: Some Dating Considerations," *Peritia* 9 (1995): 356.

121 Ní Mhaonaigh, "*Cogad*," 377.

122 "*Tainig tairngire na n-éarlamh*," qq. 3, 5-7.

123 "*An deimhin a-nos teacht an tairrngire?*" q.4.

124 "*La i dTeamhraigh ag Toirdhealbhach*," q. 2.

125 "*Do shlán uaim, a Áth Seanaigh*," *The Poems of Giolla Brighde Mac Con Midhe*. ed. and trans. N.J. Williams (London: Irish Texts Society, 1980), q. 2.

126 "*Do shlán uaim, a Áth Seanaigh*," q. 5.

127 "*Do shlán uaim, a Áth Seanaigh*," q. 15.

128 "*Aoidhe mo chroidhe ceann Briain*," *The Poems of Giolla Brighde Mac Con Midhe*. ed. and trans. N.J. Williams (London: Irish Texts Society, 1980), q. 14.

129 "*Aoidhe mo chroidhe ceann Briain*," q. 33.

130 *The Poems of Giolla Brighde Mac Con Midhe*. ed. and trans. N.J. Williams (London: Irish Texts Society, 1980), 309.

131 "*Righe Conaire ag Cloinn Néill*," *The Poems of Giolla Brighde Mac Con Midhe*. ed. and trans. N.J. Williams (London: Irish Texts Society, 1980), q. 7.

132 "*Righe Conaire ag Cloinn Néill*," q. 12.

133 "*Brian a-nois do-ním do Mhaghnus*," *The Book of Magauran*, ed. Lambert McKenna (Dublin, Dublin Institute for Advanced Studies, 1947), no. 11, qq.1-3.

134 "*Brian a-nois do-ním do Mhaghnus*," q. 19.

135 "*Brian a-nois do-ním do Mhaghnus*," qq. 6, 15, 29.

136 "*Buaidh cagaish ar cath mBréifne*," ," *The Book of Magauran*, ed. Lambert McKenna (Dublin, Dublin Institute for Advanced Studies, 1947), no. 20, qq. 5-6.

137 "*Ní beag an léansa ar Leath Cuinn*," ," *The Book of Magauran*, ed. Lambert McKenna (Dublin, Dublin Institute for Advanced Studies, 1947), no. 22, q.8.

138 "*Millte Éire d'iomthnúdh Ghaoidheal*," ," *The Book of Magauran*, ed. Lambert McKenna (Dublin, Dublin Institute for Advanced Studies, 1947), no. 23, q.1.

139 "*Millte Éire d'iomthnúdh Ghaoidheal*," q. 20.

140 "*Do togbhadh meirge Murchaidh*," *Irish Monthly* 47, 102: qq. 1-3.

141 "*Do togbhadh meirge Murchaidh*," q. 1.

142 "*Do togbhadh meirge Murchaidh*," q. 17.

143 "*Do togbhadh meirge Murchaidh*," q. 27.

144 "*Caidhead ceithre teallaigh Teamhra*," *The Poems of Giolla Brighde Mac Con Midhe*. ed. and trans. N.J. Williams (London: Irish Texts Society, 1980), qq. 4-5.

145 "*Caidhead ceithre teallaigh Teamhra*," q. 5.

146 "*Caidhead ceithre teallaigh Teamhra*," qq. 6-7.

147 "*Caidhead ceithre teallaigh Teamhra*," qq. 23-4, 31.

148 "*Dénaidh comhaonta a chlann Éibhir*," Aithdioghluim Dana, ed. Lambert McKenna (London: Irish Texts Society, 1939), no. 26, q. 1.

149 "*Dénaidh comhaonta a chlann Éibhir*," q. 6.

150 "*Dénaidh comhaonta a chlann Éibhir*," q. 22.

151 "*Dénaidh comhaonta a chlann Éibhir*," q. 30.

152 T.F. O'Rahilly, "On the Origins of the Name Érainn and Ériu," *Eriu* 14 (1943-48): 14-21.

153 *Annals of Connacht,* s.a. 1310.

154 F.J. Byrne, *Irish Kings and High-Kings* (London: B.T. Batsford, 1973), 17.

155 *Annals of Connacht,* s.a. 1224.

156 William A. Nitze, "The Fisher King in the Grail Romances," *Publications of the Modern Language Association of America* 24 (1909): 365-418.

[157] Declan Kiberd, "Literature in Ireland," *The Oxford Illustrated History of Ireland*, ed. R.F. Foster (Oxford: Oxford University Press, 1987), 285-6.

[158] T.F. O'Rahilly, "On the Origin of the Names Érainn and Ériu," *Éigse*, 14 (1943-48): 14.

[159] O'Rahilly, "The Names Érainn and Ériu," 14.

[160] "*Ata sund senchas Muain*," *The Poems of Giolla Brighde Mac Con Midhe*, ed. and trans. Williams (London: Irish Text Society), no. 12.

[161] "*Ata sund senchas Muain*," q. 23.

[162] Séamus Mac Mathúna, "An Inaugural Ode to Hugh O'Connor?" *Zeitschrift für Celtische Philologie*. 49-50 (1997): 548-575.

[163] Mac Mathúna, "An Inaugural Ode to Hugh O'Connor?" q. 25.

[164] Mac Mathúna, "An Inaugural Ode to Hugh O'Connor?" q. 26.

[165] Mac Mathúna, "An Inaugural Ode to Hugh O'Connor?" q. 28.

[166] Mac Mathúna, "An Inaugural Ode to Hugh O'Connor?" q. 19.

[167] Mac Mathúna, "An Inaugural Ode to Hugh O'Connor?" q. 11.

[168] Mac Mathúna, "An Inaugural Ode to Hugh O'Connor?" q. 19; the translation by Mac Mathúna is faulty in this line where he states that Aodh "proclaims the banishment of the Foreigners from the world." Surely Aodh is stating that the Foreigners have invaded his world, implying the concept of "one's world."

[169] Mac Mathúna, "An Inaugural Ode to Hugh O'Connor?" q. 30.

[170] Mac Mathúna, "An Inaugural Ode to Hugh O'Connor?" q. 21-22.

[171] Brian Ó Cuív, "Poem in Praise of Raghnall, King of Man," *Eigse* 8 (1956/7): 283-301.

[172] Ó Cuív, "Poem in Praise of Raghnall," 285.

[173] Ó Cuív explains that the term "Eamhain Albhlach" no doubt stems from the Irish mythological concept of the otherworldly island or an overseas fairlyland in which immortals dwelt. He postulates that in this poem the term does in fact refer particularly to the Isle of Man since in later poems of the fifteenth century the connection is clearly made. In this poem as well, the poet makes it very clear that the island he is speaking of is the Isle of Man in qq. 8, 16, and 17; Ó Cuív, "Poem in Praise of Raghnall," 297-98.

[174] Just as there was a High Kingship in theory, Tara represents the place from where such a High King would rule. Tara was viewed as the political center of Ireland, and hence if someone made the claim to the High Kingship, they would rule Tara, and if a person ruled Tara, they should be considered High King.

[175] "*Uaisle [a-]chách ceinéal mBréanainn*," *The Book of Magauran*, ed. Lambert McKenna (Dublin: Dublin Institute for Advanced Studies, 1943), p. 141.

[176] "*Uaisle [a-]chách ceinéal mBréanainn*," q. 31.

[177] Lambert McKenna, "A Poem by Gofraidh Fionn Ó Dálaigh," *Eriu* 16 (1954): 132-9.

[178] McKenna, "A Poem by Gofraidh Fionn Ó Dálaigh," q. 4.

[179] McKenna, "A Poem by Gofraidh Fionn Ó Dálaigh," qq. 9-11.

[180] McKenna, "A Poem by Gofraidh Fionn Ó Dálaigh," q. 14.

[181] McKenna, "A Poem by Gofraidh Fionn Ó Dálaigh," q. 15.

[182] McKenna, "A Poem by Gofraidh Fionn Ó Dálaigh," q. 16.

[183] McKenna, "A Poem by Gofraidh Fionn Ó Dálaigh," qq. 24-8.

[184] McKenna, "A Poem by Gofraidh Fionn Ó Dálaigh," qq. 37-47.

[185] McKenna, "A Poem by Gofraidh Fionn Ó Dálaigh," qq. 49-53.

[186] McKenna, "A Poem by Gofraidh Fionn Ó Dálaigh," q. 57.

[187] Quiggin, "O'Conor's House at Cloonfree," q. 14; Finan and O'Conor, "The Moated Site of Cloonfree," 72.

[188] Quiggin, "O'Conor's House at Cloonfree," q. 16.

[189] Quiggen, "O'Conor's House at Cloonfree," q. 23.

[190] Simms, *From Kings to Warlords*, 44-45.

Chapter 3:
Settlement Patterns and National Identity

In a series of articles published in the late 1950's and 1960's, A.J. Otway-Ruthven first explained the general pattern of Anglo-Norman and Gaelic settlement that took place in medieval Ireland.[1] Brooks also compiled an important collection of knights' fees in Wexford, Carlow, and Kilkenny.[2] Recent work, though, especially by Terry Barry, shows the massive amount of research that still needed in the field of medieval Irish settlement studies. The greatest needs are the analysis of rural settlement, the establishment of fortification typologies, and discovering the relationship between urban areas and rural settlement.[3] Furthermore, few explanation of these patterns use modern geographical and statistical analysis.[4] Indeed, for all the data in existence regarding the medieval period in Ireland, it is striking that no real statistical analysis has been completed which comprehensively considers geographic information as historical source material.

G.I.S. and Geographic Statistics

A computer system which incorporates and integrates the collection, storage, manipulation and presentation of geographical data is commonly referred to as a Geographic Information System (G.I.S.). The development of Geographic Information Systems began in the late 1960's and coincided with the growth of increasingly functional computer systems. However, not until personal desktop computers became affordable and functional for people with minimal computer science skills did Geographic Information Systems evolve into systems realistically operated by non-computer programmers.

The significance of technological developments in Geographic Information System technology is the increasing accuracy with which it allows the researcher to analyze large, complex, and disparate sets of data. The researcher can then manipulate and update the data to create models and output in the forms of maps, graphs, and statistics.[5] MapInfo, the application used in this study, is a typical example of a modern Geographic Information System.[6] MapInfo analyzes data which has been entered in the form of a database. The database, composed of multiple fields, may consist of any sort of historical data (such as a name, date, size, or economic value), but a Geographic Information System like MapInfo also attributes geographic information to each field entry. For instance, a database might include a group of monastic houses. The database in MapInfo might include the names of each house, the date in which each was founded, and the size of the house. However, the Mapinfo database would also include a value corresponding to the position of each monastic house in the landscape. Other features, such as elevations, bodies of water, and political borders can be analyzed. Additionally, seperate databases listing features of other sites can also be incorporated into the application, allowing MapInfo to analyze the relationships between different databases. MapInfo also includes a programming language, MapBasic. It allows the user to customize project-specific sub-routines with complex statistical measurements which are not part of the core MapInfo application.

Until recently, historical studies incorporated maps primarily for illustrative or reference purposes, ascribing them to the same role as descriptive photographs or artwork. Clearly the use of maps which inaccurately reflect data can easily and incorrectly sway scholarly arguments. Issues such as the scale of the map used, the size and form of the points used to represent sites or features, and even the colors used to indicate regions and areas can make an incredible impact upon the reader's perception of the data.[7] One way to avoid this problem is to create the maps only after performing geographic and spatial statistical analysis, such that the map is the product of rigorous analysis. Instead of creating traditional maps that elicit subjective opinions concerning the data, geographic and spatial statistical analysis forces the researcher to isolate the statistically significant data, then present it using charts, informational illustrations, as well as maps.

The techniques used for geographic and spatial analysis were first proposed in Clark and Evans' seminal article discussing the possible use of plant ecological analysis for archaeology.[8] The technique called "Nearest Neighbor Analysis" measures the distribution of a population's individual points or sites in a given area and determines whether that distribution departs from either a random or a regular distribution. Debates over the relevance and statistical validity of Nearest Neighbor Analysis began shortly after Clarke and Evans' articles first appeared. Getis remarked that the procedure could prove faulty if two points were each other's nearest neighbor.[9] Clarke and Evans' themselves discussed the problem of the boundary in Nearest Neighbor Analysis; the result of the analysis can vary dramatically if the area under analysis is expanded or shrunk. One might imagine a cluster of points in a county which, within the area of the county, seem rather evenly distributed, but that, within the area of the country incorporating that county, seem very clustered indeed.

In Nearest Neighbor Analysis, "r" designates the distance between each pair of points, "n" designates the the population of points, and the density of points is designated as "p" for a given area "A". The formula for p is thus

$$p = (n-1) / A \qquad (3.1)$$

and the mean nearest neighbor distance, r(o), is given by the formula

$$r(o) = \sum r/n. \qquad (3.2)$$

For a random distribution of points, the expected mean nearest neighbor distance, r(e), depends only on the density of the points and is given by the formula

$$r(e) = 1 / (2 \sqrt{p}). \qquad (3.3)$$

A ratio, R, indicates the randomness of the observed distribution, and is computed as

$$R = r(o) / r(e). \qquad (3.4)$$

For a random distribution, R=1; for a clustered distribution R<1, approaching zero in extreme cases; and for a distribution which is evenly dispersed R>1, reaching a value as high as 2.1419 in extreme cases.[10] A random distribution indicates that the distribution of points is randomly spread across the given area A. Some of these points might appear clustered with other points, but in this case, the distribution is considered statistically clustered. On the other hand, in a clustered distribution, the opposite is true. If the R value approaches zero, either the distribution of points is found in isolated pairs in the area A or the points are found in a small number of clusters in the area A. An even distribution means that the points lie equidistant from one another across the landscape. The pattern is considered neither random nor clustered.

The above formulae prove reliable for testing whether a group of points is clustered. However, they do not test the significance of that clustering. For instance, a group of three points might return an R value suggesting clustering, but the significance of that clustering could be called into question if the area in question is very large. Ian Hodder and Clyve Orton suggest using the Normal distribution to test the significance of R. The standard error (σ) of r(e) is

$$(r(e)) = 0.26136 / \sqrt{(np)} \qquad (3.5)$$

and the test statistic is

$$C = (r(o) - r(e)) / (r(e) \qquad (3.6)$$

which is then compared to a table of Normal distribution at a chosen significance level. For this study, all tests were performed at the .001 significance level, meaning that if the returned value for C was greater than 3.2 or less than -3.2, the distribution would be expected to occur by chance one time in 1,000 variations. At this point, if C is in fact greater than 3.2 or less than -3.2, the null hypothesis (that the R-value returned is not significant and occurred strictly by chance) can be rejected.[11] That is, we can then be confident that the degree of clustering (R) thus calculated is statistically significant. It is therefore possible to find that an R value suggests a high degree of clustering within a group of points, but that its C value proves that the degree of clustering, while very strong, is not significant statistically.

Once established that a given set of points is in some way clustered, it then must be explained how and why they are clustered. To this end the Chi Square method of analysis is fundamental to test the relevance of geographic influences upon the distribution of points. If the total area under consideration is A, and if within this total area, a sub-category area, a, is classified as a particular type of area within A, it is possible to measure the number of sites, n, of a group, N, that lie within a, and then to measure the number of sites, n, which lie in the other sub-categories of A. If the number of expected sites (r(i)) found within the area sub-category a(i) is computed using

$$r(i) = N \, a(i)/ A \qquad (3.7)$$

then the Chi Square value is

$$X^2 = \sum \, ((n(i) - r(i))^2 / r(i)). \qquad (3.8)$$

The Chi Square analysis implies that, for any given portion of the total area, a proportional number of points in that sub-area should also exist. If the number of points varies significantly from that relative proportion, we can say that the Chi Square value will be large enough to reject the null hypothesis for each study. That is, the tendency of certain points to be clustered in certain areas is statistically significant.

This analysis is useful for a variety of applications.[12] Buffers can be created around given features to test whether points appear significantly closer to the features. To test whether a point type is significantly associated with a differing point type, concentric circles can be drawn around differing points. For instance, to test whether certain monastic houses were in proximity to towns, MapInfo could be used to draw a series of concentric circles around towns at one kilometer, five kilometers, and ten kilometers. The area in each of these concentric circles would be considered a zone for Chi Square analysis

resulting in an expected and observed number of sites for each zone. Elevation zones can also be used to test whether points significantly exist within a certain elevation.[13]

Other methods to determine spatial distribution borrow from more traditional methods of statistical analysis. One such method is time-series analysis. In time-series analysis, a series of values obeserved during a given period of time are regressed against year increments. For instance, the number of new religious houses founded in Ireland in a series of twenty-year increments can be regressed against the twenty-year increments. A time series trend can be charted using a computer statistical analysis package[14], and can return coefficients for each twenty-year increment and coefficient constant. The trends for the chart are computed by the formula

Trend=Coefficient Constant+(Coefficient for Year*Year)
(3.9)

and are then plotted against the years. The resulting chart shows a line representing the overall trend across the time span in question. For instance, as mentioned above, the number of new houses founded by a monastic order in twenty-year increments could be regressed against time. The resulting chart shows a line with either a positive or a negative slope, and would therefore show a positive line (meaning the order founded significantly more houses over time) or a negative line (meaning the order had not founded significantly more houses over time).

A final method of spatial analysis discussed here compares the clustering of dissimilar points from two seperate data sets. Several methods for this type of analysis have been proposed, including the concentric circle method previously described. To test the relationship between two sets of points, a series of concentric buffer zones are created around one set of points. First, the area inside and outside the buffer zones are measured. Then the expected number of points is derived given the total area and the total number of points (as in the method used to calculate a Chi value for the relevance of proximity to rivers or of elevation in settlement). A further method of comparing two sets of points is to construct a Chi Square contingency table in which the nearest neighbor for each point is entered into the table on the basis of its being a like

Scale of Map	Level of Error	Scale of Map	Level of Error
1:1,200	±3.33 ft.	1:12,000	±33.33 ft.
1:2,400	±6.67 ft.	1:24,000	±40.00 ft.
1:4,800	±13.33 ft.	1:63,360	±105.60 ft.
1:10,000	±27.78 ft.	1:100,000	±166.67 ft

TABLE 3.1: MARGINS OF ERROR FOR VARIOUS MAP SCALES

(Source: Foote, Kenneth, and Huebner, Donald. "Error, Accuracy and Precision." The Geographer's Craft Project. (Austin, The Department of Geography, University of Texas at Austin: 1995). For a map with a scale of 1:12,000, for instance, any given point or line on that map would be reliably located within a margin of error of plus or minus 33.33 feet.)

or unlike point. A Chi Square value is returned showing any significant pattern in the distribution of the two sets of points.[15]

Error in Geographic Information Systems

In the last decade, the users of Geographic Information System technology rarely considered the problems of error, accuracy and precision in the collection and manipulation of geographic data.[16] Indeed, one of the main problems with modern Geographic Information System technology is that after viewing what appears to be clear and meaningful maps and analyses the user may lose sight of the nature of the evidence. Since the early 1990's, though, error, inaccuracy and imprecision are generally recognized as able to actually define whether a project can be successful and worth undertaking.[17]

The essential problem that leads to error and inaccuracy in using Geographic Information Systems lies in the strength of the systems themselves.[18] The systems consider huge amounts of data with accuracy and speed by analyzing relationships between seemingly different groups of data. For instance, it might be possible to analyze points that represent towns in one data set and another data set's points that represent monastic houses or lines that represent elevations in another dataset. The product of that analysis, however, is only as valid as the data sets, and these are composed of data with varying degrees of accuracy.

Accuracy refers to "the degree to which information on a map or in a digital database matches true or accepted values. [It is] an issue pertaining to the quality of data and the number of errors contained in a data set or map."[19] Accuracy, for instance, refers to the validity of the data in terms of how the particular Geographic Information System handles the data (including issues such as processor error, errors in mathematical formulae, and the age of the data entered). Precision, on the other hand, refers to "the level of measurement and exactness of description in a G.I.S. database."[20] The level of precision in the construction of a Geographic Information System analysis is the degree to which the researcher measures the position of points, lines and areas to particular fractions of a unit of measure. The two factors, while distinct, are also inter-related; it is possible for data to be quite accurate, but lack precision. A surveyor might record a data set accurately and another researcher might analyze that data using impeccable statistical analysis; if the precision is less than what the researcher's project requires, the results can be meaningless. A surveyor can record data that are accurate but are only precise to ±1 mile; if the researcher who uses these data is concerned with a 10-mile square area, this level of precision will negate any results. It is also possible for a data set to be very precise but not accurate at all. The data set might be recorded at ±1 meter, but then the researcher might use faulty mathematical operations (for instance typing "+" instead of "-" in a formula); the Geographic Information System might calculate areas using an inaccurate operation; or surveyors might incorrectly record the data that they observed.

One type of error in accuracy particularly pertinent to any study is positional inaccuracy. This type of error is due to the inherent variance in the degree of representation for which a given map may be responsible. Any map merely represents reality, and hence always includes a certain amount of error due to the impossibility and impracticality of creating a 1:1 scale map. This degree of error is based upon either the scale of the map or the precision of the points or areas plotted on that map. Various map scales have particular precisions which can govern the size of the project for which the map may be used, as shown in Table 3.1. These varying levels of precision mean that a point plotted on a map, instead of representing a "precise" location in real space, actually represents a "probable" location given the scale of the map.

In addition to the map's precision in terms of scale, the data set coordinates are precise only to the degree to which the coordinates were recorded. In the coordinate system of the Irish National Grid used by the Ordnance Survey in the county archaeological surveys of Ireland (used throughout this study), the coordinates are recorded using a letter followed by a four-digit number. The letter represents a particular 100 kilometer square area, while the four following numbers represent the coordinates within that 100 square kilometer area. The level of precision for most published county archaeological surveys produced by The Office of Public Works is limited to 100 meters ±10 meters.

Other sources of data, as well, were not created for use with Geographic Information Systems and are therefore rather dubious material if converted for spatial analysis using a digitizing tablet or a scanner. One such resource is the map of political boundaries for the year 1300 in Goddard Orpen's *The Normans in Ireland*.[21] While most boundaries represented in this map are simply borders of several modern Irish counties (particularly those counties within the province of Leinster), other boundaries appear more suspicious in terms of their actual accuracy; the borders in the western portions of Ireland constantly fluctuated. As well, the map's scale would prevent any local analysis at the county level but might prove useful for an analysis of the whole island. Often, though, these imprecise maps (which were not to be used in geographic statistic analysis) are the only maps available to the scholar of medieval Ireland.

Other maps that have been utilized for this study were created by the Ordnance Survey of Ireland. These include *The Map of Monastic Ireland*, with a precision of 1 kilometer ± 100 meters and the four sheet *Map of Ireland* at the 1:250,000 scale, with a precision of about 1 kilometer ± 100 meters. The Royal Irish Academy *Atlas of Ireland* also includes many useful maps and an index of place names including Ordnance Survey coordinate accurate to 1 kilometer ± 100 meters.

Related to the concept of error in scale and precision, the ability to zoom in and out on a map using Geographic Information Systems can lead to misunderstanding. A map digitized at the 1:100,000 scale, once on the screen, can be viewed by zooming in and out to virtually any distance from the earth. Regardless of that distance, the scale of the map does not actually change. The zoom feature on a G.I.S. might be compared to a magnifying glass used to look at a paper map; no matter how close one gets to the paper map, the scale remains constant, and hence the accuracy of the map remains the same regardless of how the map is reduced or expanded. As well, features found on digitized maps often misrepresent reality since the lines differentiating various elevations do not usually reflect the gradual or even radical changes actually occuring in the landscape. Similarly, digitized sources often do not take into consideration the fact that flat projections (such as the Irish National Grid) misrepresent the locations of points on a spherical planet.[22]

Both cartographic studies and geographic studies share many of these possibilities for error; however, when these sorts of error apply to a Geographic Information System, the level of error is compounded. Several layers of data are considered simultaneously, and each layer brings its own margin of error to the project's total level of error. This chapter uses several methods to alleviate the problems of error and precision. First, statistical analysis includes compensation for data discrepancies through the use of higher p values for the analysis. For this project, all tests will be conducted at the .001 significance level, meaning that if a value exceeds a critical value for the relevant type of statistical analysis, the chance that the particular event occurred randomly is one in a thousand. The level of significance commonly employed in statistical analysis is .01; Terry Barry, for instance, used this level due to the greater chance for particular patterns to prove significant. Due to the high level of significance required for the .001 level, those patterns would be much less apparent.[23] Second, while most databases for this study include errors of precision, the errors are minimized when mean values are considered for each individual database. For instance, in the nearest neighbor analysis, the most important factor is the mean distance to the nearest like neighbor; this value will not differ significantly due to precision errors, particularly if the database is of considerable size. If the database has fewer files, that chance of error increases.

Sources of Data and Digitizing

The data used for this study represent a cross-section of settlement types in medieval Ireland.[24] However, the reliability of different of data types varies, and forces the acceptance both of assumptions regarding the data and of the employment of different analytic types. A Geographic Information System can analyze data in point, line or area format. Data in an area format might include a county, state, or field system, while data in a point format might include a building, structure, or historic site. Line data can refer to rivers, political borders, or coastlines.

The types of sites included in the various databases for this study include both secular and religious foundations. A motte and bailey earthwork fortification is a large earthen mound (the motte), often with an earthen rampart (the bailey) enclosing a small courtyard. The motte might be topped by a wooden structure, while the motte and the bailey usually included a palisade of timber for protection. The motte and bailey earthworks are often assumed to predate most stone castles and as temporary military strongpoints, although, as will be explained later in this chapter, this view is currently being challenged. The nobility built stone castles as centers for both military and administrative activity. Early stone castles of Ireland, noted for their large keeps, contained halls from which nobles exercised their authority. Later, as castles were built further and further west near the colonial frontiers, different designs suggest a stronger emphasis on military protection (such as the use of drum towers at the corners and at the main gate house, as at Roscommon castle) and a lesser emphasis on administrative activity. In certain areas, particularly urban areas such as Dublin and Limerick or frontier areas such as Athlone, the Crown built castles known as royal castles. These royal castles acted as the centers of royal authority in Ireland, with Dublin Castle in particular serving as the center of English rule in Ireland throughout the middle ages.

Several articles, gazetteers and books address the settlement of motte and bailey fortifications. Goddard Orpen's map of mottes in Anglo-Norman Ireland provides a rough numerical estimate of mottes in medieval Ireland but does not include a site listing nor any real information regarding the patterns of settlement for the mottes.[25] On the other hand, Glasscock, does include a gazetteer in his article regarding motte and bailey settlement in Ireland.[26] His listing does not include any information such as proximity to rivers, elevations, dates of settlement, or proximity to

other types of settlement, and, since several of the entries are clearly inaccurate, must also be cross-referenced with the relevant county archaeological inventories that exist. Glasscock's work has been substantially updated in two articles by Kieran O'Conor; O'Conor suggests the existence of far more mottes in Ireland than Orpen or Glasscock assumed.[27] Using county inventories and the lists by Glasscock and O'Conor, a database of motte and baileys was constructed for this study. H.G. Leask's work on Irish castles serves as a starting point for any discussion of castles and fortifications in Ireland, but Tom McNeill and David Sweetman's recent books concerning castles and lordship in medieval Ireland provide excellent additional data.[28] Each castle's coordinates can be found in the county inventories where they exist while information such as construction date can usually be located in various source calendars for medieval Ireland or in the Irish annals.[29] The various calendars of documents relating to Ireland are summaries of medieval Irish documents, and because of the fire at Dublin's Public Record Office during the Irish Civil War, they are often all that remain of medieval Ireland's Anglo-Norman administrative records. The annals of Ireland, generally written by Gaelic clerics in monastic settings, record various event that for a particular year, death notices, and the erection or attack of castles.

As the colony developed from the earliest stages of the arrival of the Anglo-Normans in the late twelfth century, towns and boroughs also developed in areas where castles and political structures were established. A town is usually characterized by the presence of a defensive wall around the town, a church, and some sort of bureaucratic center. The bureaucratic center, at least initially in the settlement of the Anglo-Normans in Ireland, was often a motte and bailey structure; later, a castle became the administrative center of the political structure in the colony. A borough, while similar to a town in many physical ways, is different from a town in that a legal sanction was awarded to a borough by which it was allowed to have a market. B.J. Graham has written extensively on the nature of boroughs in medieval Ireland and in a 1977 article provides a gazetteer that lists medieval boroughs and the dates at which the boroughs were established, along with material concerning market status.[30] He comments that the list certainly has its share of problems due to inequality of extant sources, but, as this study will later show, the list's distribution corresponds to the distribution of the other sets of Anglo-Norman data sets, which suggests that perhaps his list is not too far off the mark.

The Gaelic people's settlements in Ireland are often very difficult to identify. Archaeological identification as yet does not differentiate between later Gaelic settlements and those in existence before the Anglo-Norman's arrival. It has often been assumed that as the Anglo-Normans expanded their colony in Ireland, they used and re-used sites previously occupied by Gaelic settlements. This seems to be a plausible argument when studying motte and bailey settlements or castles, but lacks sufficient evidence when interpreting the complexities of mottes built upon ringforts.[31] Many Gaelic sites mentioned in the Irish annals are only identified by a placename and lack reference to any distinguishable features in the modern landscape which corresponds to the medieval site. This is not surprising since the particular military tactics used by the Irish in the middle ages centered around hostings into enemy territory followed by retreat into friendly territory; fortifications were considered refuges for cattle and non-combatants, not as tools of occupation. In fact, the Irish considered fords and bridges far more strategic since these sites allowed access across the rivers which served as border areas.[32] Nevertheless, the sites mentioned in the annals do provide record of Irish attacks upon Anglo-Norman castles (often unrecorded by the Anglo-Normans) and those castles which were successfully captured by the Irish. A further topic discussed at the end of this chapter is the use of the word *longphort* in the annals; it is often translated as "stronghold," and was a common term used in the annals of pre-Norman Ireland. The term was rarely used in the thirteenth century but increased in popularity during the fourteenth century. There do not seem to be any court records from any of the Gaelic kings which would document when and where fortifications or settlement were established, nor are there clear remains of settlement in terms of fortifications or villages.[33] One solution to this problem in terms of using a Geographic Information System is to create a database of references to those fortifications, settlements, and incursions in the Irish annals. However, the use of the annals in this way can prove very problematic. Most annals focus on a particular area geographically or on the fortunes of a particular royal family. The *Annals of Connacht*, for instance, focus on the Kingdom of Connacht and its royal families, the Ó Conchobhair and Mac Diarmata among others, while the *Annals of Ulster* are primarily concerned with the Ó Néill and Ó Domhnaill in Ulster. Nevertheless, sufficient overlap exists between the different collections of annals to provide a fairly comprehensive picture of Gaelic settlement in medieval Ireland. In creating databases using the annals, one finds references to the same act repeated

in different sets of annals which are therefore considered multiple references to the same event. For instance, the *Annals of Connacht* might report that a castle was attacked in the year 1250, and the *Annals of Loch Cé*, a member of the same family of annals, might report the same event.[34] In these cases, one would make a single entry in the database itself.

The combination of Gwynn and Hadcock's *Medieval Religious Houses, Ireland* and the individual county archaeological inventories published by the Office of Public Works provides outstanding sets of data concerning religious houses in Ireland.[35] In fact, these data are probably the most thorough because they include not only the names and locations of religious houses but other important data such as the years of foundation and dissolution, the names of the original patrons, and in some cases, economic data from taxations and tithes. Religious houses in medieval Ireland are easily displayed and analyzed because of the pioneering efforts of Gwynn and Hadcock. Their work, divided into chapters discussing each of the religious orders in medieval Ireland, adapts easily to statistical and G.I.S. usage. For each house, categories were entered for house name, religious order, years of foundation and dissolution, county, diocese, and, finally, the Irish National Grid X and Y coordinates. The data for all fields excepting the coordinates came from Gwynn and Hadcock while data for the coordinates was found in either the *Ordinance Survey Map of Monastic Ireland* or the Office of Public Works county archaeological inventories.[36] A certain lack of precision was accepted in the X and Y coordinates taken from the Map of Monastic Ireland (which is accurate to the nearest kilometer) as compared to the county inventories (which are accurate to 10 meters). This particular problem will be alleviated as more inventories are published.[37]

The county inventories also list many parish churches for the various diocese in medieval Ireland. As well, the fourteenth century church taxation and valuations identify the medieval parish churches for each diocese. However, these sources still to do not provide an accurate glimpse of the nature of the church at the local level in Ireland, as many of the medieval parish churches are still not identified in the landscape.[38]

While collecting data and creating databases for statistical geographic analysis was a matter of finding the relevant collections of material, using that material in meaningful ways required having maps and digitized features to compare the relationships between all of those sites and the landscape. For this survey, several features were chosen which would then be used for analysis with the relevant databases created from the historic material as described above.

Finding a collection of digitized geographic material for Ireland was impossible at worst and cost-prohibitive at best. The best solution for this lack of digitized data lay in digitizing the material from easily accessible printed maps. A map of Ireland without any features was included with the MapInfo package, so the real problem was locating the other data. Using the 1993 Ordnance Survey 1:250,000 series map and a 12x12 Calcomp digitizing pad, the 300 meter and 120 meter elevations were digitized. B.J. Graham names several rivers of primary importance to boroughs for economic and trade purposes: the Shannon, Boyne, Suir, Barrow, Liffey, Blackwater, and Slaney Rivers. These rivers were digitized from the same map as above using the same digitizing pad. Since the precision of the digitizing pad is greater than the accuracy of the map, the level of error in these digitized samples corresponds to the level of error of the map used for the digitizing. In this case, the 1:250,000 maps is therefore accurate to a level of about one kilometer. Another geographical factor tested for its relevance to the founding of religious houses was proximity to a coastline. The area within 10 kilometers of the Irish coast was designated as another buffer zone. Next, both the area of this coastal buffer and the area of the inland region within this buffer were calculated.

Historical Background

In 1169 an Anglo-Norman force led by Robert fitz Stephen and acting for Richard de Clare, the Earl of Stiguil arrived in Ireland. They came from southern Wales and landed in County Wexford at the request of Diarmait MacMurchadha, the deposed King of Leinster. Later, after his marriage to the daughter of MacMurchadha and the subsequent death of MacMurchadha in 1171, de Clare found himself heir to the kingship of Leinster which he promptly claimed against several Irish challengers.[39] King Henry II, who had initially authorized de Clare's venture in support of MacMurchadha, arrived in Ireland later in 1171 and forced the submission of de Clare and the other Anglo-Norman nobles. After Henry re-granted the lands back to the barons, he reserved the town of Dublin and the other seaports of southeastern Ireland to royal control. Henry left in 1172, never to return.

After Henry's departure, the Anglo-Norman nobles began to expand their kingdoms to the north, west and south of Ireland. John de Courcy and Hugh de Lacy gained prominence in Ulster due mainly to limited Gaelic opposition.[40] The relationship between the western Irish kings and the Anglo-Normans was complicated by Henry II's establishment of the Ó Conchobhair as the king of Connacht as his vassal by the Treaty of Windsor in 1175.[41] Under this arrangement, the then king of Connacht, Ruaidrí Ó Conchobhair, would become the king of the western regions which were as of yet unconquered by the Anglo-Normans. Ruaidrí Ó Conchobhair, however, abdicated in 1183, and his successors fought among themselves for several generations until Cathal Crobderg Ó Conchobhair gained the throne. In 1215, King John of England granted Connacht to Cathal and his heirs for good service. After a series of long wars, though, Connacht officially passed to the de Burghs in 1227.

The twelfth and thirteenth century settlement that took place in Ireland may be best understood in terms of the framework of lordship.[42] The king controlled the more urban areas of Dublin, Waterford, and Cork while Anglo-Norman rulers progressively progressively sub-infeudated the march regions. However, because the lords were primarily concerned with acquiring lands that were profitable and arable, they never achieved a comprehensive level of settlement in the march regions. Hence, even in the eastern regions of Ireland little occupation took place above the 120-meter elevation and in the boggy lowlands. For the citizens and lords of Dublin (the capital of the lordship), the Gaelic lords living just south of Dublin in the Wicklow Mountains were a constant threat and annoyance as they regularly raided and plundered the southern outskirts of Dublin.[43]

During the two centuries which concern this study it is possible to discern three distinct periods of settlement. Each of the three periods is associated with particular types of settlement, and with those particular types of settlement are found particular types of patterns. The first period spans the years 1180-1250 and covers the initial incursion of the Anglo-Norman settlers. The types of settlement associated with this first period are the motte and bailey earthworks, the early castles established as the centers of administration and power for the lords, monasteries of the continental variety (including Cistercians, Praemonstranians, Augustinians, and the military monastic orders), and the coastal Norse towns first captured by the lords then claimed for the English Crown. The second period of settlement, 1250-

1320, spans a period of intensification of settlement with little real expansion of the colony's area. Towns and boroughs were established throughout this period in the already settled areas of the colony, and larger castles were constructed on the perimeter of the colony by lords or by the Crown itself. Though mottes and other earthwork fortifications were likely still used and constructed, the extent of their continued use into the late thirteenth and fourteenth centuries is still debatable.[44] While in contrast to the earlier period when continental monastic orders became established throughout the colony, in this second period, few new monasteries were founded. However, a large number of friaries were founded in proximity to towns and boroughs. The third period, 1320-1400, may considered one of decline due to the clear lack of any new building, either secular or religious. Although no new, major castles were built, some scholars have observed that at this time tower houses make their first appearance in the Irish landscape.[45] While this decline is clearly observable in the Anglo-Norman evidence, the level of decline has not been established with regard to the Gaelic regions of Ireland.

Analysis of Data

Early Settlement, 1200 to 1250 In the early twentieth century Orpen observed that the Anglo-Normans arriving in Ireland during the late twelfth century built castles and earthwork fortifications to establish their authority, much as the Normans invading England nearly a century earlier.[46] Usually identified by a large earthen mound, the mottes were often as high as 10 meters, surrounded by a palisade, and topped by a wooden tower. In some cases a palisade also topped a bailey, or earthen bank and ditch. The relationship between those motte and bailey structures and the stone castles (for which usually exists more historical and archaeological evidence than their earthen counterparts) still presents questions. McNeill points out clear cost differences in money and time in the construction of a stone castle as opposed to a motte. He also states that the stone castles might be equated with the lordship's caput, while the mottes were probably associated with the lower level local lords.[47] Nearest neighbor analysis returned an R-value of 0.7422, which suggests clustering, and a C score of -9.0249, which shows that the clustering is indeed significant.

This significant level of clustering warranted a closer examination of the relationship of the motte settlement pattern with other geographic features. Table 3.3 shows

the relationship between mottes and rivers. The rivers digitized (following Graham's article on boroughs) proved significant due to their size and usefullness for colonists'.[48] Buffer regions of 1 km., 5 km., 10 km., and 15 km. were drawn within MapInfo, and then MapBasic was used to count the number of mottes within each region. The null hypothesis, that no relationship exists between the settlement of mottes and the areas around rivers, is easily rejected given the returned Chi value of 574.07. Therefore, we can say that mottes tend to be located significantly closer to rivers than might be expected in a random distribution.

The distribution of mottes in Ireland clearly shows a significant tendency in the eastern regions of Ireland. This in itself is not surprising, since these are the regions in which the Anglo-Normans first settled. Illustration 3.1 shows this distribution. The number of mottes according to elevation is given in Table 3.4. Again, the null hypothesis, that there is no significant relationship between elevation and the settlement of mottes, is rejected with a Chi value of 26.87. The distribution of mottes in relation to elevation therefore proves significant and shows a clear tendency towards lowland settlement (below the 120 meter elevation).

McNeill argues convincingly that while twelfth and thirteenth century military methodology certainly included the construction of castles in conquered lands, their administrative needs also played a significant role in the use of these castles in the newly conquered lands. The major castles built as *capita* for the major lords in Ireland display significant weaknesses, suggesting that perhaps the major role of the castle in medieval Ireland was administrative rather than military.[49]

A database of castles created for this study uses McNeill's work as a secondary source and Giraldus' *Expugnatio Hibernica*, *Song of Dermot and the Earl*, and *The Calendar of Documents Relating to Ireland* as primary sources.[50] The distribution map of these castles confirms McNeill's position that the castles were primarily administrative centers. The castles seem dispersed among the counties establies by the Anglo-Normans. For the castles built in the twelfth century, an R-value of .758 was returned with a C score of -1.73066, suggesting that the castles built in the earliest period may be best described as approaching a clustered distribution; however, the returned R value was not significant in any way. This probably owes to the small number of castles in the database given Ireland's area as a whole. The castles of the early thirteenth century, however, seem to be clustered. The returned R-value of 0.3004 with a C score of -4.635 confirms this and shows that the clustering is in fact significant.

The database of stone castles for this first period indicates numbers fewer than 30; this means that the clustering analysis might be less significant than other tests. The results of the river analyses for this period show a significant relationship between these castles and rivers (see Tables 3.6 and 3.8). The castles built in the early thirteenth century (which were found to be clustered in the analysis above) exhibited locations not only by rivers, but also, in particular, by the Shannon River. No significant relationship existed between these castles and elevation as noted in Tables 3.7 and 3.9.

The monastic reforms of the Irish Church that began in the twelfth century were enhanced by the plantation of Cistercian monasteries throughout the colony. Anglo-Norman lords founded many of these monasteries, but Gaelic lords founded several in the western and southern regions of Ireland.

The cluster analysis applied to Cistercian monasteries shows that, given the area of Ireland, the houses were not significantly distributed as proven by the R value of 1.06 and the C score which did not exceed 3.2. These values mean that there is no significant clustering of Cistercian monasteries given the area of the island of Ireland. Nevertheless, there are other geographic factors to consider which might be significant in understanding where the monasteries were likely founded.

As with the motte and bailey analysis, the total number of Cistercian monasteries was then analyzed in terms of elevation. The returned Chi value of 12.03 shown in Table 3.11 does not allow the rejection of the null hypothesis, ie., that there is no relation between the settlement of Cistercian monasteries and elevation.

When the Cistercian monasteries were analyzed in comparison to the major rivers, a Chi value of 44.644 was returned. This allowed for the rejection of the null hypothesis that there is no relationship between the settlement of Cistercian monasteries and proximity to rivers. This proximity is, in fact, significant, and, given the expected values for the areas around the rivers, the numbers found in the 1 kilometer and 5-kilometer zones greatly exceed expected values. In other words, the

analysis shows that the relationship between Cistercian monasteries and rivers was not only significant but exceptionally related.

In addition to the Cistercians, monastic orders associated with the Anglo-Norman lords included the military monastic orders, particularly the Knights of the Temple and the Hospitaller Knights. These orders of knights founded houses in close proximity to localities first settled by the Anglo-Normans and often received rich endowments from the greater lords themselves. Moreover, the overwhelming majority of these houses were founded during this initial invasion period; all but two of the 36 houses were established before 1220. Since the two contemporaneous orders shared similar organizations and functions, they will be considered together for purposes of this study.

The houses of the Templar Knights and the Hospitaller Knights show significant clustering, with a returned R-value of 0.6391 and a C score of -4.199. The clustering clearly reflects the relationship between the settlement of these houses and the early Anglo-Norman colony. The houses of the orders existed almost exclusively in the southeast portion of the island where the most intensive settlement took place as indicated by the motte analysis. In fact, the R-value of 0.6391 shows an even greater degree of clustering than indicated for the motte and bailey earthworks. The scores returned from other types of analyses also proved significant, meaning that military monastic orders proved not only clustered significantly, but clustered in lowland areas with fairly close proximity to major Irish rivers.

Given the seemingly significant number of military monastic houses located close to the coast, Mapinfo proved useful once again in studying settlement. Using MapInfo, a coastal buffer zone of 10 kilometers was created. The number of houses in the internal and external regions were compared with the expected values and a Chi Square value is returned. The data in Table 3.16 show that this distribution is in fact significant, given the Chi square value of 14.65. Therefore one may confidently state that the military monastic orders were significantly located in close proximity to the coast, to major rivers of Ireland, and the lower elevations.

The above analyses all point to several facts concerning this early period of settlement. First, and perhaps foremost, the level and limit of settlement can be deduced

TABLE 3.2: MOTTE NEAREST NEIGHBOR ANALYSIS

R Value	0.742255
C Value	-9.0249

where n=336

TABLE 3.3: MOTTE ASSOCIATION WITH MAJOR RIVERS

REGION	OBSERVED	AREA	EXPECTED	(O-E)*(O-E)/N
1 km	17	2447	9.894	5.103
5 km	69	8977	36.296	29.465
10 km	99	10705	43.283	71.719
15 km	137	8887	35.932	284.266
outside 15k	14	52084	210.592	183.523
TOTAL	336	83100		
			Chi Square=	**574.077**

TABLE 3.4: MOTTES BY ELEVATION

ELEVATION	OBSERVED	AREA	EXPECTED	(O-E)*(O-E)/N
below 120	220	44890	181.504	8.164
120-300	116	34587	139.846	4.066
above 300	0	3623	14.648	14.648
TOTAL	336	83100		
			Chi Square=	**26.879**

TABLE 3.5: NEAREST NEIGHBOR OF CASTLES BEFORE 1250

Castles	R	C	n
12th Century	.758	-1.73066	13
13th Century	.3004	-4.635	11

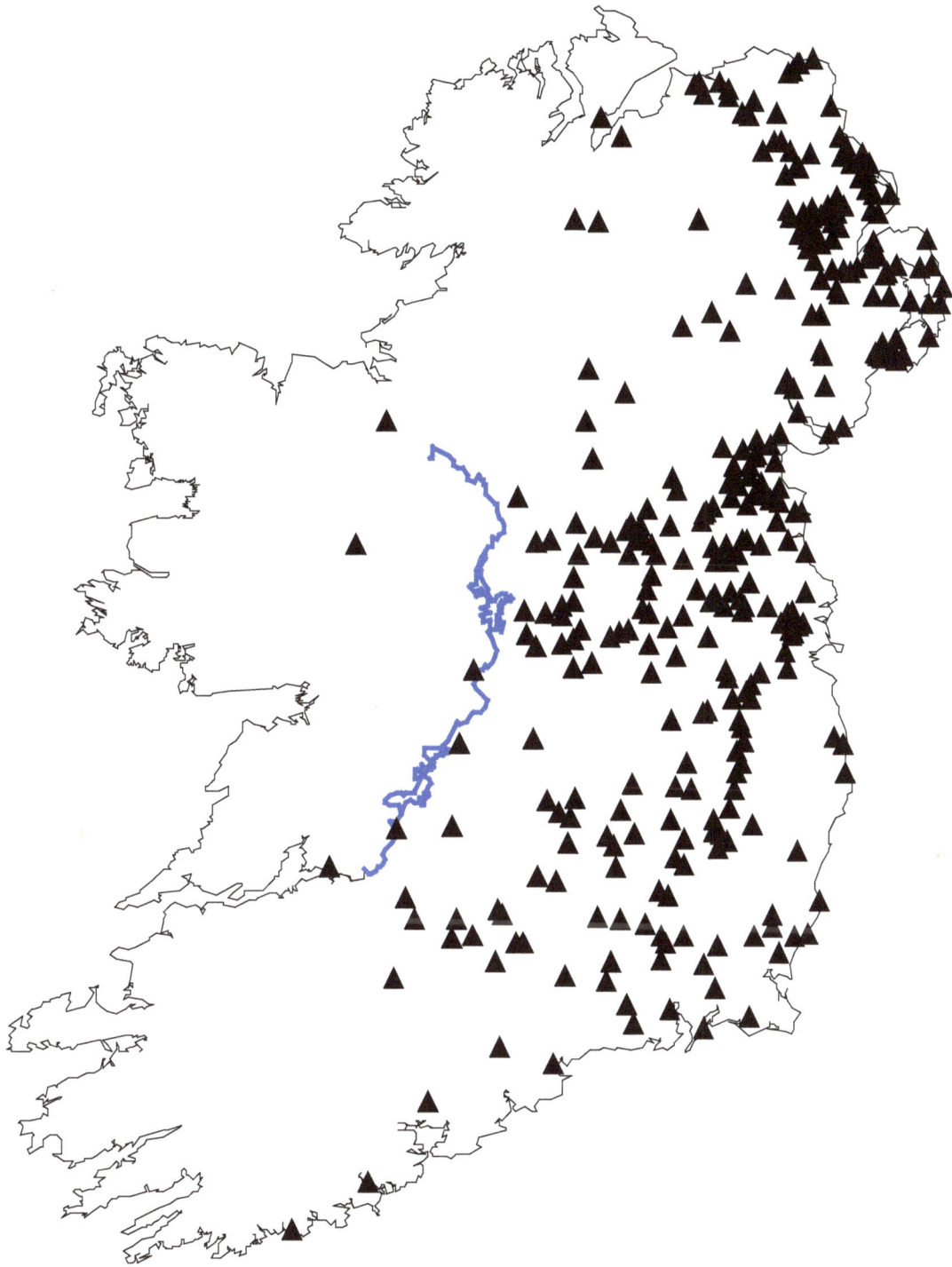

Figure 3.1: Mottes in Medieval Ireland, after Glasscock and O'Conor

TABLE 3.6: TWELFTH CENTURY CASTLES AND MAJOR RIVERS

Buffer	Number	Area	Expected	(O-E)*(O-E)/N
1k	4	2447	0.382	34.179
5k	3	8977	1.404	1.813
10k	3	10705	1.674	1.048
15k	1	8887	1.390	0.109
outside 15k	2	52084	8.147	4.638
Total	13	83100		
			Chi Square=	**41.789**

TABLE 3.7: TWELFTH CENTURY CASTLES BY ELEVATION

Area	Number	Area	Expected	(O-E)*(O-E)/N
below 120m	8	44890	7.022	0.136
120m-300m	5	34587	5.410	0.031
above 300m	0	3623	0.566	0.566
Total	13	83100		
			Chi Square=	**0.734**

by considering the distribution map of motte and bailey structures. Second, the Cistercians, a monastic order associated with the Norman-French religious reform of the eleventh century, are not necessarily significantly located within any particular region. However, the military monastic orders seem to have been a vital part of the initial arrival of the Anglo-Normans, as their houses are located in significant relationship to the coastal areas which would have been the points of incursion for the Anglo-Normans. Finally, the castles built in association with motte and bailey structures show the same tendencies towards lowland and river settlement. They were not significantly clustered in the early half of this period because they were primarily built as *capita* for the major political boundaries of the early colony. However, in the second half of this period, the newly built castles appear significantly near the Shannon River valley and close to what might be considered the frontier region of the colony.

The Middle Period, 1250-1320 Intensification of settlement characterizes this next period medieval

Ireland. After the initial gains of the early period of the colonization, and after subsequent ventures into Connacht and Munster, the Anglo-Normans strengthened those initial gains by establishing towns, boroughs, and markets in the conquered territories.

Boroughs are a type of settlement that is suited to this study because the boroughs themselves appear in the historical records and because those boroughs are easily identifiable with modern place-names.[51] As with the other types of settlement investigated in this study, the boroughs were tested in their relationship to those major rivers following Graham's 1977 article on boroughs. The result was a very strong correlation between the construction of boroughs and proximity to those rivers.

Several tests were performed which analyzed the relationship between the settlement of boroughs and the settlement of motte and bailey earthworks. Hodder has suggested that a variation of the Chi Square analysis can be used, but this form of analysis has difficulties because

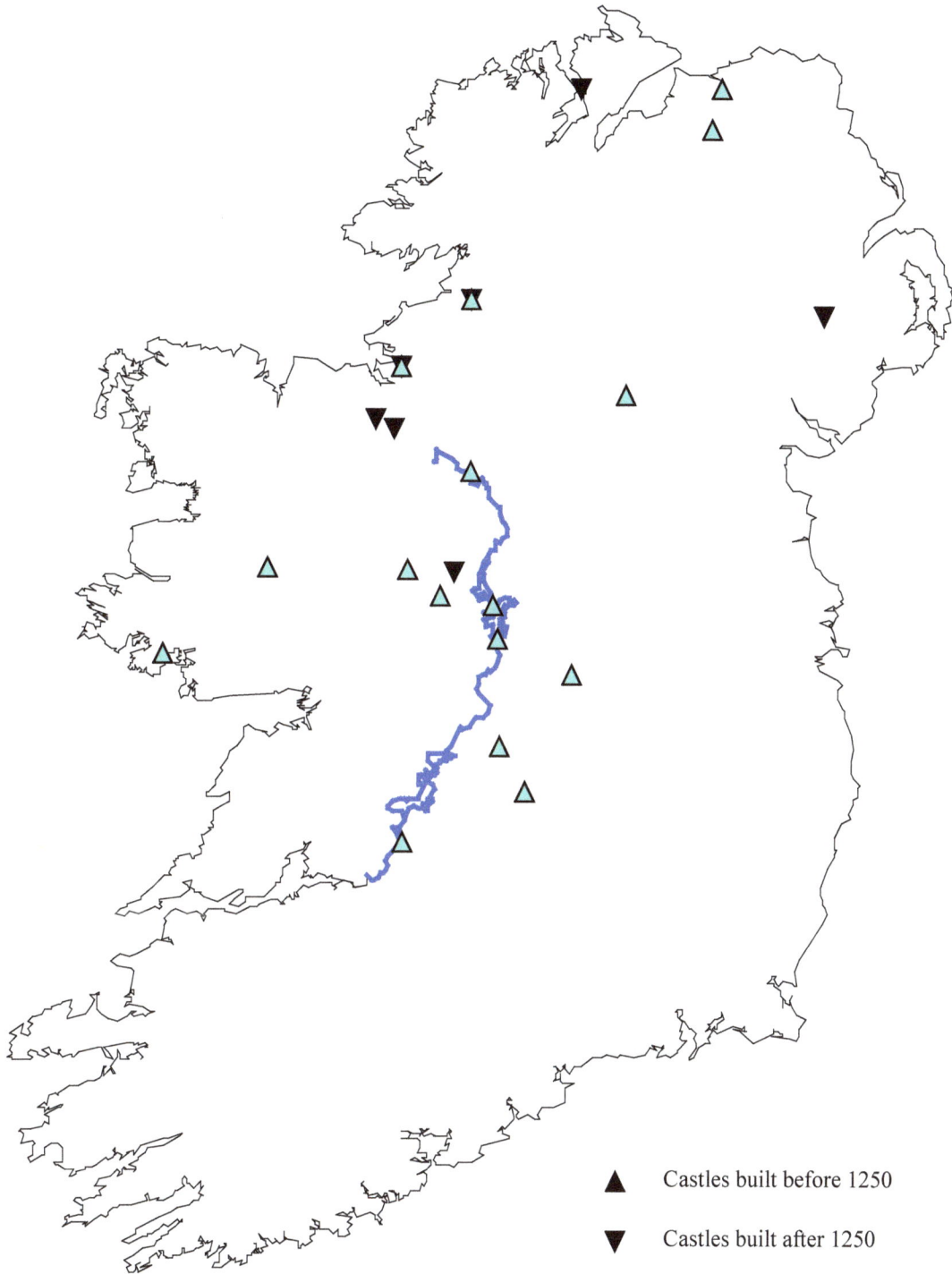

Figure 3.2: Castle Building in Medieval Ireland

TABLE 3.8: THIRTEENTH CENTURY CASTLES AND MAJOR RIVERS

Buffer	Number	Area	Expected	(O-E)*(O-E)/N
1k	5	2447	0.323	67.505
5k	1	8977	1.188	0.029
10k	2	10705	1.417	0.239
15k	1	8887	1.176	0.0264
outside 15k	2	52084	6.894	3.474

TABLE 3.9: THIRTEENTH CENTURY CASTLES BY ELEVATION

Zone	Number	Area	Expected	(O-E)*(O-E)/N
below 120m	8	44890	5.942	0.712
120m-300m	3	34587	4.578	0.544
above 300m	2	3623	0.479	4.820
Total	13	83100		
			Chi Square=	**6.077**

TABLE 3.10: CISTERCIAN MONASTERIES CLUSTERING

R	1.06
C	0.92

where n=47

TABLE 3.11: CISTERCIAN MONASTERIES BY ELEVATION

Zone	Observed	Area	Expected	(O-E)*(O-E)/N
below 120m	37	44890	25.389	5.309
120m-300m	10	34587	19.561	4.673
above 300m	0	3623	2.049	2.049
Total	47	83100		
			Chi Square=	**12.032**

TABLE 3.12: CISTERCIAN MONASTERIES BY PROXIMITY TO RIVERS

Zone	Observed	Area	Expected	(O-E)*(O-E)/N
1km	8	2447	1.383	31.627
5km	11	8977	5.077	6.909
10km	1	10705	6.054	4.219
15km	5	8887	5.026	0.000
outside 15k	22	52084	29.457	1.888
Total	47	83100		
			Chi Square=	**44.64**

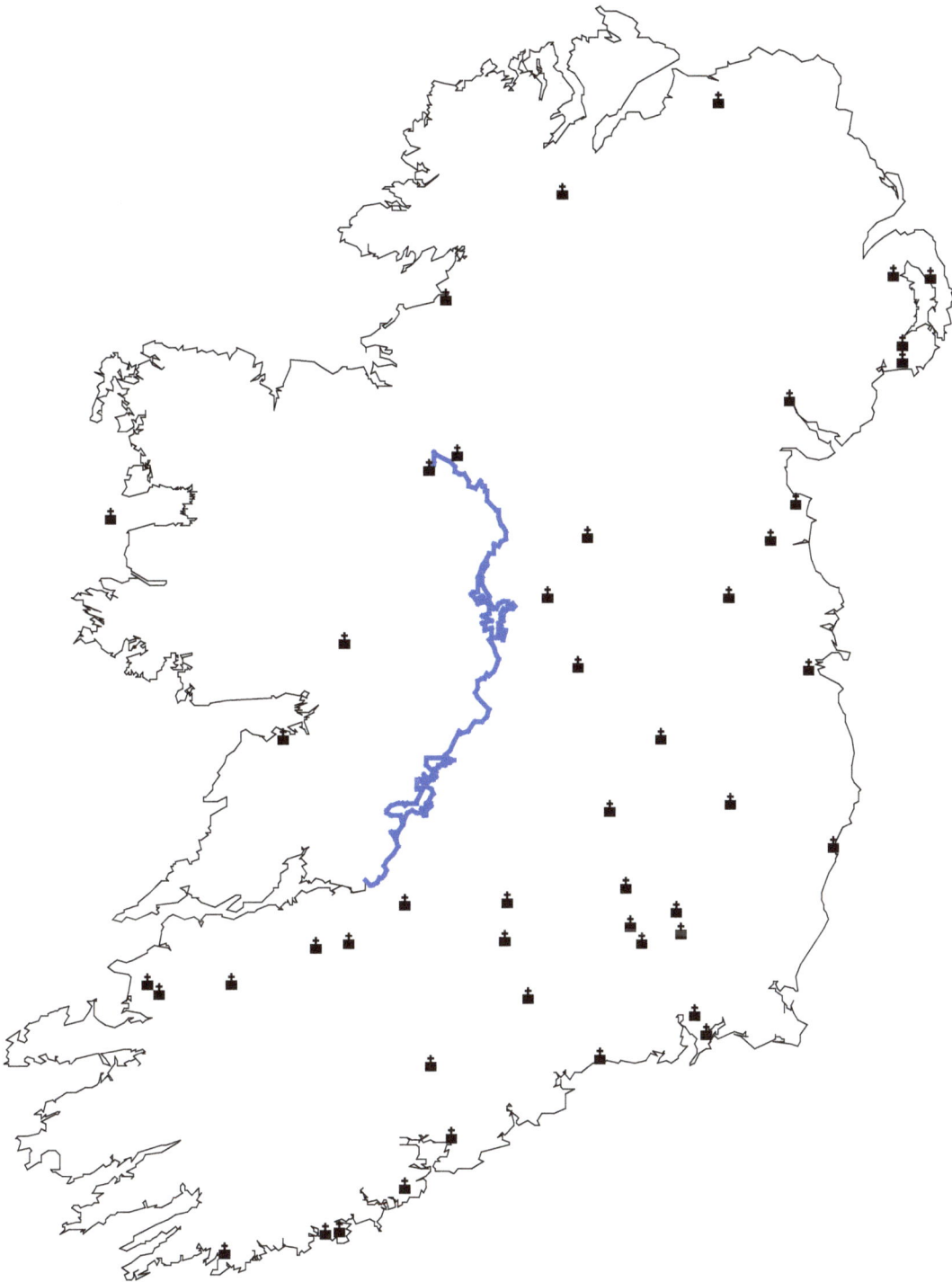

Figure 3.3: Cistercian Monasteries in Medieval Ireland

it is based upon the construction of a grid of quadrats (or squares) which are then used to measure the number of like for the comparison between mottes and boroughs yielded a Chi Square value of 50.038, which allows the rejection of the null hypothesis, that there is no correlation between the settlement of mottes and boroughs in proximity to each other. In other words, we can safely conclude that during this middle period boroughs were likely to be founded in close proximity to motte and bailey earthworks.

Another method of analyzing the relationship between mottes and boroughs is by creating buffer zones around each motte of one and five kilometers. The number of boroughs found in those zones was compared with the number that would be expected in each zone given the area of each zone. The result was a Chi Square value of 713.135, which would easily allow the rejection of the null hypothesis that there is no correlation between the settlement of boroughs and mottes. In fact, this large score is attributable to the large number of boroughs located within one kilometer of a motte.

The Anglo-Normans built very few new castles in this period. References to the construction of castles in the annals suggest that while in the early period about 15 new castles were constructed along the frontiers of the colony, the number of new castles constructed after the first 40 years of the thirteenth century declined to a total of eight for the next 140 years. The chart in Illustration 3.10 also shows that in this period the number of references to attacks on Anglo-Norman castles increased dramatically. One way to show whether there is a statistical relationship between these factors is by conducting a correlation and regression analysis. However, a correlation analysis of the number of constructions sites and the number of different sites for each given quadrat is problematic since the size of the quadrat greatly affects the resulting Chi Square value.[52] Hodder also suggests constructing a contingency table using the nearest neighbor method to measure the distance to the nearest like neighbor and nearest unlike neighbor. The resulting contingency table of castles and the number of castles destroyed returned a score of 0.181. For correlation analysis, a score of 1.00 would suggest a perfect positive correlation (as one set of values increases, the other set increases), while a score of -1.00 would suggest a perfect negative correlation (as one set of values increases, the other set decreases). Thus, while the graph seems to suggest that as the number of castles constructed decreased the number of castles attacked increased, this assumption is not statistically valid. Nevertheless, the

geographic distribution of these castle constructions and attacks is significant. The distribution of these castles is significantly associated with the Shannon River basin, which would suggest that in this middle period new castles were built on the frontier of the colony as buffers to the Gaelic regions of the island, and even further as staging points for attacks and settlement in Connacht.[53]

The Franciscan and Dominican Friars arrived in Ireland during the second quarter of the thirteenth century. The initial foundations appeared in the Anglo-Norman's coastal towns, but after 1250, over 20 foundations existed across Ireland. By the end of the period with which this study is concerned, more than 50 houses existed in Ireland. The majority of houses (42, to be precise) were founded in the 1250-1320 period. Franciscan and Dominican houses were primarily founded in the urban areas of continental Europe and England. To test whether this tendency occurred in medieval Ireland, the two Chi Square methods of analysis previously described were employed. Each Franciscan and Dominican data set was compared to the distribution of mottes and the distribution of boroughs using the concentric circle method as well as the like and unlike nearest neighbor method.

The first method of cluster analysis yielded two highly significant Chi Square values. For the relationship between Franciscan friaries and mottes, the returned value was 82.60. The relationship with boroughs gave a returned value of 150.085. Both values easily allow the rejection of the null hypothesis that there is no relationship between the settlement of Franciscan Friaries and both mottes and boroughs (this is no surprise since it has already been shown that mottes and boroughs existed in close proximity). The alternate method of Chi Square analysis which uses concentric circles around a given point also yielded significant values. The numbers of friaries within a one-kilometer radius around each of the mottes was only four, but the expected value was a mere 0.694. The values for the other zones were fairly close to the expected values, meaning that the significance lies in the closest proximity of the friaries with mottes.

The very small expected value of 0.335 friaries within one kilometer of the boroughs caused a huge Chi Square value of 1822.021. The number of Franciscan Friaries found within one kilometer was 25, nearly 75 times the expected value. The expected number of friaries located outside the five kilometer zone was 30 and lower than the expected value of 51 but, as can be seen in Table 3.23, the high

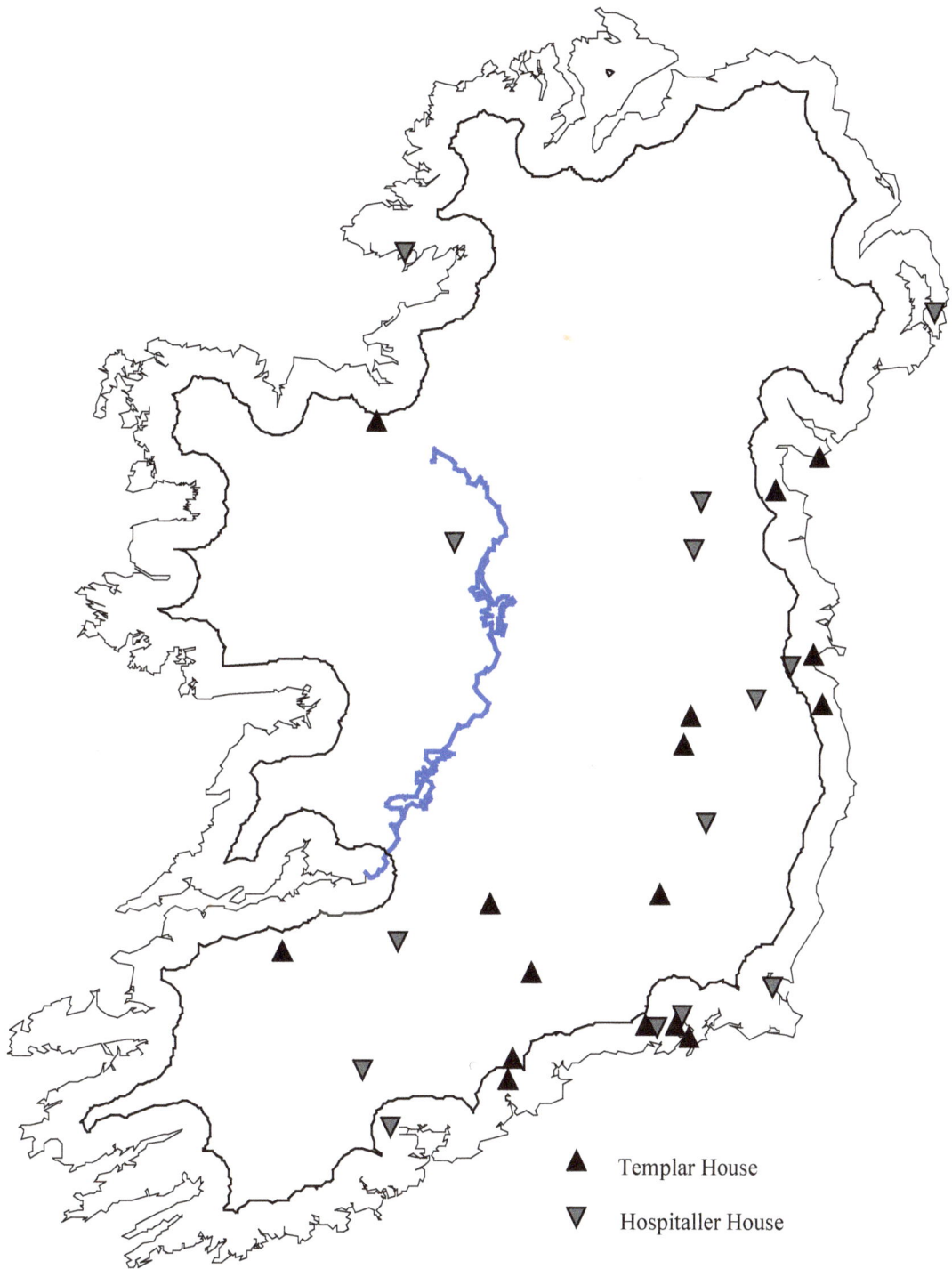

Figure 3.4: Military Monastic Order in Medieval Ireland with Ten Kilometer Coastal Buffer

TABLE 3.13: CLUSTERING OF MILITARY MONASTIC HOUSES

R value	0.6391
C score	-4.199

where n=36

TABLE 3.14: MILITARY MONASTIC HOUSES BY PROXIMITY TO RIVERS

Zone	Number	Area	Expected	(O-E)*(O-E)/N
1k	3	2447	1.0600	3.550
5k	12	8977	3.888	16.916
10k	6	10705	4.637	0.400
15k	4	8887	3.849	0.005
outside 15k	11	52084	22.563	5.926
Total	36	83100		
			Chi Square=	**26.799**

TABLE 3.15: MILITARY MONASTIC HOUSES BY ELEVATION

Zone	Number	Area	Expected	(O-E)*(O-E)/N
below 120m	29	44890	7.022	68.780
120m-300m	7	34587	5.410	0.466
above 300m	0	3623	0.566	0.566
Total	36	83100		
			Chi Square=	**69.813**

TABLE 3.16: MILITARY MONASTIC HOUSES AND THE COAST

Zone	Number	Area	Expected	(O-E)*(O-E)/N
Inland area	16	57718	26.393	4.092
10km buffer	22	24382	11.149	10.559
Total	38	83100		
			Chi Square=	**14.652**

Chi value is attributable mainly to the number of friaries found within one kilometer of the boroughs. The number actually located in that area, 25, is much greater than the expected number, 0.335.

The analysis for the Dominican Friaries resulted in very similar findings; extremely high Chi Square values show clustering between the Dominican Friaries and mottes and boroughs, allowing the rejection of the null hypothesis that there is no relation between the settlement of Dominican Friaries and mottes or boroughs. In short, then, it can be said that a very strong correlation existed between the creation of the new houses of friars in towns and areas that had already been settled by the Anglo-Normans. Typically, the new friaries were clearly found in close association with already established settlement. This reflects the apostolic and urban *modus operandi* of the Franciscan and Dominican Orders as opposed to the more monastic and contemplative goals of the Cistercians who often located their monasteries in remote settings. Indeed, this data reflects this difference in attitudes towards settlement since the association of friaries with boroughs shows a trend towards urban settlement.

The Final Period, 1320-1400 Because of the changing nature of secular settlement in Ireland throughout the entire period of this study, it is difficult to make any sort of comprehensive statistical analysis over all three periods. What can be analyzed across all three periods, though, are the changes in monastic settlement because accurate numbers and locations of monastic houses built throughout the medieval period exist.

A database consisting of all known monastic houses in medieval Ireland was constructed and then sub-divided according to decade. A second database tracked the number of new foundations per decade for each monastic order. The relevance of recording the number of new foundations is the supposition that the level of expansion of a particular order, in terms of the actual number of new houses established and in terms of those new houses being established in new geographic areas, can be measured by the number of new foundations of that order. During the early period, for instance, the Cistercians and military monastic orders gained prominence throughout the colony. Later, as the Franciscans and Dominicans arrived in Ireland, the Cistercians and military monastic orders ceased to expand with new houses; apparently benefactors began to favor the Franciscans and Dominicans and their more urban orientation. These orders, too, eventually

ceased to expand as the entire colony receded during the fourteenth century. When viewed as a whole, the medieval monastic orders of Ireland display a decline which began during the thirteenthc century. The level and degree of decline of new monastic foundations in Ireland in the Middle Ages is clearly shown in a time series chart. As shown in Figure 3.8, the overall trend line for all monastic orders slopes down at a steep angle; the individual orders themselves display a less marked decline. The difference between the monastic whole and the individual orders lies in the relatively low numbers of individual houses as compared to the higher number of total monastic houses. Most striking, then, is the very clear downward trend of monastic orders as a whole.[54]

Because of the changing nature of secular settlement in Ireland throughout the entire period of this study, it is difficult to make any sort of comprehensive analysis using, for instance, mottes and boroughs, aside from proving that the density of settlement in Leinster, for example, increased during the first two sub-periods of this study. Those two types of settlement are fundamentally different and represent two different responses to particular needs in the colony, one military and administrative, the other economic. But the notable point to consider in this third period is that there was very little new secular settlement in Ireland throughout the period. No significant castles appeared, and quite clearly by the end of the fourteenth century the medieval Anglo-Norman colony in Ireland contracted. The accepted explanations for the decline in colonial expansion and, in fact, decline of the colony itself, center around three factors. First, two natural calamities, famine in the second decade of the fourteenth century and plague in the middle of the century struck Ireland just as they did the rest of Europe. Second, Edward Bruce, brother of Robert Bruce of Scotland, led a campaign in Ireland in the second decade of the century that devastated portions of north and eastern Ireland.[55] And third, the number of new peasants in Ireland declined at the end of the thirteenth and throughout the fourteenth century. As a result, Anglo-Norman lords were unable to establish towns and boroughs in newly gained territories in the west during the late thirteenth century.

Gaelic Settlement Patterns, 1200-1400 In the later Middle Ages several continental pilgrims traveled to Ireland to visit St. Patrick's Purgatory and other pilgrimage sites in Ireland.[56] While on pilgrimage to St. Patrick's Purgatory on Lough Derg, Raymond de Perelhos commented that the Irish did not live in permanent structures but seemed

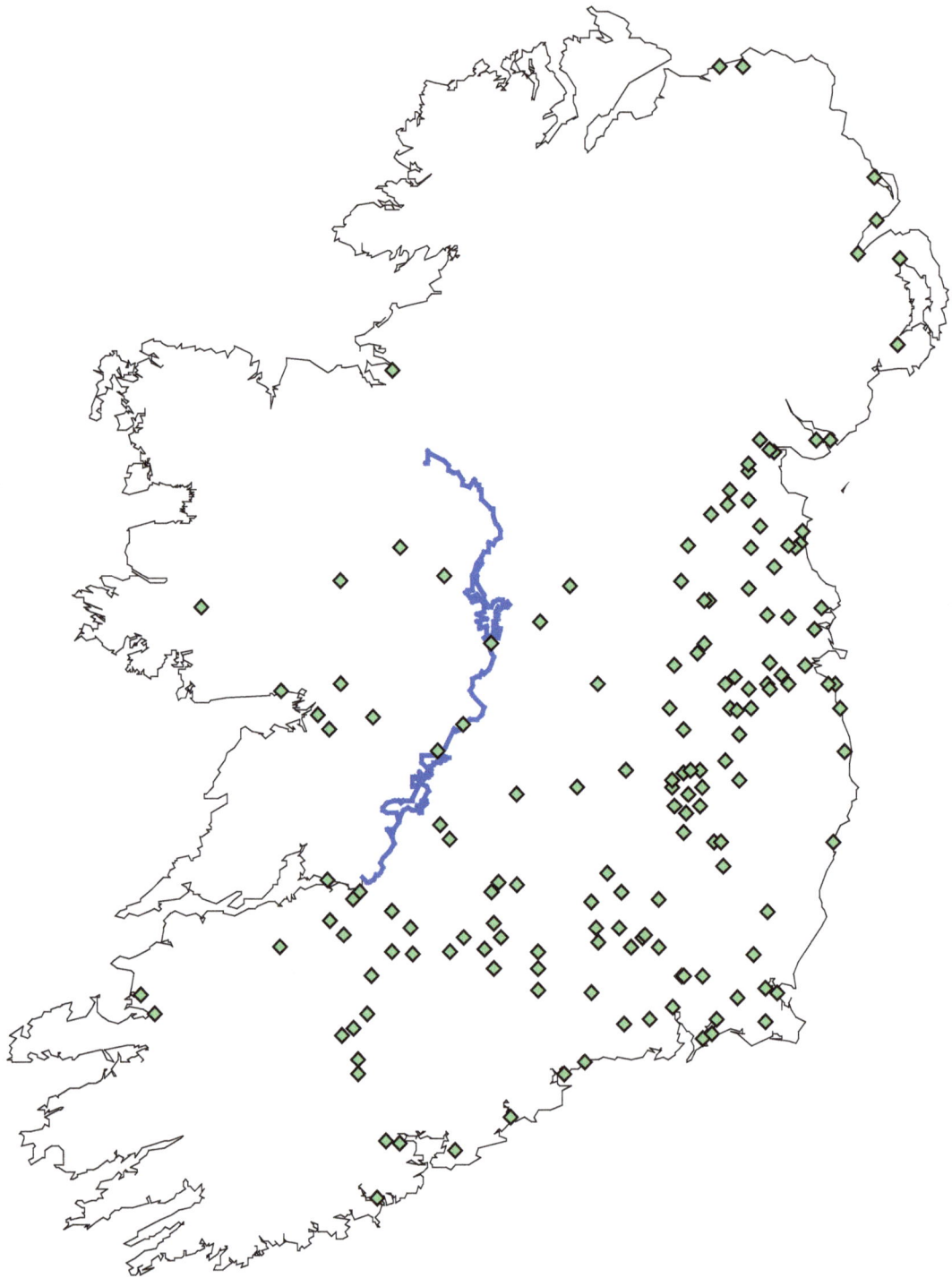

Figure 3.5: Boroughs in Medieval Ireland (after Graham)

TABLE 3.17: BOROUGH AND RIVER ASSOCIATION

Zone	Number	Area	Expected	(O-E)*(O-E)/N
1k	24	2447	4.740	78.237
5k	36	8977	17.392	19.908
10k	32	10705	20.740	6.113
15k	20	8887	17.217	0.449
outside 15k	49	52084	100.908	26.702
Total	161	83100		
			Chi Square=	**131.41**

TABLE 3.18: ASSOCIATION OF MOTTES AND BOROUGHS

Base Point

Nearest Neighbor		Motte	Borough
	Motte	235	60
	Borough	98	101

Chi Square=50.038

TABLE 3.19: BOROUGHS FOUND WITHIN PROXIMITY TO MOTTES

Zone	Number	Area	Expected	(O-E)*(O-E)/N
within 1km	30	978	1.318	624.107
1km-5km	52	15156	20.426	48.801
outside 5km	30	66966	90.255	40.226
Total	112	83100		
			Chi Square=	**713.135**

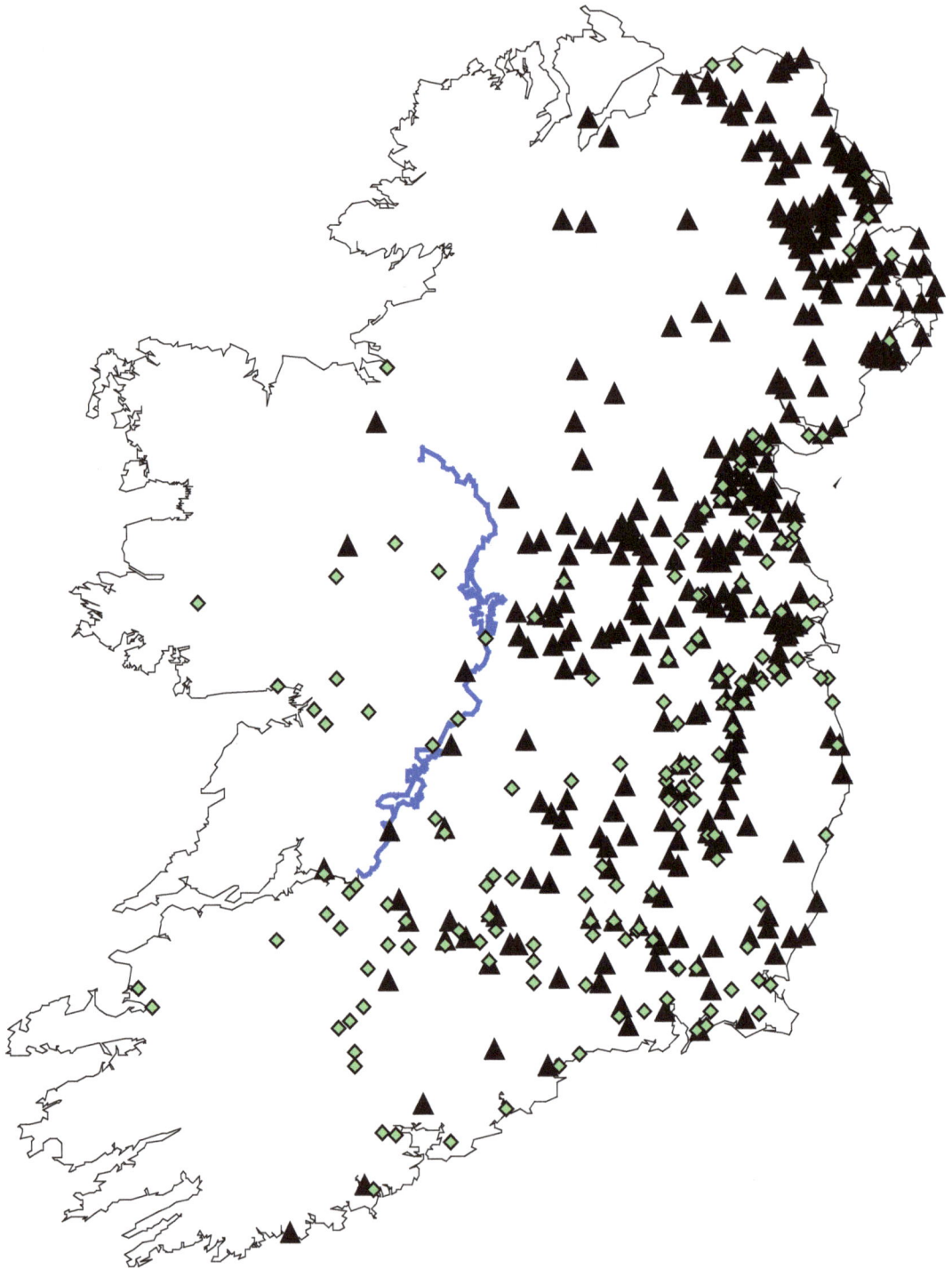

Figure 3.6: Mottes and Boroughs in Medieval Ireland

TABLE 3.20: CLUSTERING OF FRANCISCAN FRIARIES AND MOTTES

Base Point			
		Motte	Franciscan
Nearest Neighbor	Motte	293	22
	Franciscan	40	37

Chi Square=82.620

TABLE 3.21: CLUSTERING OF FRANCISCAN HOUSES AND BOROUGHS

Base Point

		Borough	Franciscan
Nearest Neighbor	Borough	15	161
	Franciscan	44	0

Chi Square=150.085

to prefer structures constructed of wattle and daub. This description of structures in which the Irish lived bears resemblance to the comments of Giraldus Cambrensis, who defined the kings of Ireland as inferior because they resided in wooden structures instead of stone castles.[57] However, this statement of Giraldus is questionable, given the fact that some of the Irish lords did indeed live in fortified, permanent structures.[58] Giraldus seemed, in fact, more intent upon branding the Irish as an inferior race than in clearly describing the structures in which the Irish lived. Nevertheless, it is striking that other commentators, such as Raymond de Perelhos, observed the Irish manner of settlement as clearly different from that of the rest of Europe. Other vistors to Ireland who were not pilgrims made similar claims; Abbott Stephen of Lexington, when investigating the Cistercian monasteries of Ireland in the early thirteenth century, noted that the kings of Ireland dwelt in small wooden huts (see Chapter Four for further detail concerning Stephen of Lexington).[59]

Ó Corráin has argued that the provincial kings did inhabit fortified structures in the pre-Norman period,[60] and later the Anglo-Normans and the Irish reused many of these structures. However, these fortified sites were clearly not castles, nor were they "proto-castles." Given the Irish propensity for cattle raids and small scale skirmishing, these structures were more than likely used as symbols of kingship and not as real administrative or military centers. They might even be considered enclosures on a large scale, similar to the Irish ringfort which probably served more as a cattle enclosure than a major defensive earthwork.[61] When describing these settlements, Irish annalists often used the word *longphort*, a term which may be translated as "stronghold" or "encampment," as opposed to *caislen*, which was generally used in reference to castles, and, in particular, stone castles built by the Anglo-Normans. In Freeman's edition of the *Annals of Connacht*, the term *longphort* alternatively describes a stronghold or an encampment, depending upon the particular context of the usage. If the reference is to a raiding party or an incursion into a neighboring region, Freeman translates *longphort* as "encampment," but if the reference describes a royal

TABLE 3.22: FRANCISCANS WITHIN MOTTE ZONES

Zone	Number	Area	Expected	(O-E)*(O-E)/N
within 1km	4	978	0.694	15.736
1km-5km	10	15156	10.760	0.053
outside 5km	45	66966	47.545	0.136
Total	59	83100		
			Chi Square=	**15.926**

TABLE 3.23: FRANCISCANS WITHIN BOROUGH ZONES

Zone	Number	Area	Expected	(O-E)*(O-E)/N
within 1km	25	473	0.335	1811.428
1km-5km	4	9908	7.0345	1.309
outside 5km	30	73192	51.965	9.284
Total	59	83100		
			Chi Square=	**1822.021**

TABLE 3.24: DOMINICAN FRIARIES AND MOTTES

Base Point

		Motte	Dominican
Nearest Neighbor	Motte	10	333
	Dominican	29	0

Chi Square=268.551

TABLE 3.25: DOMINICAN HOUSES AND BOROUGHS

Base Point

		Borough	Dominican
Nearest Neighbor	Borough	8	161
	Dominican	31	0

Chi Square=151.449

TABLE 3.26: DOMINICAN FRIARIES AND MOTTES

Zone	Number	Area	Expected	(O-E)*(O-E)/N
within 1km	6	978	0.470	64.943
1km-5km	11	15156	7.295	1.881
outside 5km	23	66966	32.233	2.645
Total	40	83100		
			Chi Square=	**69.469**

TABLE 3.27: DOMINICANS IN PROXIMITY TO BOROUGHS

Zone	Number	Area	Expected	(O-E)*(O-E)/N
within 1km	21	473	0.227	1895.177
1km-5km	3	9908	4.769	0.656
outside 5km	16	73192	35.230	10.497
Total	40	83100		
			Chi Square=	**1906.331**

site, he translates *longphort* as "stronghold." This seems a reliable distinction; however, regardless of differing contexts, the underlying meaning of the term *longphort* is one of an impermanent structure.[62] As well, for a brief time in the late twelfth century, the Ó Conchobhair kings of Connacht built fortifications (including castles and bridges) as part of a strategy for controlling access to and from Connacht.[63] During this period, though, the use of the term *longphort* rarely occurred. The term is then used with frequency in the late thirteenth century (when *caislen* is no longer used to describe the structures built by the Irish kings but is instead used to describe Anglo-Norman stone castles exclusively). This suggests that there was a temporary shift in the strategy employed by the Ó Conchobhair kings to control Connacht.

The fact that the Irish rarely built permanent structures creates great difficulties in gathering and inputting data useable in a Geographic Information System database. Compared to the Anglo-Norman material, often documented in both historical records and found in the archaeological record, the settlements of Gaelic Ireland are seldom identified. When they are identified, the settlements equate with the highest levels of Gaelic society, perhaps even the provincial level. This state of affairs, according to McNeill, raises several points.[64] First, and foremost, one wonders whether the Irish did not feel sufficiently threatened to build defensive structures. Instead, it might be more pertinent to consider the few Gaelic lords who actually built permanent structures, thus suggesting that these Gaelic lords felt most threatened. Second, given the continued tradition of raid and counter-raid as a military strategy in Ireland, lordship in an Irish sense did not depend upon the imposition of a hierarchical network of fortified administrative centers. An Irish king's reign was dependent upon military success and the marshalling of often conflicting branches of a royal family, and not upon the prestige associated with centralized strongholds. Kenneth Nicholls would apparently agree with this idea when he states that the twin factors of a highly mobile population (which corresponds to the Gaelic military practices of raid and counter-raid) and of the flimsy nature

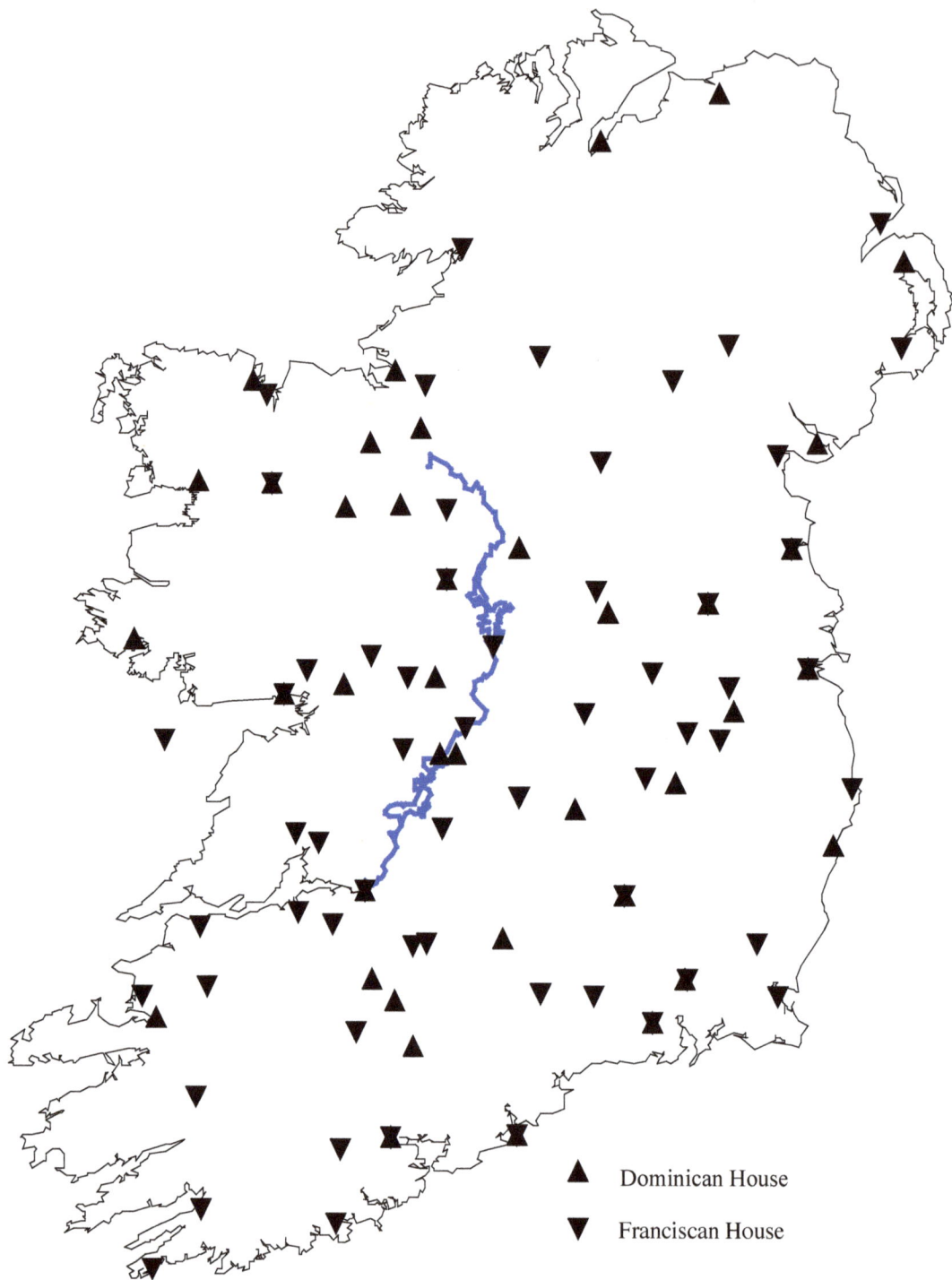

Figure 3.7: Dominican and Franciscan Houses in Medieval Ireland

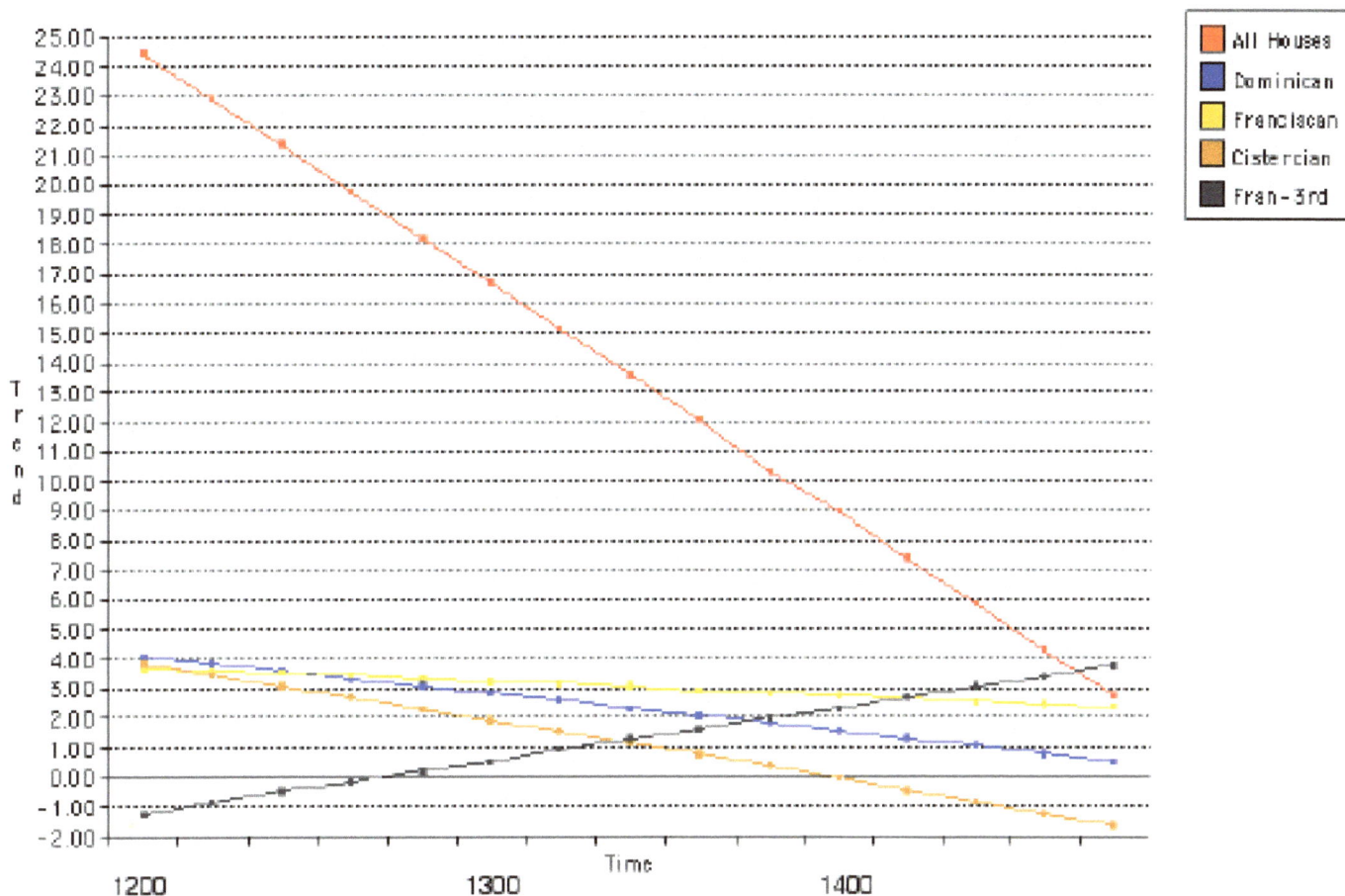

Figure 3.8: Trend Lines Illustrating the Foundations of New Monastic Houses in Medieval Ireland

of the typical Irish dwelling have caused problems in the interpretation of Gaelic settlement in the later middle ages.[65] O'Conor posits that the Gaelic lords in the western and highland regions had settled on some of the island's poorest soil. These rocky and boggy types of soil were particularly unsuited for the use of mounted armored warriors. If the castle is understood as a landscape feature that denies the ability of mounted knights to control land, then the castle is a response to the heavily armored knight. O'Conor suggests that Gaelic lords built so few castles or fortifications because the land that they inhabited was already defensible against large scale attack.[66]

At this point in the study, G.I.S. was used to deduce in a systematic and statistical manner whether the raids and incursions of the Irish might reveal a statistical geographic tendency. The same database used to organize the castle data derived from the annals may be used to show the location of castles attacked by the Irish and when these castles were attacked. Chart 3.2 displays the incedence of attacks in increments of 20 years, revealing that the

number of castles attacked peaked in the middle of the thirteenth century. Castles attacked in the fourteenth century number less than 10, although a slight increase occurred towards the middle of the fourteenth century. These findings prove quite significant, since many historicans and archaeologists mark the beginning of the colony's decline in the early fourteenth century. The collapse of the colony is attributed to economic decline after the famine, the invasion of Edward Bruce in 1315, and finally the plague in the middle of the fourteenth century.[67] Instead, the instability of the colony appears to have begun as early as the middle of thirteenth century, and resulted from the Anglo-Norman inability to hold and control land in the west and north and from counter attacks by the Irish kings. Furthermore, the number of attacks in the fourteenth century, being less than 10, suggests that those major social calamities--famine, Bruce invasion, plague--also caused a decrease in the attacks made by the Irish since those calamities affected the Irish (although to a lesser extent in terms of the plague). The annals are notably difficult sources with which to work; but the fact

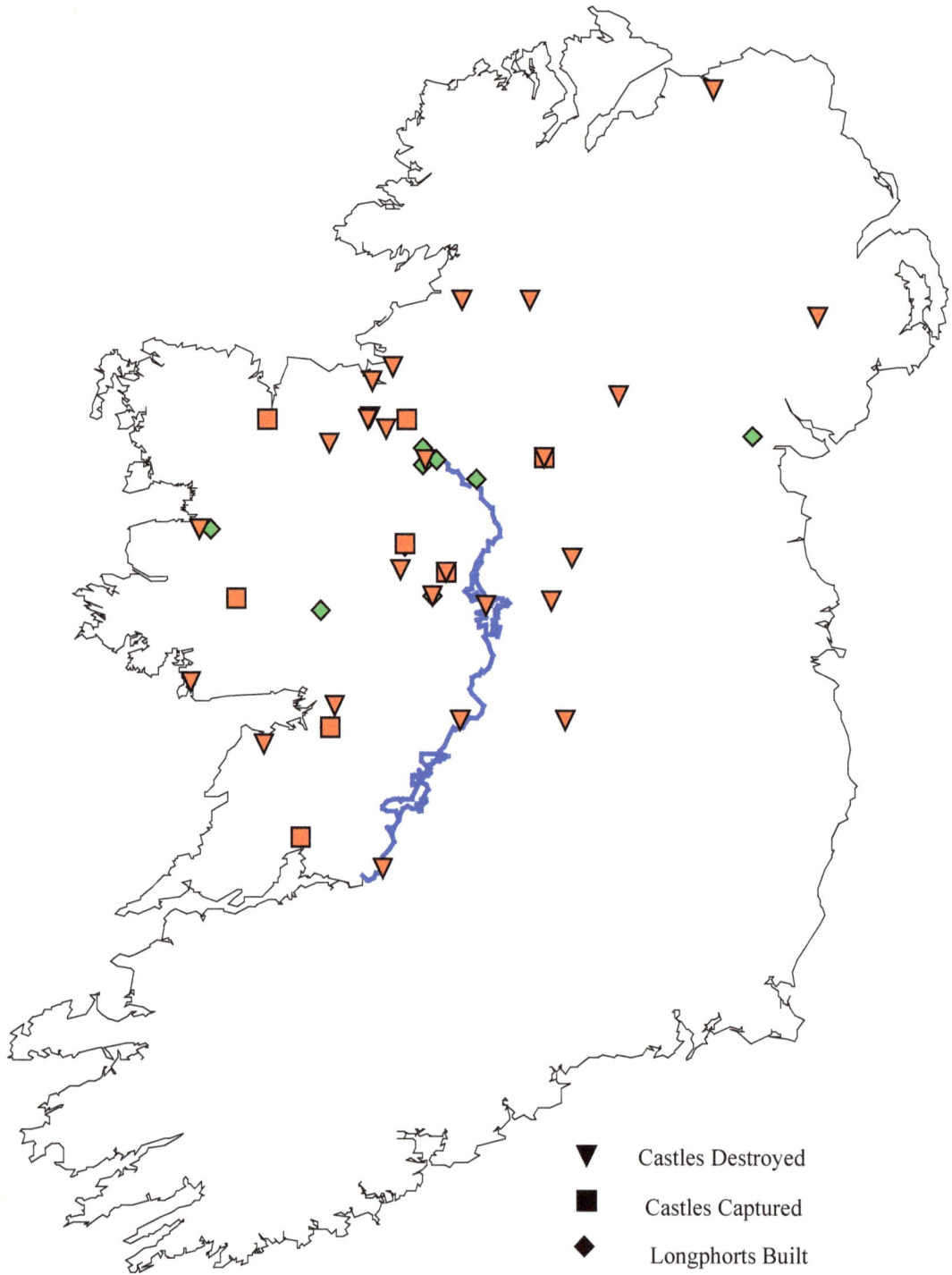

Figure 3.9: Annalistic References to Attacks upon Castles and the Construction of Gaelic longphort

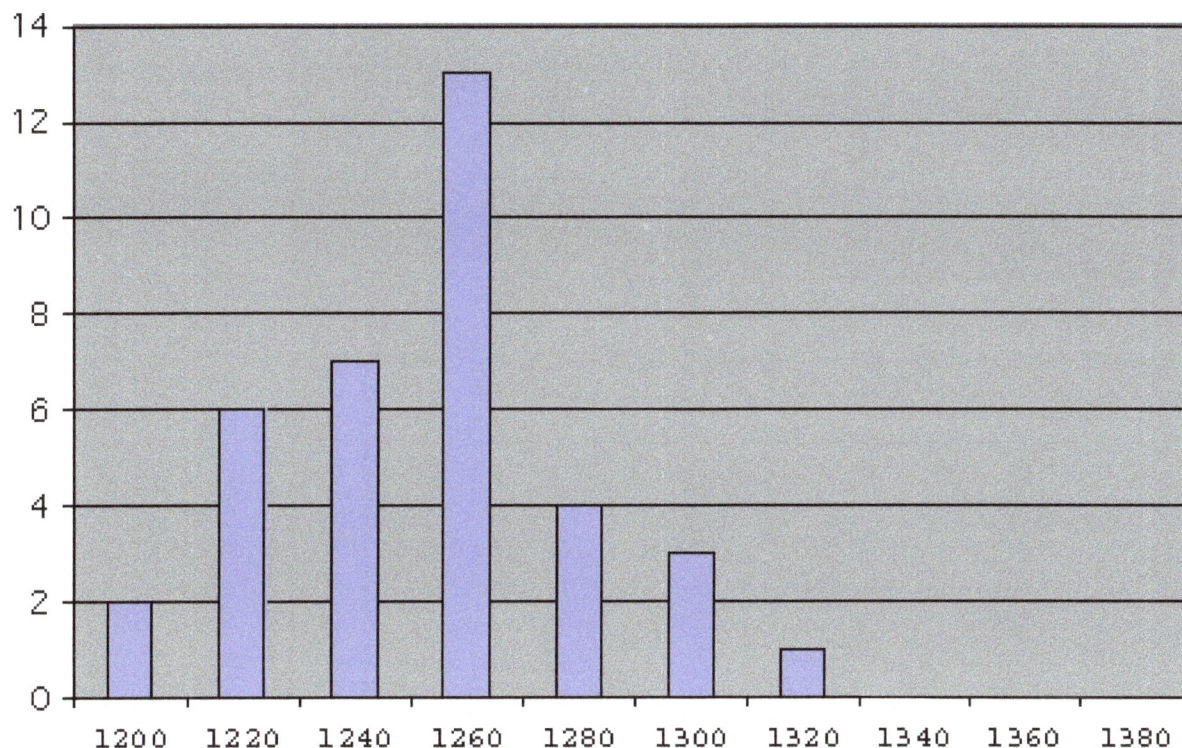

Figure 3.10: Number of Reported Gaelic Attacks upon Anglo-Norman Castles in Twenty Year Increments

remains that the references to attacks on castles were significant enough to actually record. Though the forces involved in such attacks were small, and the incidents themselves were sometimes recorded in one set of annals and not another (which reflected a particular groups need to provide a running history of its accomplishments in battle), these references ultimately prove important in their categorization of castle sites inhabited at the time, castles which were important enough to attack, and geographic territories under contention.

The monastic and apostolic orders in Ireland often recorded the founder of a particular house or friary which provides information about whether the founder was of Anglo-Norman or Gaelic background. The relevance of this distinction blurs in the period after that which this study is concerned. In the fifteenth and sixteenth centuries, descendents of the Anglo-Norman lords such as the Fitzgerald Lords of Kildare were said to have become "more Irish than the Irish themselves" and were often criticized for being not quite English. However, the relevance of the distinction between Anglo-Norman and Gaelic founders was marked during the thirteenth and fourteenth centuries.

In the mid twelfth century the Cistercians first came to Ireland before the Anglo-Normans arrived in the 1170's. Irish kings often supported new Cistercian foundations in order to gain the support of the Church, thus enhancing their own authority. By 1171, Gaelic lords supported 15 Cistercian abbeys in Ireland, while after 1171 a further 22 were founded by both Gaelic and Anglo-Norman lords. Of those 22, Anglo-Norman lords founded seven, while Irish kings founded the remaining 15 (four of which failed by 1228). Many of those 22 appeared in regions subsequently absorbed by the Anglo-Norman colony. As they colonized these regions, the Anglo-Normans endeavored to also sieze the authority of these abbeys. The situation worsened in 1217 with the deposition of the abbot of Mellifont after he violently refused to admit Cistercians sent to make a visitation to the abbey. In 1227, all involved Irish Cistercian abbots were deposed after they were accused of being part of a conspiracy. After Stephen of Lexington purged the abbeys of Mellifont and Jerpoint, abbots were forced to shift their affiliations to non-Irish mother houses (see Chapter Four).[68]

Relative to the Continental and English abbeys, the Cistercian abbeys of Ireland existed in poverty. Furthermore, after the Order's troubles in the early thirteenth century, few new abbeys were founded in Ireland. This is often attributed to a general decline in available field and farm workers in the middle of the thirteenth century.[69] By the time the Black Death arrived in the mid-fourteenth century, many abbeys had few monks and no lay workers. Clearly, the Cistercians in Ireland, whether founded by Irish kings or Anglo-Norman lords, fell into decline as early as the 1240's.

During the continued decline of the Cistercians, the Franciscan and Dominican Friars arrived in Ireland. The Franciscan and Dominican friaries showed a significant tendency to be founded in established towns and boroughs. However, of the 17 friaries founded by the Irish, eight were not located in towns or boroughs. For the Franciscans, this was exemplified by the overt administrative division between Irish and Anglo-Norman custodies in 1325.[70] In 1327, Edward III ordered that the annual payment of alms to the friars of Athlone should be transferred to the friars at Cashel since the friars at Athlone were primarily Irish. The Franciscan Order continued to expand in Ireland; but, despite efforts of the government in Dublin to curtail development in Irish areas, the Franciscans in the fourteenth century were often associated with the rebellious Irish (see Chapter Four).

Conclusions

The decline of the Anglo-Norman colony is a well-established fact; people living in the colony in the thirteenth and fourteenth centuries would have agreed. However, this analysis shows that the decline actually began earlier than often supposed; before the famine of the early fourteenth century, the Bruce invasion of 1315, and the arrival of the bubonic plague in the middle of the fourteenth century. The causes of the colony's decline are clearly complex, and not easily discerned by geographic analysis; in other words, the geography itself did not cause the decline in the colony. However, the analysis shows that the initial period of Anglo-Norman colonial expansion ended around 1250 and the decline in expansion resulted in a general decline in the fortunes of the colony itself.

This study has shown that the settlement of motte fortifications were statistically significantly located in proximity to each other, in association with rivers and in low elevation areas. While some have suggested that mottes may in fact have been occupied well into the late thirteenth and perhaps even into the fourteenth century,[71] it is still clear that mottes reflect the initial pattern of

settlement by the Anglo-Normans since these structures acted as the local level of administrative government. Related to this settlement of mottes is the fact that castles constructed early in the history of the colony are not clustered and not significantly located in any area. This is due to the nature of the stone castle as a higher level bureaucratic center. But in the middle of the thirteenth century, the Anglo-Normans began building new castles significantly clustered around rivers. As well, these castles were located particularly in close proximity to the Shannon River basin. These newer castles, like Roscommon castle, tend to display a greater concern for military control as opposed to administration.

The settlement of religious houses in the early period is primarily characterized by the settlement of Cistercian monasteries; there was no significant clustering of these monasteries in medieval Ireland, but they were significantly located near rivers and in lowland areas. The military monastic orders were found significantly clustered close to the coastal areas of initial colonial settlement. This all suggests that the general pattern of Anglo-Norman settlement was essentially related to lowland settlement in the eastern half of Ireland. This area was very similar in agricultural quality to the more fertile regions of England and the Continent, and that comparison certainly drew the attention of settlers in this early phase.

This is also why boroughs are not only significantly found in proximity to rivers but also in proximity to mottes. Boroughs, which were towns that had achieved official market status, would of course have been located close to regions in which agriculture would have played a major economic role in society. But in this period there are very few new castles or fortifications built by the Anglo-Normans, and the castles that had been built in the previous period came under increasing attack from the Gaelic lords in the west and north. When the new communities of Dominicans and Franciscan Friars came to Ireland in the thirteenth century, they too were significantly located near mottes and boroughs. In other words, they were found in that same lowland setting and were often located in the boroughs themselves. These facts considered together point to the fact that in the second period of this study the colony did not expand but rather became more dense in areas that had been initially settled by the original Anglo-Norman settlers in the late twelfth century.

Conversely, this study has also shown that the Irish kings made concerted and significant efforts to attack the colony early in the thirteenth century. These attacks should be considered from two different perspectives. First, while the lands to the north and west were settled by Anglo-Normans early in the thirteenth century, there did not seem to be a massive infusion of settlers from England, as there had been in Leinster. The power of the Irish kings in these regions, while often significantly less than the King of England, the Justiciar in Dublin, or even most of the Anglo-Norman lords, was nevertheless great enough to enable them to raid the colony almost at will. Second, these attacks were a form of establishing lordship for the Irish just as establishing power centers was for the Anglo-Normans. The Irish king was noted for his individual prowess in battle, his ability to raid and prevent counter-raids from his enemy, and his ability to gain wealth from those raids, as was shown in the analysis of the political ideology found in bardic poetry in Chapter Two of this study. He was not noted for his ability to build large and extensive castles, nor was he noted for his ability to employ strong administrative systems of government. As well, as O'Conor has suggested, the terrain and geography may have been used as a strategic advantage by the Gaelic lords against the Anglo-Normans. It is no coincidence, then, that there is a lack of settlement evidence for the Irish in this period; the nature of lordship for the Irish was radically different from the Anglo-Normans' lordship.

One final thought: this study is based upon data that was compiled during the latter part of the 1990s, a time when massive amounts of data were being compiled, digitized, and made functional for GIS analysis. This conclusions of this portion of this study, while ultimately valid in terms of the methodology and technique employed to reach those conclusion, must be considered tentative if only because more sets of data will be available by the end of the first decade of the new millenium.

[1] A.J. Otway-Ruthven, "The Medieval County of Kildare." *Irish Historical Studies.* XI (1959), 181-99; "Knight Service in Ireland." *Journal of the Royal Society of Antiquaries of Ireland.* LXXXIX (1959), 1-15; "The Character of Norman Settlement in Ireland." *Historical Studies V.* (1965), 75-84.

[2] E. Brooks, *Knights' Fees in Counties Wexford, Carlow, and Kilkenny* (Dublin: Irish Manuscripts Commission, 1950).

[3] T.B. Barry, "Late Medieval Ireland: the Debate on Social and Economic Decline, 1350-1550." In *An Historical Geography of Ireland.* ed. B.J. Graham, L.J. Proudfoot. (London, Academic Press, 1993), 99.

[4] Barry and Graham have used statistical analysis in some of their works regarding ringworks and medieval towns respectively, but these studies are limited exclusively to the use of Chi Square analysis for measuring the relevance of settlement in certain zones, as this study does later in this chapter. These studies are also limited by the fact that they were not able to consider multiple sets of data because the measurements were made by hand and not with computer analysis packages. See T.B. Barry, *The Medieval Moated Sites of South-East Ireland: Counties Carlow, Kilkenny, Tipperary, and Wexford* (Oxford: British Archaeological Reports, 35, 1977).

[5] David J. Maguire, *Computers in Geography.* (New York, Longman Scientific and Technical Press, 1989), 172.

[6] MapInfo for MacIntosh, Version 3.01 (Troy, New York); MapBasic for MacIntosh, Version 3 (Troy, New York). It should be noted that when this thesis was begun in 1995 version 3.01 was the most up to date version of the software. Since then, MapInfo Corporation has continued to develop MapInfo for Windows, but stopped production of MapInfo for Macintosh at version 4.0. I opted to continue using version 3.01 because, first, I had already created a sizable amount of databases using 3.01, and, second, I had created a number of MapBasic programs that would only work with version 3.01.

[7] The best introduction to this cartographic issue is Mark Monmonier's recent works on expository cartography. See Mark Monmonier, *Mapping It Out: Expository Cartography for the Humanities and the Social Sciences* (Chicago: University of Chicago Press, 1993), 242.

[8] P.J. Clark and F.C. Evans, "Distance to Nearest Neighbour as a Measure of Spatial Relationships in Populations." *Ecology,* 35 (1954): 445-53. See also L.R. Dice, "Measures of the Amount of Ecologic Associations Between Species." *Ecology* 26 (1945): 297-302.

[9] A. Getis, "Temporal Land Use Pattern Analysis with the Use of Nearest Neighbor and Quadrat Methods," *Annals of the Association of American Geographers,* 54 (1964): 391-9;

[10] Ian Hodder and Clive Orton, *Spatial Analysis in Archaeology* (Cambridge: Cambridge University Press, 1976), 40-41.

[11] Hodder and Orton, *Spatial Analysis in Archaeology,* 40-41.

[12] Hodder and Orton, *Spatial Analysis in Archaeology,* 224-225.

[13] Barry has used a similar method in analyzing medieval moated sites in south-eastern Ireland (Barry, *The Medieval Moated Sites of South-East Ireland: Counties Carlow, Kilkenny, Tipperary, and Wexford*), using elevation and soil qualities as factors in determining the settlement of moated sites.

[14] MINITAB for Macintosh, Version 8, Minitab Incorporated: 1992.

[15] Hodder and Orton, *Spatial Analysis in Archaeology,* 204-207.

[16] Kenneth Foote and David Huebner, *The Geographer's Craft Project* (Austin, Department of Geography, University of Texas at Austin, 1995): 1.

[17] Mark Monmonier, *How to Lie with Maps* (Chicago: University of Chicago Press, 1996), 43-54

[18] Foote and Huebner, *The Geographer's Craft Project,* 2.

[19] Foote and Huebner, *The Geographer's Craft Project,* 3.

[20] Foote and Huebner, *The Geographer's Craft Project,* 3

[21] G.H. Orpen, *Ireland Under the Normans, I-IV,* (Oxford, Oxford University Press, 1911-20).

22P.A. Burrough, *Principles of Geographical Information Systems for Land Resource Assessment* (Oxford: Clarendon Press, 1990).

23Barry, *The Medieval Moated Sites of Southeastern Ireland*, 21.

24 In most cases, the data sets used for this study were compiled by the author using information gathered from textual sources. Where possible, these data sets were cross referenced with data sets from the Irish Archaeological Inventory Site and Monument Record.

25Orpen, *Ireland Under the Normans, Vol. I-IV.*

26R.E. Glasscock, "Moated Sites and Deserted Boroughs and Villages: Two Neglected Aspects of Anglo-Norman Settlement in Ireland" in *Irish Geographical Studies*, ed. N. Stephens and R.E. Glasscock (Belfast, 1970): 162-77.

27Kieran O'Conor, "Irish Earthwork Castles," Fortress 12 (1992): 1-12; idem, "The Later Construction and Use of Motte and Bailey Castles in Ireland: New Evidence from Leinster," *Journal of the Kildare Archaeological Society* 17 (1987-91): 13-29.

28 Tom McNeill, *Castles in Ireland* (New York: Routledge, 1997); David Sweetman, *The Irish Castle* (Dublin, 1999).

29*Calendar of Documents Relating to Ireland.* Ed. H.S. Sweetman, 5 Vols., London (1875-86); *Annals of Connacht.* Ed. A. Martin Freeman, Dublin, Dublin Institute for Advanced Studies, (1944); *The Annals of the Kingdom of Ireland by the Four Masters.* 7 vols., Dublin (1848-51); *The Annals of Loch Cé.* Ed. W. M. Hennessy, 2 Vols., Rolls Series, London (1871); *The Annals of Ulster.* Ed. W. M. Hennessy and B. MacCarthy, 4 Vols. Dublin (1887-1901).

30B.J. Graham, "The Towns of Medieval Ireland," in *The Development of the Irish Town* (New Jersey, Rowman and Littlefield, 1977).

31 T.B. Barry, *The Archaeology of Medieval Ireland.* (London, Routledge, 1987), 37.

32Thomas Finan, "Annalistic References to Medieval Irish Fortifications: A G.I.S. Approach," forthcoming.

33For the earlier periods of Irish medieval history archaeologists have been at pains to explain where exactly the population actually lived. The most likely solution is that even into the thirteenth century the Irish lived in nucleated farmsteads with wooden structures, perhaps in raths. These structures, of course, would not appear without archaeological excavation because the wooden structures would have rotted quickly in the moist Irish climate, and would only appear as post-holes. O'Conor has offered further hypotheses (see Kieran O'Conor, *Settlement and Society in Medieval Gaelic Ireland.* Discovery Program Monographs, 4: 1998) but the issue will not be resolved without extensive excavation in regions that have had historically seen little comprehensive analysis.

34 Gearóid MacNiocaill, *The Medieval Irish Annals.* (Dublin: Dublin Historical Association Medieval Irish History Series, No. 3, 1975), 29-36.

35Gwynn and Hadcock, *Medieval Religious Houses, Ireland* (London: Longman Publishers, 1988).

36 See Thomas Finan, The Nation and National Identities in Medieval Ireland, 1200-1400 (Doctoral Dissertation, The Catholic University of American, Washington DC, 2001), Appendix B.

37The Office of Public Works, Ireland, has been publishing the county archaeological inventories at the rate of two per year. As of 1997, the Archaeological Survey of Ireland had published nine of the thirty two counties, with the field surveys completed for a further thirteen counties. See O'Conor, T*he Archaeology of Rural Settlement in Medieval Ireland*, 12-15.

38 Add reference to sinead ni ghabhlains article and the churches of Offally book.

39The three classics of studies of medieval Irish history, Orpen, *Ireland Under the Normans, Vol. I-IV.* Oxford: Oxford University Press (1911-20); Edmund Curtis, *A History of Medieval Ireland.* (Dublin: Maunsel and Roberts, 1923), and Otway-Ruthven, *A History of Medieval Ireland,* are now supplemented by Robin Frame, *Colonial Ireland, 1169-1369* (Dublin: Helicon, 1981); Art Cosgrove, *Late Medieval Ireland, 1370-1541* (Dublin: Helicon, 1981); and Sean Duffy, *Ireland in the Middle Ages* (Dublin: Gill and MacMillan, 1997).

40Frame, *Colonial Ireland*, 26.

[41] Marie-Terese Flanagan, *Irish Society, Anglo-Norman Settlers, Angevin Kingship* (Oxford: Oxford University Press, 1989), 229-272.

[42] Frame, *Colonial Ireland,* 70.

[43] Otway-Ruthven, *A History of Medieval Ireland*, 201.

[44] Kieran O'Conor, personal comment.

[45] See C.T. Cairns, *Irish Tower Houses, a Co. Tipperary Case Study.* (Athlone, 1987); and O'Conor, The Archaeology of Medieval Rural Settlement in Ireland, 102. At the present time, it seems that the tower house should be considered an example of the mingling that occurred between the Anglo-Norman and Gaelic peoples, in that the tower house brings the Anglo-Norman use of stone together with the need for small scale defense of personal property. The idea of the tower house, according to O'Conor at least, is more similar to pre-Anglo-Norman, Gaelic settlement types, like crannogs (natural island fortifications) and the *longphort*. Nevertheless, it seems that an insignificant number of tower houses (compared to the hundreds that have been identified) were constructed before 1400.

[46] N.J.G. Pounds, *The Medieval Castle in England and Wales* (Cambridge: Cambridge University Press, 1994), 54-71.

[47] McNeill, *Castles in Ireland*, 56-58.

[48] B.J. Graham, "The Towns of Medieval Ireland."

[49] McNeill, *Castles in Ireland,* 76-78.

[50] This information was entered into a database based upon the textual information provided by the relevant source (probably date of construction, name, etc.). The coordinates entered for each site was recorded from the Discovery Series maps published by the Irish Ordnance Survey.

[51] Graham, "The Towns of Medieval Ireland," 29-30.

[52] Hodder and Orton, *Spatial Analysis in Archaeology*, 202-204.

[53] Finan, , "Annalistic References to Medieval Irish Fortifications: A G.I.S. Approach," forthcoming.

[54] The rise in the trend of the Franciscan Friars represents a rise in the number of friaries for the Franciscans, but this may be misleading since in the late fourteenth and fifteenth centuries the houses established were Franciscan Third Order friaries. The rise in the Third Order Franciscans is a topic which is outside the time period with which this study is concerned, that is, between 1200 and 1400, but it may be relevant to the discussion of nationalism in Early Modern Ireland because those friaries were established in predominantly Gaelic areas.

[55] Sean Duffy, ed., *The MacMillan Atlas of Irish History* (New York, MacMillan Press, 1997): 42-43.

[56] J.P Mahaffy, "Two Early Tours of Ireland," *Hermathena*, XVIII, no. 40 (1914): 3-9.

[57] J. Dimock, *Giraldus Cambrensis Opera*, vol. 5., Rolls Series (London), 182.

[58] McNeill, *Castles in Ireland*, 15.

[59] O'Dwyer, *Conspiracy of Mellifont*, 31.

[60] Donnchadh Ó Corráin, *Aspects of Early Irish History.* 68-70.

[61] Mathew Stout, *The Irish Ringfort* (Dublin: Four Courts Press, 1996), 32-33.

[62] *Dictionary of the Irish Language*, s.v. *longphort.*

[63] John Ryan, *Toirdelbach O Conchubair, (1088-1156), King of Connacht, King of Ireland Co Fresabara* (Dublin: National University of Ireland, 1966), 11-13.

[64] McNeill, *Castles in Ireland,* 168.

[65] Nicholls, Kenneth. "Gaelic Society and Economy in the High Middle Ages." *New History of Ireland, Vol II.* Oxford University Press (Oxford): 403.

[66] O'Conor, *Settlement and Society in medieval Gaelic Ireland*, 97-99.

[67] Duffy, *Ireland in the Middle Ages*, 134.

[68] O'Dwyer, *The Conspiracy of Melifont*, 34-41.

[69] Gwynn and Hadcock, *Medieval Religious Houses,*

Ireland, 117-118.

[70] Gwynn and Hadcock, *Medieval Religious Houses, Ireland,* 237.

[71] Personal comments, Terry Barry and Kieran O'Connor, 1999.

Chapter Four:
Nationality and The Medieval Church in Ireland

Acute national conflict occurred within the church in thirteenth and fourteenth century because concurrent but vastly different understandings of its function and structure existed. According to John Watt, the northern episcopal province of Armagh, the church was divided between regions known as "*ecclesia inter Anglicos*" and "*inter Hibernicos.*" This division reflected that each province was unified under one archbishop, but was in reality fragmented both geographically and ethnically.[1] Watt showed that while the local churches in Armagh managed to coexist, they nevertheless experienced clear divisions along national lines as described by thirteenth and fourteenth century writers.

One problem in studying ecclesiastical organization during thirteenth and fourteenth century Ireland occurs because definitions for terms such as "Irish church" or "the church in Ireland" are rarely defined.[2] For purposes of this study, the term "Irish church" refers to that particularly self-conscious part of the medieval Roman Catholic church in Ireland concerned with issues which included institutional control, patronage, and specific issues of reform (such as marriage laws), even if those practices were not unique to Ireland in this period. The term "the church in Ireland" shall refer to that institutional Church from England which was brought to Ireland as part of the Anglo-Norman settlement. These two definitions are essentially based upon Watt's evidence for the division of the church in fourteenth century Ulster[3] and were understood by both fourteenth century Anglo-Norman and Irish commentators as indicative of Ireland's ethnic divisions.

However, these divisions remained somewhat blurred. While geographical areas such as Connacht remained part of the "Irish church" throughout this period, many "Irish church" areas were still part of the "church in Ireland" in an institutional and organizational sense. Ireland was divided into four episcopal provinces in the twelfth century. Those areas more heavily settled by the Anglo-Normans[4] tended to adopt characteristics of the English church despite technically belonging to the "church in Ireland."

The "Irish church" and the "church in Ireland" existed as parts of a wider, Western European church organization; hence the term "church" is often employed to define that wider Church organization. Ireland, like England and numerous other regions of Europe, made up the international body known as the medieval Roman church.[5] The "English" church of the middle ages is often defined as those regions subject to Canterbury and York, despite that other regions, such as the March of Calais, the four Welsh bishoprics, and Scottish bishoprics, variously came under the jurisdiction of Canterbury and York as well.[6] In Ireland, although part of a wider, international church, the boundaries of the four provinces which constituted the church in Ireland remained surprisingly constant.

Pre-Norman Reforms and the Organization of the Church

Before considering the church during the thirteenth and fourteenth centuries, a review of the twelfth century Irish church reforms is necessary. This century was important for the development of a self-conscious Irish church. The church in Ireland defined the geographic island of Ireland as the perimeter of the church. The Irish church appeared sufficiently self-conscious to view itself as different from other Roman Catholic regions; nevertheless, the church considered itself part of the more universal Church.[7] This double identity was no different from other regions of medieval Europe, including England. Unique to Ireland, though, were the circumstances of colonization and the divisions, both ethnic and geographic as discussed in Chapters Two and Three, existing in medieval Ireland.

The unique national identity of the Irish church in the twelfth century results from this tension between "being like" and "being different." The practices of the Irish church, particularly concerning marriage and certain other sacramental practices, clearly contradicted the practices encouraged by the Gregorian reforms of the Roman church.[8] The Irish church's institutional structures also exhibited archaic features such as hereditary ownership of church lands by individuals (*erenach*) from particular families.

The twelfth century reform of the Irish church was both part of the wider Gregorian reforms of the eleventh century and part of a more localized reform movement within the Irish church.[9] The reform movement's origins prove difficult to trace, but several factors contributed to a reawakening within the Irish church. The relative peace enjoyed on the Continent during the eleventh century allowed pilgrims from Ireland to undertake journeys to Rome. Such pilgrimages, undertaken by notable royal personages such as Maolruanaidh Ó Maeldoraidh, *rí in tuascirt* ("king of the north [of Ireland]") in 1026,[10] Sitric King of the Norsemen in Dublin,[11] and Flaithbertach Ó Néill,[12] indicate a widening world view on the part of Irish culture, and hence the Irish Church.

King Sitric may also claim responsibility for extending the Irish church's world to Canterbury, as suggested by Watt, since the establishment of the diocese of Dublin may relate to a pilgrim's promise made by Sitric in Rome.[13] Regardless of the origin of the relationship between Dublin and Canterbury (the details in this period are completely unclear), by 1074 the people of Dublin assured Archbishop Lanfranc that they remembered Canterbury's favor in establishing the see of Dublin. In that year, Lanfranc consecrated Bishop Patrick of Dublin, which formalized the link between Dublin and Canterbury through the supplication of the Dublin see to Canterbury.[14] Not only was the relationship between Canterbury and Dublin formalized, but it was based upon a formal submission of Dublin to Canterbury. This submission followed York's submission to Canterbury in 1072 after Lanfranc informed Pope Alexander II that, from the time of Augustine and Bede, Canterbury had exercised authority over York. Lanfranc stated that his "predecessors exercised primacy over the Church of York and the whole island which men called Britain and over Ireland as well."[15] By gaining the right to ordain the bishop of Dublin[16] and to make a formal claim of authority over Ireland (although Dublin was never the primatial see of Ireland), Lanfranc bolstered his own primatial claim to all of Britain, including York (hence, northern England), and managed to extend his claim to Scotland and Ireland.[17] Watt suggests that the claims made over Ireland should be seen as a by-product of Canterbury's attempt to gain authority over York, both of which were included in a litany of areas controlled by Canterbury.[18]

Similar to King Sitric in Dublin, the kings of Munster also made overtures to Canterbury later in the eleventh and early twelfth centuries. On one occasion they attempted to gain a bishop for Waterford, and on another they hoped to gain a bishop at Limerick. Both were important trading towns for the Ó Briain kings of Munster, and the prestige associated with acquiring additional bishops within Munster drove the Ó Briain kings to gain bishops at these economic centers. But even at the turn of the eleventh century there were difficulties in finding a legitimately ordained native Irish bishop to perform an ordination. We can not concretely say whether this was an issue until later in the twelfth century; John of Salisbury remarks that delegates of the Irish church and secular leaders requested a legate from the Holy See because they did not have any archbishops.[19] The Irish church and the secular leaders of Ireland may have recognized some sort of inadequacy in the method by which bishops were consecrated in Ireland. John of Salisbury's comment, though, probably refers to the desire of the Irish church to receive official papal sanction for the institutional reforms that would be promulgated at the Synod of Rath Breasail.

In 1101, Muirchertach Ó Briain, King of Munster, called the first major reforming synod of the twelfth century at Cashel, the then-capital of Munster. According to *Chronicon Scotorum,* the men of Ireland held a synod at Cashel in 1101, and at this synod Muirchertach Ó Briain gave the Rock of Cashel to the church without any lay encumbrance. The *Annals of the Four Masters* comment that men from *Leath Mogha* ("the land of the south") attended this synod and refer to the award of Cashel to the church.[20] Neither the *Annals of Inisfallen* nor the *Annals of Ulster* mention this gathering. Muirchertach called the gathering with the clear notion of making the meeting a Munster event. Thus it is not surprising that the annals of other geographic regions do not mention the event. While the synod supposedly included the entire church in Ireland, it was attended only by those clergy from the southern regions which Muirchertach controlled.

The decrees from the synod are found among the genealogical records of Síol Briain (the O'Brien dynasty) which were included as an appendix to O'Grady's text of *Caithréim Thoirdhealbhaigh.*[21] In one sense, the decrees do not differ from other reform measures throughout the Western church at this time. Continental synods also made decrees addressing the problem of simony, clerical celibacy, and the freedom of the church . However, the synod did address situations particularly found in Ireland;

a specific example was that an *erenach* (or "hereditary abbot" who managed and maintained the lands and resources of an Irish monastery) should neither be a lay or married person. The text as it reads indicates that the title in question is an *airchinnech*, which, according to Kenney and Gwynn, reflects a shift from the Latin term *abbas* to the Irish *airchinnech*.[22]

Unlike the Synod of Cashel, which was not included in many of the the Irish annals, the annals all refer to the Synod of Rath Breasail in 1111. According to the annals, the assembly took place under the leadership of Muirchertach Ua Briain (referred to as *árd ríg nÉrend* ["high king of Ireland"] in the *Annals of Innisfallen*, and as leader of the men of *Leath Mogha* ["the south of Ireland"] in the other annals), Cellach, *coarb*[23] of Patrick, and Maol Muire Ó Duinnín, a high ranking bishop of Ireland.[24] Each annal clearly reflects bias in listing the two clerical leaders; in the *Annals of Ulster*, Cellach is titled *coarb* of Patrick and is followed by Maol Muire Ó Duinnín who is called "noble senior of Ireland."[25] *Chronicon Scotorum, the Annals of Innisfallen*, and the *Annals of Tigernach*, refer to Maol Muiré Ua Dunáin as *árd espug Érenn* ("high bishop of Ireland") and secondarily note Cellach.[26] The titles and listings applied to particular kings and clerics implies that different annals favored different leaders.

The annals reflect their political biases in these references in that the annalists tend to place their local kings and prelates in higher regard than did neighboring annalists. However, all of the annals agree that the actual number of bishops, clergy, and lay persons attending the Synod numbered in the hundreds. The *Annals of Ulster* state that 50 prelates, 300 priests and 3,000 *mac n-ecalsa*[27] attended. *Chronicon Scotorum* states that 58 bishops, 318 priests, 28 deacons, and countless other clerics participated. The Synod must have been a large affair, and, unlike the Synod of Cashel ten years earlier, with its bias towards the southern regions of the church in Ireland, it included individuals from the whole island.

The other factor gleaned from these references is the number of prelates and bishops (at least 50) then in Ireland; at the same time in England, there were less than 20 bishops, while Wales had only four. This density of Irish bishops posed clear challenges for a church bent on reform; in addition to the improper consecration of many bishops, dozens ministered regions not viable as dioceses in the Continental sense. According to tradition, the area served by the bishop should include a sizeable population;

however, in Ireland the area served was often the size of a larger *tuath*.[28] On the other hand, Colman Etchingham suggests that the high number of bishops in eleventh and twelfth century Ireland could result from including the *com-episcopi*, auxiliary bishops without any territorial see, within the count of bishops with territorial sees.[29] The Irish, according to Etchingham, must have possessed a different concept of diocese; one not based upon an inherently territorial dimension.

While the Synod of Cashel primarily concerned itself with the clerical behavioral reform, especially as it related to marriage practices and ecclesiastical jurisdiction, the Synod of Rath Breasail exclusively addressed the diocesan structure of the Church in Ireland. Geoffrey Keating, the sole source for the decrees of the Synod, copied material concerning the Synod of Rath Breasail and the Synod of Kells-Mellifont ten years later from the now lost *Book of Clonenagh*.[30] Keating prefaces his remarks with a rationale for the structure established at Rath Breasail: just as 12 bishops were fixed under Canterbury in the south of England and 12 bishops were fixed in the north under York, 12 bishops were fixed in the northern and southern halves of Ireland.[31] Apparently the prelates at Rath Breasail were somewhat familiar with the letter of Pope Gregory the Great (cited by Bede in *Historia Ecclesiastica*) which instructed Augustine of Canterbury to create a two-fold structure between Canterbury and York. Yet, this structure is not simply an adaptation of the English model; the division of the Irish church into two provinces reflected a recognition of the traditional two-fold division of Ireland into *Leath Mogha* ("land of the south") and *Leath Cuinn* ("land of the north"). The writers of the annals used these terms when they described the geographic origins of individuals who attended synods or fought in battles.[32]

The Irish church traditionally considered Armagh in the north as the primatial see of Ireland, with Cashel a relatively new see; therefore, the creation of Cashel as the see of *Leath Mogha* posed difficult issues for the Synod.[33] Limerick profited from the arrangement, since Muirchertach Ó Briain resided in Limerick and it was the see of the papal legate, Giolla Easpuig. The synod easily divided Leinster into five bishoprics. In *Leath Cuinn*, the church provisionally established the dioceses of Connacht. Keating describes a provision for Connacht stating that if the clerics "...do not agree [on the number or place of dioceses in Connacht], we approve of any division that will satisfy them, but provided there be only five bishops in Connacht."³⁴ Apparently, the clerics were not in accord regarding the number of dioceses for Connacht. The division of Armagh, however, proved a simpler proposition and the diocese maintained the original boundaries and divisions throughout the period of this study.

In restructuring suffragan sees, the synod envisioned Armagh and Cashel each with 12 sees beneath them in deference to the pattern established in England. As Gwynn notes, Cashel has only 11 suffragan sees in the list, six in Munster and five in Leinster.³⁵ Perhaps the reformers at Rath Breasail anticipated Dublin's inclusion in the hierarchy in the near future and hence did not want to cause problems by creating six sees in Leinster. Nevertheless, Dublin retained strong ties with Canterbury, as shown in 1121 when, only twenty years after the Synod of Rath Breasail, the people of Dublin sent Gregory to Archbishop Ralph of Canterbury for consecration. Archbishop Ralph was told that the bishops of Ireland were jealous of Dublin because Dublin did not want to subject itself to Armagh's rule.³⁶ After returning to Dublin to find the gates closed against him, Gregory returned to Canterbury for an unknown period. During that time, Cellach, the *coarb* of Patrick, claimed the see of Dublin. Gregory later returned to Dublin to take back the see, and in 1121, Dublin was made a diocese of Cashel.

The Synod of Kells-Mellifont, held in 1152, met to implement further reforms of the diocesan structure of the Church in Ireland and to request for the church in Ireland formal papal recognition through the granting of *pallia* to the sees of Armagh and Cashel as the metropolitans in Ireland. However, Malachy's mission as given by the pope failed when Malachy became ill and died at Clairvaux while visiting his friend Bernard. In response to growing demands from Ireland, Pope Eugenius III sent Cardinal John Paparo to Ireland bearing not two *pallia* but four. Eugenius' reasoning in sending four *pallia* instead of two is unclear. In the subsequent forty years after the Synod of Rath Breasail, dramatic shifts in the secular power structures of Ireland occurred. In particular, when Muirchertach O'Brien fell ill in 1114, the Ó Conchobhair kings of Connacht began the climb to prominence which would last beyond the next century. Toirrdelbach Ó Conchobhair, who came to the throne in Connacht in 1106, marched on Dublin in 1118 and was crowned king. He made his bid as High King of Ireland by weakening neighboring opposition and securing the support of the people of Dublin.³⁷ By the middle of the century, though, he faced a severe challenge from a northern

king, Muirchertach Mac Lochlainn of Cenél nEógain. Muirchertach secured the submission of Diarmait Mac Murchada, overlord of Dublin and king of Leinster.

Several factors support the logic behind the creation of the two new metropolitan sees during the political atmosphere of this time. Toirrdelbach himself was a great benefactor of the church since he established a number of churches and monasteries in Connacht. The Ó Conchobhair dynasty in Connacht could therefore claim the right to a metropolitan see within their territory, but Toirrdelbach Ó Conchobhair and Muirchertach Mac Lochlainn both sought to secure the support of the people of Dublin.³⁸ Dublin, by this time, was integrated economically into Irish society, and was no longer considered by the Irish as a town inhabited by foreigners.

Most secondary literature surrounding the reform movements of the twelfth century in Ireland point out that the main impetus behind the movement was to align the church in Ireland with the rest of the church in Europe. Duffy has even suggested that part of the reason behind Muirchertach Ó Briain's push towards reform in the church bordered on vanity. Muirchertach did not want to "...preside over a country out of step with the rest of Europe..."³⁹ and that his international prestige hinged upon the status of the church. No doubt the church wished to reform itself in order to fall into step with Continental Christianity.

This self-conscious attitude with which the members of the church hierarchy in Ireland regarded themselves against the rest of Latin Christianity illustrates a growing concept of unified self-image. The church in Ireland was understood as distinct from other regions of Europe. That self-image may be considered a national self-image since it incorporates several different levels of identity. First, the geographic boundaries of the island referred to as "Ireland" are retained as the defining border of the four provinces together. In other words, Ireland was considered an entity itself and did not include neighboring islands (such as the Isle of Mann). The Synod of Cashel did not even consider Dublin a diocese, but by the end of the twelfth century, it too was incorporated into this geographic frame. Second, although the church eventually divided itself into four provinces, clerics at Rath Breasail desired only two areas in recognition of the tradition in place since the early Christian period. Eventually, the Synod of Kells-Mellifont divided Ireland into four metropolitan sees reflecting the mythological and political division of Ireland.

Laudabiliter and the English Church

In 1155, Henry II, just one year into his reign, requested and obtained a papal bull from Pope Adrian IV now referred to as *Laudabiliter*. In the bull, Adrian authorized Henry to "...enlarge the boundaries of the Church, to proclaim the truths of the Christian religion to a rude and ignorant people, and to root out the growths of vice from the field of the Lord."[40] Modern historians have wondered why Henry delayed his action upon the bull, since the Anglo-Norman lords first arrived in Ireland in 1169 and Henry II himself arrived in 1171.

In his new edition of *The Church in Medieval Ireland*, John Watt argues that the relationship between the Church at Canterbury and the arrival of the Anglo-Normans in 1169 and of Henry II in 1171 has been over-exaggerated in recent years.[41] He cites the work of Flanagan[42] and Frame[43] (and hence O'Doherty[44] and Bethell[45]) as proponents of a "Conspiracy of Canterbury," as he puts it, in which Canterbury (whose relationship with the Dublin diocese evaporated once Dublin became one the four provinces of the church in Ireland) influenced Henry II to invade Ireland.[46]

Flanagan, on the other hand, suggests that Canterbury's reaction to the Synod of Kells-Mellifont, where the Irish Church clearly established an independent episcopal structure that did not include any sort of relationship with Canterbury, was the impetus for the acquisition of the papal bull *Laudabiliter* represented . Flanagan also posits that most twentieth century Irish historians pass over O'Doherty's thesis that the idea for the invasion originated with Canterbury and not Henry. O'Doherty would contradict the accepted modern nationalist view that the invasion of Ireland by the Anglo-Normans was guided by the English Crown itself; the invasion, according to Flanagan, was interpreted as "colonial and malevolent in intent towards the Irish."[47] She also mentions that most of the major twentieth century Irish medievalists (including F.X. Martin, Otway-Ruthven, and Lydon) have in fact followed Orpen's view that Henry was essentially an opportunist who saw a new colony for the taking when Diarmait Mac Murchada approached Henry in 1166-67.[48]

Countering Flanagan's assertions Watt states that what is fundamental to the argument of the "Canterbury conspiracy" to invade Ireland is Canterbury's claim to primatial authority over the Irish church. This claim of authority would date back into the eleventh century. According to Watt, the evidence provided in the twelfth century for the conspiracy never includes any sort of Canterbury primacy over the Irish church, which, in essence, negates the argument. Since Canterbury did not make a direct claim to primacy, it would seem that Ireland was not a great concern of Canterbury.[49]

This debate concerning the role played by the English Church at Canterbury in the bull *Laudabiliter* is based upon different readings of the same events. However, both positions have a common factor: both look to apply a consistent, clear motivation behind the actions of Henry II and Canterbury over the course of 30 years. During those 30 years, Henry II's intentions towards Ireland changed considerably.

At the Council of Winchester, called by Henry II after his coronation, clerics within the English Church suggested that Henry invade Ireland.[50] While Flanagan acknowledges Canterbury's interest in such a venture due to Canterbury's claims of primacy over Irish episcopal sees (negated after the Synod of Kells-Mellifont), more likely Canterbury was concerned with the issue of primacy over the sees of the British, Welsh, and Scottish churches and feared that their case in Rome would be weakened by an independent Irish church.[51] The tradition of Canterbury's claim of primacy over Irish sees dates to the eleventh century when some Irish bishops were consecrated by Canterbury, but the claim was bolstered by Lanfranc's interpretation of Bede which states that Augustine of Canterbury was bishop of the provinces of Gaul and of Britain. Lanfranc likely assumed that Ireland was one part of the province of Britain.[52]

During the mid-twelfth century Canterbury was concerned with the actions of the Irish church. Several chroniclers concerning the papal legation made by Cardinal Paparo to Ireland in 1151 reflect this concern. Robert of Torigny stated that the mission was denied access to England because the mission injured the customs and dignity of Canterbury which had customarily received the submission of the bishops of Ireland.[53] John of Salisbury met Paparo in Rome and recorded a very negative view of him. He offers that Paparo schemed with the king of Scotland to gain metropolitan status for St. Andrews.[54]

By 1155, John of Salisbury stated in his *Metalogicon* that he was responsible for attaining the bull *Laudabiliter* for Henry II. Pope Adrian IV granted the request based upon the interpretation of the *Donation of Constantine* which grants the Holy See sovereignty over all islands. According to this interpretation, Ireland as an island would be subject to Rome, and the Pope could grant dominion over the island to Henry II.[55] Pope Adrian sent a gold ring with an emerald as a sign that he had invested Henry as the rightful ruler of Ireland.[56] John of Salisbury also happened to be the secretary for the archbishop of Canterbury, and because of this relationship John was no doubt working more for the see of Canterbury than his king.

In his statement regarding his acquisition of *Laudabiliter*, however, John of Salisbury did not mention Canterbury's primacy over Ireland. Shortly after spending time with Pope Adrian in Rome in 1156, John returned to England with *Laudabiliter* in hand.[57] We do not know if the bull was ever given to Henry, or, if so, what his reaction was. If requested by Canterbury, the bull was a failure. The Irish church retained independence, but Henry II gained a justification for invading Ireland, ie., to reform the church in Ireland.

By the time Henry II arrived in Ireland nearly twenty years after *Laudabiliter* was granted, *Laudabiliter* and the claims of the church at Canterbury of primacy over the Irish church had become moot points. Henry II may have entertained the notion of adding Ireland to the vast Angevin realms early in his reign, but the twenty years delay in acting on the idea suggests that it ranked low in his priorities. Even Diarmait Mac Murchada's request for aid in 1168 was met with his ambivalence; Henry accepted Mac Murchada's submission, but delayed action until 1171. When Henry realized that the Anglo-Norman settlers in Ireland were establishing lordships in Ireland essentially without him, Henry decided that intervention in Ireland at the highest level had become a necessity.[58]

To establish his lordship over Ireland, Henry needed to exert control in the most comprehensive and thorough manner possible. He forcibly secured the submission of the Irish kings and the Anglo-Norman settlers by arriving in Ireland at the head of an army larger than anyone in Ireland could muster. If Henry did receive *Laudabiliter* two decades earlier, he more than likely recalled the bull's claims and the suggestions made by Canterbury concerning the Irish church because it provided a means by which he could also gain the submission of the Irish church. On the other hand, if Henry did not receive *Laudabiliter*, perhaps clerics from Canterbury with knowledge of the bull may

have brought it to his attention. By promoting himself as the Christian crusader in a land that was portrayed as rife with corruption and abuse, Henry could bolster his claims of lordship over Ireland while at the same time gaining sanction from the church. Further, as shown in Rome's letters to Henry, Henry stood to gain the support of an Irish church still concerned with internal reform and which saw him as the best means for the reforms' ultimate achievement.[59]

The Post-Norman Church

Concerning Henry II's motivations, Watt stated that they were "…quite secular in nature and had no more to do with Church reform or the primacy of Canterbury than had the Donation of Constantine or a ring from the pope in authorizing his [Henry II's] assertion of lordship over Ireland."[60] Watt later modified this view. While the motivations behind the invasion were political and had more to do with growing lordships in both the Welsh Marches and in the colony in Ireland under the control of Richard de Clare, an important religious element still contributed to the invasion.[61]

The Second Synod of Cashel, called by Henry in 1172, revealed that religious element. Henry's aim in calling the Second Synod of Cashel may be considered from three different perspectives. First, Henry needed to gain the submission of secular rulers in Ireland. To this end, his army would have outclassed every army fielded by either Gaelic king or Anglo-Norman baron, and it is difficult to imagine anyone not submitting to such an overt display of power. Such a show of force would be further enhanced by Henry exhibiting both secular and religious lordship over all parts of his dominion. Second, he needed to secure the support of the Irish hierarchy by asserting his authority as the overlord of Ireland who would lead the reform movement in Ireland. Finally, Henry needed to assure Pope Alexander III that the church in Ireland would be better after his invasion, and that he would forward the reforms of that church through his personal leadership. In gaining the support of the church in Ireland, Henry gained the support of the Pope which, in turn, provided the spiritual justification for his overlordship.

Giraldus Cambrensis, Roger of Howden, and Ralph of Diceto all refer to the Synod but vary in their descriptions.[62] Giraldus lists some of the statutes while Roger of Howden merely states that the Synod took place to ensure practices of the Irish Church would conform to the practices of the English Church. *The Annals of St. Mary's Abbey, Dublin* also mention the Synod's statutes; however, these annals list seven canons while Giraldus mentions an eighth, that the Irish Church should conform in practice to the English Church.[63] The addition of the eighth canon in Giraldus was not his invention since Roger of Howden also mentioned that the Synod's primary concern was instituting the practices of the English church in the Irish church. All the major church officials in Ireland (with the exception of the Bishop of Armagh, Giolla Meic Liac Mac Diartmata, who took ill at the outset of the Synod) attended the Synod; Donatus of Cashel, St. Laurence O'Toole of Dublin, Catholicus of Tuam, and the papal legate, Christian, bishop of Lismore, are known to have gathered at Cashel. These bishops all affirmed the decrees of the Synod.

The content of the decrees bears strong similarity to the decrees of the earlier twelfth century Irish reform synods. Irish marriage customs still proved incompatible with the established marriage canons of the post-Gregorian church,[64] and certain sacramental practices, including the precise location at which baptism and the teaching of children should take place, continued to pose problems for the church in Ireland.[65] The prelates also stipulated that good Christians should pay tithes to their local parish and that lands of the church should be free from all exactions, including, in Giraldus' account, the exaction of *coign*, or free billeting for soldiers and servants on church lands.[66] The sixth decree describes the process by which every good Christian should make a last will and testament, and upon a good Christian's death, how the lands and goods should be divided. The seventh decrees that every good Christian should be buried with masses, vigils and all due ceremonies. In the Annals of St. Mary's Abbey, the list of decrees ends here; those listed by Giraldus conclude with the statement that all divine offices "…shall henceforth be celebrated in every part of Ireland according to the forms and usages of the church of England."[67]

Because Roger of Howden stated that the focus of the Synod as the alignment of Irish church practice with English church practice, this eighth decree was to be expected. Giraldus also included a commentary on the final decree, stating that it is by divine Providence that Ireland has received her lord and king from England. The cause of Henry coming to Ireland was to root out the wickedness that had prevailed in Ireland for a long period of years. Giraldus, a firm supporter of Henry II and

critic of the Irish, was probably revealing that support and criticism in his commentary.[68]

Pope Alexander III received some version of the decree since he himself sent three letters in response to the bishops and kings of Ireland and to Henry. Ralph of Diceto did not refer to any effort to inform the pope while Giraldus only vaguely referred to letters being sent to Alexander.[69] Roger of Howden, however, stated that letters of submission were sent to the pope before the synod.[70] Alexander claimed that the bishops informed him of the spiritual condition of the Irish people in a series of letters and that other trustworthy individuals offered accounts of the Church as well.[71] The bishops advised Alexander that the Irish as a people (*gentem*) were barbarous, uncivilized and ignorant of the divine law ("…*barbarum, incultam, et divine legis ignarum…*").[72] Alexander viewed the arrival of Henry as the salvation of the Irish people and therefore gloried in his victory and triumph. He instructed the bishops to support the king in his endeavors and to lay censure upon anyone failing to uphold their oath to support the king.

Alexander also wrote to the kings and princes of Ireland, stating that they must hold true to their oaths of fealty to Henry. By supporting Henry, they would be supporting both the church and the whole people of Ireland.[73] Alexander's letter to Henry describes a condemnable society. He writes that the Irish marry their stepmothers, live with their brother's wife while the brother is still alive, practice concubinage with their sisters, and even marry their own daughters after putting their wives away. Alexander also mentions that the Irish eat meat during Lent, refuse to pay tithes, and in general disrespect the churches of God.[74] While particular to Ireland and the type of society existing in Ireland, the problems which Alexander describes were similar to problems found in most of the Roman church following the wider eleventh and twelfth century reforms of the church.[75]

No sources for the Synod mention Henry's use of *Laudabiliter* to support his status as over-lord of the Irish church, the Anglo-Norman barons, or the Irish kings. In truth, he had no need. The Second Synod of Cashel was important because it formally established a reality that practically already existed. The church in Ireland supported Henry because he seemed to be the best vehicle of achieving the reforms that the church had been striving to attain for the previous century. The secular leaders in Ireland had no choice but to submit to Henry because of his military strength. While *Laudabiliter* was later dragged out as support for Anglo-Norman rule and as evidence that the Anglo-Normans had not fulfilled their obligations in ruling Ireland in the *Remonstrance*[76] of the Gaelic kings of Ireland. At the Second Synod of Cashel Henry did not have to bring out *Laudabiliter* because it was simply not necessary, or he never actually received the bull in the first place.

Ethnic Bias in the Church in Ireland

The bishops and archbishops of Ireland all agreed that Henry II was the best leader for the reform of the church in Ireland. Even those church members in regions not heavily settled by the initial wave of Anglo-Normans supported him. On the surface, the church in Ireland seemed unified: the diocesan system was firmly established, the method by which bishops and archbishops were to be elected was standardized, and the church retained its own geographic integrity as an independent entity distinct from Canterbury and England.[77] The meager evidence of the colony's first thirty years suggests that there was little, if any, conflict within the church in Ireland.

However, by the end of the fourteenth century, that stability changed dramatically. Most scholars have assumed that a crisis in the church in Ireland developed as a direct result of the parallel overall decline of the colony. The decline, according to these scholars, began in the early fourteenth century with the famine and Bruce invasion and accelerated with the arrival of the plague in the middle of the century. Evidence from the early thirteenth century (which is nearly contemporary with the evidence regarding Gaelic attacks upon the colony discussed in Chapter Three of this text), suggests that later conflicts within the church in Ireland resulted directly from local and personal conflicts that were described by contemporaries in national language. In other words, conflicts over land use and ownership on an island with a limited supply of arable land often developed into conflicts involving the church that were described in national language.

During the reigns of Henry II and his son John, who served as Lord of Ireland before becoming king, the church in Ireland formally adopted the English method of electing bishops and archbishops. The process of filling ecclesiastical offices was standardized, and it seems that the church in general was pleased with the process, as chapters were free to elect individuals to occupy sees as they saw fit.[78] Henry II and John never expressed any desire for racial or ethnic exclusion as long as the pattern of election established by the Irish and English churches was followed.[79]

However, in 1217, William Marshall, regent in England and lord of Leinster, ordered the justiciar in Ireland, Geoffrey de Marisco, to enforce a policy of exclusion whereby Irish candidates to any see in Ireland should be denied. The archbishop of Dublin, Henry of London, who also served as the papal legate and had previously served as justiciar in Ireland, was to assist in executing this policy.[80] The mandate was clear and unambiguous: "The King commands the justiciary of Ireland that he do not allow any Irishman to be elected or promoted in any cathedral church in that country, as disturbance might thereby ensue."[81] Whether this mandate reflects an overt policy change by the church in Ireland or a personal power-play by several barons who held lordships in Ireland, though, remains uninvestigated.

As justiciar, Geoffrey de Marisco involved himself in the elections of bishops in the diocese of Ardfert and Killaloe. The chapter at each diocese had canonically elected an Irish candidate. When de Marisco, as justiciar, attempted to force his candidates (one of whom was his nephew) into the sees, the archbishop Donnchadh of Cashel complained to the Holy See that de Marisco infringed not only upon the church but upon the established English patterns of elections. Honorius III ruled in favor of Donnchadh and the Irish candidates, and plainly condemned the policy of racial exclusion in Ireland.[82]

Aubrey Gwynn suggested that the policy of exclusion originated with Henry of London, who met with William Marshall at Oxford after returning to England from Rome on the news of King John's death.[83] Otway-Ruthven, though, oberved that Henry of London was on good terms with the Irish bishops. Henry had recently returned from the Lateran Council with the archbishop of Tuam. Otway-Ruthven suggested that perhaps the source of this policy is Geoffrey de Marisco.[84] On the other hand, Watt prefered to describe a mesh of family, political and territorial relations behind the policy of exclusion which prevents a clear conclusion that leads to who was responsible for the policy.[85]

While fundamentally correct that the mandate against Irish clerics resulted from personal conflicts over territory, Watt underestimates the true nature of the mandate's background. Each of the three individuals supporting the mandate (Henry of London, William Marshall, and Geoffrey de Marisco) stood to gain immensely by controlling the elections of bishops and archbishops. However, each man was also involved in personal disputes which would have influenced him to support the mandate.

In 1214, the senior members of the Marshall family seized land from the diocese of Ferns. As a result of this seizure, Albinus, then bishop of Ferns, excommunicated Marshall.[86] Though contested, the excommunication was upheld by the Pope, and an interdict was additionally laid upon Marshall's lands. Marshall actually died while excommunicated, but the dispute continued for the next decade. In 1218, Honorius III himself wrote to Albinus of Ferns and Henry of London in an attempt to make peace between the bishop and William Marshall the Younger.[87] The lands were not returned until Philip de Prendergast restored the lands to Ferns.

William Marshall and Geoffrey de Marisco, as justiciar, disputed the elections of two bishops to the sees of Killaloe and Ardfert. The chapters at each see elected Irishmen but the results were set aside as invalid because the Crown had not granted license. This elective manner of Irish bishops dates to the reign of Henry II, who stated that no election was to take place without royal permission.[88] Alternate Anglo-Norman clerics were supplied for the sees at Killaloe and Ardfert but, upon appeal by the Irish canons, Rome granted the sees to the previously elected Irish candidates.

As Watt shows, Marshall and de Marisco were both involved with the town of Killaloe.[89] William Marshall held interests in nearby areas and attempted to construct a castle at Killaloe in 1207, but was rebuffed by the bishop of Killaloe who owned the land.[90] Also, Geoffrey de Marisco, who was related to Henry of London by marriage (his son had married Henry's niece), administered the lands of the Butlers during the minority of Theobold Walter Butler. The Anglo-Norman candidate to the bishopric of Killaloe, Robert Travers, hailed from a family of tenants of the Butlers. Travers was supported by the unnamed deputy of the Archbishop of Cashel (who had been living in exile in France due to infringements upon the liberty of Cashel) and was actually ordained by three bishops, but in the meantime the chapter had elected their Irish candidate, who went to Rome to protest the election. While Rome sided with the chapter, Travers retained possession of lands associated with the see until 1226. De Marisco's influence obviously assured Travers' bishopric.

In addition to the Butler's lands in Killaloe, Geoffrey de Marisco also involved himself intimately with the civil wars in Connacht that had erupted after the death of Cathal Crobdergh. De Marisco's actions against Killaloe and Ardfert might then be seen as part of a wider plan of expanding his control over disputed territories. In order to secure his place as King of Connacht, Cathal Crobdergh consistently bargained with the Anglo-Norman lords and kings. After negotiating an arrangement with King John by which Cathal would pay 300 marks every year for the lands of Connacht aside from Athlone, Cathal hoped that his son Áed might succeed him upon his death, since the grant was made to Cathal and his heirs for good service.[91] Áed was expelled from Connacht by other factions of the dynasty but then gained the aid of de Marisco who sent a large force to help Aedh in 1225. Due to the influence of the de Burgos, who also held a charter for Connacht, de Marisco was forced to summon Áed to an inquest to investigate the nature his service to the Crown and the Dublin government. Áed agreed to meet de Marisco's son at Athlone, but, reportedly remembering past Anglo-Norman treacheries, proceeded to burn and plunder Athlone. Richard de Burgo was granted Connacht, and Áed was murdered while attempting to reconcile his position with Geoffrey de Marisco.

The 1217 mandate to disallow Irish bishops or archbishops thus relates less to national identity than to personal politics. The Marshals certainly felt a personal vendetta against Irish prelates after the exommunication of William Marshal and the rejection of Marshal's plans to build a castle at Killaloe.[92] Henry of London supported Marshall's plan and never contradicted efforts to support an Anglo-Norman hierarchy. Similarly, Geoffrey de Marisco, as justiciar and a lord in Ireland, displayed a consistent pattern in supporting potential allies against other lords. Pre-existing distinctions between Anglo-Norman and native Irish existed in the minds of the mandate's creators and enforcers. Working within a powerful institution, those individuals applied those pre-existing distinctions to enforce a law of discrimination.

The Church and the Legal Status of the Irish

While the motivations behind the mandate of 1217 stem from personal conflicts painted in national language and the results institutionalized ethnic discrimination, change occurred in the late thirteenth and fourteenth centuries. The colony changed considerably between 1217 and 1270, when David MacCarwell, the Irish-elected Archbishop of Cashel, first proposed the purchase of a grant of English Common Law for "all the Irish of Ireland." During the thirteenth century, the protracted civil wars in Connacht continued between the various branches of the Ó Conchobhair dynasties with Anglo-Norman lords often taking sides. In 1260 the sons of several Irish kings, including Áed Ó Conchobhair and Tadhg Ó Briain, banded together under the leadership of Brian Ó Néill to form a confederation that recognized Ó Néill as the High King of Ireland. Scottish mercenaries made their first appearance as supplemental support to Irish kings in the late thirteenth century. MacNeill suggested that the change in the colony began with a growing sense of identity on the part of the Irish and a deeply felt sense of oppression.[93] However, Lydon has said that these events, while indicative of a growing sense of identity, can only be understood in terms of early thirteenth century racist attitudes.[94] Anglo-Norman lords clearly based their discrimination upon personal conflict over the possession of land and territory rather than on outright racial animosity.

The Anglo-Norman colony often reacted to these events of the thirteenth century with mixed and haphazard responses. The confederation of Irish princes in 1260 was apparently defeated by a group of local levies and not by a formal army led by the leading magnates of the day. Two years later, in response to more trouble in Connacht, John de Verdon raised a large army to assist Walter de Burgo against Áed Ó Conchobhair. No battle occurred, however, since the parties made peace later that same year.[95] Additionally, the southwest experienced renewed conflict at the hands of the Mac Carthaigh; Fineen Mac Carthaigh defeated the army of the justiciar William de Dene at Callan.[96]

After the occurence of these significant events, David MacCarwell, archbishop of Cashel, requested the grant of Common Law for the Irish. The Irish certainly felt a legal disadvantage, especially those Irish living within the area where Common Law was firmly established. Most legal actions raised by an Irishman could be defeated in practice if the defendant alleged that an Irishman had initiated the action (see Chapter Five).[97] A common complaint by the Irish in the thirteenth century was the debate concerning whether a person could be convicted for killing an Irishman.[98] The use of native law by some Anglo-Normans in paying *éraic* (a blood fine in Irish law) as compensation

for murder as opposed to the Common Law sentence of execution complicated the issue still further.[99]

The English chancery bestowed individual grants of Common Law, and thus it seems unlikely that MacCarwell's proposition was met with overt hostility from Henry III. MacCarwell initially offered a sum of 7,000 marks for the grant.[100] The Crown apparently expected a far greater sum, since the fee was raised to 8,000 and then 10,000 marks according to later documents.[101] Otway-Ruthven commented that MacCarwell's motives for the request of the grant were clear enough. The Irish would have wanted to hold their lands with the English laws of inheritance, to obtain dower for their widows, and to protect themselves from the harsher penalties of the Common Law as it existed in Ireland.[102] MacCarwell firmly believed that the Common Law purchase would benefit both the Irish living within the colony and those living within the areas where brehon law (the Irish system of laws) was more prominent. He was willing to expel from the church any Irish who did not accept the law and promised to excommunicate those who continued to disturb the peace of the land.[103]

MacCarwell's interest was not limited to the elevation of status of his fellow Irish through a grant of Common Law. Henry III protested MacCarwell's election to the see on the grounds that MacCarwell supposedly associated with known enemies of the crown. His actions revealed a marked antagonism towards the Anglo-Normans living in Cashel.[104] In addition, MacCarwell, who had become a Cistercian later in life, was responsible for the restoration of Mellifont as a mother house to other Cistercian houses in Ireland, even though Mellifont had become nearly exclusively Irish. Later, by 1321, Mellifont actually refused to admit English members.[105] MacCarwell was clearly a complex figure, and to categorize him merely as a supporter of Irish national or racial sentiment does not reflect that complexity. Hand has described MacCarwell as the "…last representative of those native churchmen who retained something of the hopes with which the twelfth-century reformers greeted the Normans."[106] MacCarwell proposed the idea of the grant knowing that it would strengthen his position as a cleric and the position of the church in Ireland. MacCarwell no doubt hoped to replace the practice of Irish brehon law with English law, since brehon marriage laws had posed problems for the reformers of the Irish church since the twelfth century.[107]

MacCarwell's request for Common Law failed. Although Edward apparently encouraged the idea of granting

Common Law to the Irish on grounds that the laws practiced by the Irish were "detestable to God," he ultimately left the final decision concerning the grant to the Anglo-Norman lords in Ireland who seem to have quashed the grant.[108] Firm evidence concerning the initiative disappears after 1280, although in that year, a parliament was held where the issue was probably discussed.[109] The proceedings of this gathering state that no decision could be reached because most of the great lords were out of the country. MacCarwell's supporters, the bishops of Emly and Killaloe, died in 1281, and while MacCarwell maintained that he had widespread support for the grant, the deaths of the two coincide with the grant being denied. Since the final determination of the grant of Common Law was left to the Anglo-Norman lords, and since the lords present at that 1280 parliament refused to consider the motion, the Anglo-Norman lords probably were responding to recent events in Ireland.

During the period between the quest for the grant of Common Law and the Statutes of Kilkenny in 1366 the colony deteriorated even further. The Anglo-Norman lords attempted to solve the growing problems of the colony by legislating parliamentary statutes unique to Ireland, notably in the Statutes of Kilkenny (See Chapter Five). The effective area controlled by the Anglo-Normans had shrunk considerably, such that the Ó Briain made a claim to be kings of Munster in the south-west, the Mac Murchadha revived their claim to Leinster, and the de Burgh lords in Connacht had begun to adopt Irish customs, language, and even law (see Chapter Five). Against this backdrop the Anglo-Norman lords adopted the Statutes of Kilkenny. Clauses 13 and 14 of the Statutes of Kilkenny, which declared a policy of exclusion of Irish participation in the activities of the church at all levels, resuscitated the issue of Irish clerical status. They required any beneficed Irish clergy living among the Irish to demonstrate knowledge of English. In English regions, no Irishman was to be admitted by provision or collation into any cathedral, collegiate church, or benefice in churches. Moreover, religious houses situated in lands controlled by the English were not to admit Irish members.[110] A secular parliament that could legislate ecclesiastical matters was unique to Ireland in the middle ages. In England, during the fourteenth century, the distinctions between secular and ecclesiastical jurisdictions were more pronounced, although secular and religious rights were often contested.[111] Thus, the level of authority placed in the hands of local lords in Ireland greatly exceeded any central authority in Dublin or London.

The Statutes of Kilkenny indicate the level of decay reached in the colony. By 1366, the lines between Irish and Anglo-Norman blurred. The new divide was drawn between those people in support of the English Crown and those against him. The Statutes declared that anyone who did not support the king was an outlaw and degenerate, and, therefore, anything and anyone associated with such a person should be considered outlaw and degenerate.[112]

Elements of the church leadership in Ireland disputed the authority of the Crown from the late thirteenth century. MacCarwell encouraged the renewal of Mellifont as a motherhouse, again at a time when it primarily housed Irish monks and Irish sympathies. A parliament gathered at Kilkenny in 1310 that declared that the profession of any native Irish religious, monk, canon or friar who lived among the colonists should not be accepted, although this statement was quickly countermanded by the king under pressure from Rome.[113] When Edward Bruce invaded Ireland in 1315, Franciscan friars in the west of Ireland numbered among his strongest supporters and called for open rebellion in support of their own nation.[114]

This move towards a formal policy of clerical exclusivity reflected the Anglo-Norman lords' attititudinal changes during the previous one hundred and fifty years. By the mid-fourteenth century, Anglo-Norman lords viewed the church in Ireland as a major contributor to the decline of the colony. Especially after the Bruce invasion, the Anglo-Normans attempted to resolve many colonial problems through the institution of racial exclusivity.

Religious Orders and Ethnic Conflict

The Cistercian monastery of Mellifont was founded in 1142 through the assistance of St. Malachy, formerly archbishop of Armagh. Malachy was a close friend of St. Bernard of Clairvaux. During a stay at Clairvaux on a journey to Rome, Malachy had asked Bernard for help in establishing the order in Ireland. Clairvaux became the motherhouse for Mellifont, and, within five years, the Cistercians established two more monasteries as daughter houses to Mellifont. By the end of the century, 23 monasteries claimed Mellifont as their motherhouse.

The Anglo-Norman settlement at the end of the century contributed to the spread of Cistercianism in Ireland. While the number of monasteries that looked to Mellifont as a mother house grew to 29, the number of monasteries founded by Anglo-Norman lords reached 10.[115] In the early thirteenth century, tensions arose within the order in Ireland over the divide between monasteries related to Mellifont and those related to English and Continental houses. In the first decade of the thirteenth century, the Cistercian General Chapter of the order sent official visitors to the Irish Cistercians in an attempt to resolve the disputes. These visitations failed to dispel the conflicts erupting between Gaelic and Anglo-Norman houses. In 1216, a further visitation was denied admittance at the gates of Mellifont and was obstructed by a riot at Jerpoint, another major Cistercian monastery. By 1226, the General Chapter declared Mellifont the source of a great conspiracy and called for Stephen of Lexington to lead a more vigorous visitation. The Cistercians at Citeaux called Mellifont's activities a "Conspiracy," in the sense that seditious members of the order kept secret the hostilities dividing the Cistercians in Ireland from the wider order.

Just as the 1217 mandate against Irish clerics has been used to show the Anglo-Norman lordship's determination to eliminate any sort of Irish influence in the church in Ireland, so too was the "Conspiracy of Mellifont" taken as an example of the ethnic conflict existing from the outset of the colony.[116] Bitter conflict between the Irish Cistercians and the General Chapter's reformers sent from France clearly did take place. Yet, interpretations of this conflict often contain extreme bias.

In the late 1960's and early 1970's, Barry O'Dwyer investigated the "Conspiracy of Mellifont" as a theme in several articles and a short monograph.[117] He also published an edition of the letters of Stephen of Lexington.[118] However, several clear inaccuracies exist in O'Dwyer's work. He maintained that the 1217 mandate was a policy concocted by Henry III, who then sent it to the justiciar Geoffrey de Marisco. In fact the 1217 mandate was issued during Henry III's childhood by William Marshall.[119] In actuality, William Marshall, Geoffrey de Marisco, and Henry of London concocted the mandate in an attempt to control particular localities in which they held personal interests. Once aware of this policy of exclusion, the Holy See immediately condemned it and stated that no person should be limited to a church office on the basis of race or ethnic background.

Additionally, O'Dwyer erroneously deduced that the basis for the whole movement against the Irish Cistercians was an ideology of racial and cultural exclusivity within the Cistercian Order.[120] He stated that the change of the vernacular language from Irish to French in the houses in Ireland signaled a superiority of French culture to the Irish, and hence the Irish were justified in a premonition that "...everything was changing with the new social and military order."[121] O'Dwyer fails to clearly describe the Cistercian Order, founded in France, as an international order with monasteries as far east as Poland and the Holy Land. As an international order, it required a common language with which all members of the order could communicate. There were also Cistercian requirements that monasteries were to be visited by other abbots regularly and that abbots were to attend the General Chapter every year. The Cistercian Order was predicated upon the system of visitations to ensure that monasteries that proclaimed to be Cistercian were in fact practicing the Cistercian ideal of monasticism. These facts necessitated a common tongue which, due to the Cistercian mother house being located in northern France, was logically French. While this view of monasticism may have conflicted with the Irish view of monasticism and may have been an issue with some Irish Cistercians who wished to practice a modified form of Cistercianism, the fact remains that the General Chapter had justifiable cause for grave concern. The state of the Order in Ireland showed dire signs of conflict as reported by the visitors sent by the General Chapter.

Neither the chronology of events relating to Mellifont nor the visitations of Stephen of Lexington present a source of contention. As early as 1202, the abbot of Clairvaux received complaints against the state of the monastery of Maigue and its daughter houses, although the exact details concerning the problems at Maigue are not part of the record.[122] However, the *Statuta* of the general chapter held in 1216 name the monastery of Mellifont as a source of "many enormities" and state that the monastery needed to be investigated.[123] The following year the General Chapter recounts the incident at Mellifont in which official visitors were barred access to the monastery by armed lay brothers. The incident was repeated at Jerpoint, whose abbot received the support of the abbots of Baltinglass, Killeny, Kilbeggan, and Bective.[124] Further complicating the status of monasteries of the Mellifont filiation was the fact that Irish abbots had been dispensed from the annual General Chapter in 1190 and were only required to attend every four years due to the harsh travel conditions between Ireland and France.[125]

These monasteries shared the common factors of status as daughter houses of Mellifont endowed with lands by

Irish chieftains. Roger Stalley notes that since monasteries founded by Anglo-Normans usually received wealthier endowments of land, a certain amount of jealousy resulted among the monasteries established by the Irish.[126] Also, unlike the Irish foundations' ability to trace their lineage to Mellifont, the Anglo-Norman foundations were also different in that they did not share a common parentage. This placed the abbot of Mellifont in a very precarious position as leader of a group of monasteries in a land increasingly dominated by foreign powers.[127] Yet another discrepency, noticeable architectural differences, existed between the Anglo-Norman foundations and Irish foundations, since the Irish often diverged from contemporary design features of Cistercian monasteries in England and the Continent. The contrasting architectural styles employed in the different monasteries in Ireland certainly added to the divide between the Cistercians.[128]

The statutes of the General Chapters of 1219-1221 indicate that the problems in Ireland had grown to enormous levels and were found in all the monasteries of the Mellifont filiation. The General Chapter visitors to Ireland reported widespread abuses and that grave enormities existed, including destruction of property, open rebellion, and assassination plots. The 1221 General Chapter charged the abbot of Clairvaux with the reform of the Mellifont filiation and granted him full power to do so. The deputies assigned to correct the Mellifont abuses received instructions to secure the assistance of the secular powers in Ireland for the purpose of administration or to grant protection if need be. Clairvaux informed Gregory IX of the situation, stating that the Visitors chosen for Ireland were from varied backgrounds to avoid the suggestion of national bias.[129] The Visitation of 1227 led to the deposition of the abbots of Assaroe, Boyle, Fermoy, Abbeydorney and Newry. Stephen reassigned these monasteries to different parents in England, Wales, and France.

After the visitation of Stephen of Lexington in 1228, a marked increase in evidence occurs, not due to drastic change in Cistercian record keeping, but simply because of the unusual survival of Stephen's letters.[130] Stephen found that the work of the previous visitations failed almost immediately and that Irish monks violently opposed the new abbots from outside of Ireland placed in monasteries in the previous years. In one case, the newly appointed abbot of Baltinglass was pulled off his horse and denied entrance to the monastery. Maigue and Mellifont seem to have caused the most problems for the Visitors, including Stephen. Maigue had devolved into an armed camp in which hired mercenaries occupied the monastery and victuals filled the church. When excommunication failed to daunt the monks, they were then threatened with capture and imprisonment. A force, organized by Hugh de Burgh, bishop of Limerick, tore down a rampart around the monastery and invaded the monastery with some loss of life. Some rebels fled while others recanted and asked for mercy. The latter were readmitted to the community with severe restrictions.

In disciplining the recalcitrant monks, Stephen implemented a policy of re-education rather than dismissal. Because of these mandated changes, some Irish historians charge Stephen with discrimination, especially due to his comments regarding the "bestial" nature of the Irish.[131] Watt, however, defends Stephen and states that if a charge of discrimination is to be leveled at all, it must be cast upon an Order attempting to maintain a cohesive international identity.[132] According to Watt, Stephen followed the policies that had been established at the General Chapter. These policies explained that the reformation of Mellifont could be accomplished by installing foreign abbots and monks to lapsed Irish monasteries. Stephen's insistence that the Irish know Latin and French should also not be construed as cultural elitism. Stephen himself said the issue was not that the Irish monks spoke Irish, but that they also did not speak French and Latin, and therefore could not communicate with their Cistercian brethren on the Continent.[133]

The interpretation of Cistercian history in Ireland in early thirteenth century Ireland proves problematic due to the source material being written from the perspective of the Cistercian Order. Little if any evidence exists that would indicate why the Irish Cistercians would go so far as to arm their monasteries against visitation or to repel newly assigned abbots from outside Ireland. Perhaps the Irish monks in Cistercian monasteries of Irish foundation felt accutely threatened by the newer Anglo-Norman foundations which possessed more wealth, new architectural design, and, perhaps most importantly, overt alliances with the new Anglo-Norman rulers of Ireland. Additionally, the Cistercian Order's problems occurred at the same time that Anglo-Norman lords and clerics proclaimed that Irish clerics could not be appointed on the grounds that they were Irish. Historians also describe disputes over the control of church lands in nationalistic terms because individuals making claims to the lands were of different nations. Irish Cistercians, aware of these declarations against Irish clerics and faced with external observers who seemed to side with the Anglo-Normans, responded in ways that were not too dissimilar from other Irish clerics of the middle ages.[134]

During this period of greatest upheaval for the Cistercians, the Franciscan Friars arrived in Ireland. The Franciscans, like the Dominicans, founded friaries primarily in the urban areas established by the Anglo-Normans in the early thirteenth century (See Chapter Three). As preaching and apostolic orders of religious, their friaries were founded within concentrations of higher population, which, at this time, would have meant in the towns and boroughs of eastern and southern Ireland. The first authoritative mention of the Franciscans in Ireland occurred in 1233, when Henry III granted a gift to the Dublin friars so that they could repair the roof of their friary.[135] Gaelic leaders also patronized the Franciscans. The first Gaelic grants to the Franciscan Friars were at Cork (the founder was Diarmait Mac Carthaigh Mór, while the de Barrys and Prendergasts were also benefactors) and Ennis (the founder was Donatus Carbrac Ó Briain) in the middle of the thirteenth century, although the evidence for these foundations is sparse.[136] The Franciscans, like the Cistercians, enjoyed rapid growth in Ireland. But unlike the Dominican Friars, the Franciscans in Ireland enjoyed the status as an independent province. Established with their own minister provincial, Irish Franciscans were originally divided into four custodies. Initially, the custodies divided the island into four regions, three of which were allocated to regions controlled by the Anglo-Normans, with the fourth left for the Irish.[137] Later, in 1331, the province of Ireland was re-divided into the five custodies of Cork, Nenagh, Cashel, Dublin, and Drogheda. The custody of Nenagh was the largest of the five custodies and was allocated to the Irish, while the other four custodies divided the most intensively settled Anglo-Norman area.[138]

The first signs of trouble for the Franciscans occurred in 1285. The Dublin Exchequer commissioned a report concluding that no Irishman should be a bishop because they always support people of their own language (*linguam*). According to the report, the Franciscans and Dominicans also made similar distinctions and only supported people of their own language (*linguam*).[139] During this time, Nicholas Cusack, bishop of Kildare, wrote to Edward I. In his letter he stated that he had become aware of certain Irish members of religious orders who held secret meetings and talks with the Irish and their kings. Cusack also revealed that these religious orders supported revolt against the English. According to the

sermons of these friars, such revolts were justifiable by both divine and human law.[140] Although those sermons have not survived, the justification in terms of human law may refer to the assertion later made by several Irish kings in a letter to the pope known as the *Remonstrance of the Irish Princes* (1317). In the *Remonstrance,* the kings assert that the English kings had not fulfilled their obligations to rule Ireland justly as set out in *Laudabiliter.*

Both accounts of the Cork Provincial Chapter of 1291 seem to confirm this pattern of conflict. *Annales de Wigornia* describe a conflict within the chapter between two clearly defined peoples: the Irish and the English. According to the annals, the Irish arrived at the chapter armed with a certain papal bull in hand, although no mention is made of the reason for the bull. Apparently the bull caused a dispute between the Irish and the English, which quickly led to a physical conflict where many were killed and wounded. The annals conclude by reporting that the English only managed to restore order only with the help of the town of Cork.[141] The alternate source of the Cork Chapter of 1291, Bartholomew of Cotton's *Historia Anglicana,* describes the same event in equally vivid language but makes no mention of a bull as the root of the dispute. It recounts that the minister general of the Order of St. Francis, making visitations around the world, stopped in Ireland. At this time, unidentified attackers killed or wounded over 16 of the brothers, while the King of England imprisoned still more.[142]

In general, modern scholars take this incident at face value without delving into the accuracy of the sources.[143] The dubious quality of the sources is rarely mentioned.[144] The accounts appear in histories written by English Benedictine monks who did not display any fondness for the Franciscan Friars and who were not eyewitnesses to the events. *The Worcester Abbey Annals* describe the Franciscans unfavorably, referring to the betrayal of confessions and to another conflict arising over Henry Poche's burial (who was buried by the Friars after a dispute over the body with local monks).[145] The Irish annals record nothing in the late thirteenth century approximating a clash between English and Irish friars, nor do the Anglo-Norman annals, including the chronicle of Friar John Clyn.

If the incident at Cork actually occurred, it could be considered a case of national and racial strife in thirteenth century Ireland. However, the source of the conflict at the Chapter remains a question. In the case of the Cistercian conspiracy at Mellifont, the conflict originated with the internal discipline of the Order as stemming from racial divisiveness. In fact, racial divisiveness was a result of the internal discipline within the Cistercian Order. In Cork, though, only a vague reference to an unknown bull exists which seems to have been the major source of contention. Even if fictional, accounts of the Cork incident represent the English perception that the Franciscan Friars in Ireland were blatantly anti-English and anti-Crown. This report of the Cork Chapter should be ideologically linked with the references made to the Franciscan Friars by John Cusack in which he stated that the Franciscans in Ireland were causing a great deal of trouble in Irish regions. After the alleged conflict in Cork, the minister general of the Franciscan Friars, Raymond Gaufredi, visited Ireland as part of a general visit to England and Ireland. Edward I ordered the justiciar, William de Vesci, to assist Gaufredi in his visitation and to restrain any rebellious friars by whatever means necessary.[146]

These limited references to the conflict at the Cork Chapter raise doubts regarding the reliability of the two English sources. No Irish sources confirm the historicity of the event. Lydon has cast the relationship between the Franciscan friars and the invasion of Ireland by Edward Bruce in 1315 as further evidence that the Irish Franciscans openly conspired against the English and the Crown. However, of the many works evaluating the Bruce invasion's impact on the colony in Ireland,[147] none aside from Lydon's consider the Franciscan role in the invasion. Lydon states that during the winter of 1306-7, Scottish agents were busy in Ulster meeting with several religious and other persons.[148] Lydon concludes that the reference to religious persons refers to the Friars Minor in Ireland who preached support for the Bruces.[149] Other religious supported the invasion, including Adam, Bishop of Ferns, who was accused of counseling and offering aid to the Scots.[150] After the invasion, in 1315, Fergus Ardrossan and Walter de Moray were killed at the battle of Skerries and were later buried in the Franciscan Friary at Athy, suggesting that the Friars at Athy at least moderately supported the Scots invaders.[151] Friar John Clyn notes that many Irish supported the Scots; hence, they did not maintain their faith nor their support for the Crown and authority.[152] After the Bruce invasion, the appointment of Archbishops of Dublin and Cashel faithful to the Crown became a primary concern for Edward II.[153] He was successful and attained the excommunication for individuals who supported Bruce and his allies.[154]

In reaction to the subversive activities of the Friars a stream of official policies were enacted. The Franciscan Friars altered their organizational structure in 1331 to favor the Friaries in Anglo-Norman areas. The fifth custody established in that year restructured the ratio of Irish to Anglo-Norman friaries such that Irish houses made up the majority in only one of the five custodies. The other four custody's majorities were Anglo-Norman, thus the electoral capacity of the Gaelic friaries was severely diminished.[155] In the end, this exclusionary policy proved futile since the region effectively controlled by the Dublin government during the late fourteenth and fifteenth century was limited to the immediate area surrounding Dublin known as the Pale.

Conclusions

Some have assumed that the conflicts within the Church in medieval Ireland played a significant role in fostering national and ethnic conflict in medieval Ireland. This chapter, however, shows that conflicts in medieval Ireland involving the Church did not necessarily result from ethnic or racial strife.

From the outset of the Anglo-Norman settlement, Irish prelates and clerics supported the Anglo-Normans as the best possible vehicle for furthering the reform movement that the Irish had begun themselves in the twelfth century. The Irish maintained a mental, geographic image of what Ireland was; when the Irish reformers of the twelfth century set the borders of the provinces of Ireland, the collective border of the four provinces was the island of Ireland. Later, the bishops themselves accepted the English method of electing bishops by which local chapters had to seek authority to elect from the king. Throughout the thirteenth century they generally followed this method with few exceptions.

Although some scholars cite legislation which prevented Irish clerics from attaining clerical office as evidence of racial and national bias within the Church, this claim requires further clarification to be considered accurate. The first examples of this anti-Irish bias resulted from a local conflict with Henry of London, the Marshal family, and Geoffrey de Marisco on one side and the Irish bishops of the Cashel archdiocese on the other. The conflict, of a personal nature, involved claims made over disputed lands and, quite probably, personal vendettas regarding those lands. The mandate against Irish clerics, secured by William Marshall during the minority of Henry III, served as a means through which Anglo-Norman lords could exercise local authority, and is not a specific case of national strife. A similar argument exists concerning the problems in the Order of Cistercians in the early thirteenth century. The conflict, later painted as racial and nationalistic, actually resulted from internal discipline within the Cistercian Order.

These first cases of colonial strife, often described as nationalistic, launched an increasingly widespread phenomenon of conflict. The Irish clerics changed their perceptions of the Anglo-Normans as a result of personal interaction. At first, the Irish clerics welcomed the Crown and the Anglo-Norman lords as beneficial to the reform of the Irish Church. The Anglo-Normans, on the other hand, viewed the Irish with skepticism from the outset of their arrival, due to the practices of the Irish (in the Church and in their culture) which differed fundamentally from the Anglo-Norman world-view. MacCarwell's intention to replace Irish law with English law was an attempt to align Irish marriage laws with the Roman tradition.[156] This plan failed not due to any institutional policy made by the Crown but because local magnates in Ireland (many of whom were absent from the pertinent parliament) preferred to ignore the issue.

After the mid-thirteenth century, a shift in perceptions occurred between Irish clerics and Anglo-Norman clerics and lords. The Irish clerics tended to view Anglo-Normans with increasing skepticism and hostility while Anglo-Normans continued to view Irish society as barbaric and the Church (in Irish regions) as corrupt. At this time, the Franciscan Friars arrived and began to prosper in Ireland. Like the Cistercians before them, the Franciscans received patronage from both Anglo-Norman and Gaelic lords; by the time the Franciscans arrived in Ireland, national conflict constituted an integral aspect of the Church's internal dialogue.

This shift in perceptions, receives attention in Chapters Two and Three of this study. Chapter Two states that references to national imagery in bardic poetry increase in the middle of the thirteenth century. Chapter Three proves through settlement analysis that the colony peaked in the mid thirteenth century while Gaelic kings concertedly attacked the colony. Before the Anglo-Norman colony, the national dimension of the church in Ireland was experienced insofar as it was defined as a particular geographic region. Because of ethnic conflict and rivalry in the church after the Anglo-Norman arrival,

a nationalistic church evolved. This evolution resulted due to the ethnic and cultural differences between Gaelic and Anglo-Norman societies and the status of Ireland as a distinct geographic and ecclesiastical entity within a wider Roman church.

[1] J.A Watt, The Church and the Two Nations in Medieval Ireland (Cambridge: Cambridge University Press, 1970); J.A. Watt, "Ecclesia inter Anglicos et inter Hibernicos: Confrontation and Coexistence in the Medieval Diocese and Province of Armagh," in *The English in Medieval Ireland: Proceedings of the First Joint Meeting of the Royal Irish Academy and the British Academy*. ed. J. Lydon (Dublin: Royal Irish Academy, 1984), 46-64.

[2] Otway-Ruthven, *History of Medieval Ireland*, 126-43.

[3] Watt, "Ecclesia inter Anglicos et inter Hibernicos," 46.

[4] See Chapter Three for discussion of the geography of Anglo-Norman settlement in medieval Ireland.

[5] R.N. Swanson, *Church and Society in Late Medieval England* (London: Blackwell Publishers, 1989), 6-7.

[6] Swanson, *Church and Society in Late Medieval England*, 7.

[7] *The Historia Pontificalis of John of Salisbury.* Ed. M Chibnall (Oxford: Clarendon Press, 1956), 70.

[8] See Art Cosgrove, "Marriage in Medieval Ireland," in *Marriage in Ireland*, ed. Art Cosgrove (Dublin: Academic Press, 1987), 25-50.

[9] Aubrey Gwynn, *History of Irish Catholicism, II.i: The Twelfth Century Reform* (Dublin: Gill and Son Ltd., 1968), 1.

[10] *Annals of Innisfallen*, s.a. 1026.

[11] *Annals of Ulster*, s.a. 1028; *Annals of Innisfallen*, s.a. 1028.

[12] *Annals of Ulster*, s.a. 1030; *Annals of Tigernach*, s.a. 1030.

[13] Watt, *The Church in Medieval Ireland*, 2.

[14] *Patrologia Latina.* Ed. J.P. Migne, 150.535

[15] Lanfranc, *The Letters of Lanfranc, Archbishop of Canterbury*, ed. H. Clover and M. Gibson (Oxford: Clarendon Press, 1979), 50-1.

[16] Irish clerics still considered Dublin, a Scandinavian foundation, a town of foreigners and hence unworthy of a new diocese. Perhaps the best evidence of this point is the fact that Dublin was not present at the Synod of Cashel, nor was it considered part of the Irish episcopal hierarchy at the Synod of Rath Breasail.

[17] Flanagan, *Irish Society, Anglo-Norman Settlers*, 13.

[18] Watt, *Church in Medieval Ireland,* 4.

[19] *The Historia Pontificalis of John of Salisbury*, 70.

[20] *Annals of the Four Masters*, s.a. 1101; previously the Rock of Cashel had been the center of the Munster kingdom.

[21] *Caithréim Thoirdhealbhaigh*, ed. S.H. O'Grady, vol. XXVI (Dublin: Irish Texts Society, 1927), 174-75; Caithréim Thoirdealbhaig is a chronicle detailing the exploits of the O'Brien kings of Thomond and Munster in the thirteenth and fourteenth centuries.

[22] See Gwynn's discussion of the problem in "The First Synod of Cashel, 1101," in *The Irish Church in the Eleventh and Twelfth Centuries,* ed. Gerard O'Brien (Dublin: Four Courts Press, 1992), 158-165.

[23] The title *coarb* was used to describe the hereditary leaders of certain Irish sees that were founded by early Irish saints. The coarb of Patrick, then, is the title reserved for the bishop and later archbishop of Armagh.

[24] *Annals of Innisfallen*, s.a. 1111.

[25] *Annals of Ulster,* s.a. 1111.

[26] *Chronicon Scotorum*, s.a. 1111, *Annals of Tigernach*, s.a. 1111, *Annals of Innisfallen*, s.a. 1111.

[27] The literal translation means "sons of clerics," but it could also just as easily mean lower level clerics.

[28] A *tuath* was a term used to denote two divisions within Irish society. In one sense, it refers to the people who are ruled by a king. In the other sense, it refers to the land that the king rules. When the Anglo-Normans arrived in Ireland, there were about 150 in Ireland.

[29] Colman Etchingham, "Episcopal hierarchy in Connacht and Tairdelbach Ua Conchobair," *Journal of the Galway Archaeological and Historical* Society, 52 (2000): 13-29.

[30] Geoffrey Keating, *Foras Feasa ar Éirinn, III,* ed. Rev. Patrick Dinneen (London: Irish Texts Society, 1908), 298-307.

[31] Keating, *Foras Feasa ar Éirinn, III,* 298.

[32] See for instance *Annals of Innisfallen,* s.a. 1111.

[33] This division might extend as far back as the eighth or ninth century when *Liber Angeli* states that Ireland was to be divided between the Patrician church at Armagh and the church of Brigid at Kildare. See *The Patrician Texts in the Book of Armagh,* ed. Ludwig Bieler, Scriptores Latini Hiberniae, Vol. 10 (Dublin: Dublin Institute for Advanced Studies, 1979), 52.

[34] Keating, *Foras Feasa ar Éirinn, III,* 302-305.

[35] Gwynn, "The Synod of Rath Breasail, 1111," 187.

[36] Watt, *The Church in Medieval Ireland,* 13-14.

[37] The most recent discussion of this pattern of attaining the status of ard rí is found in Duffy, *Ireland in the Middle Ages,* 51-56.

[38] Duffy, *Ireland in the Middle Ages,* 53-55.

[39] Duffy, *Ireland in the Middle Ages,* 51.

[40] Maurice P. Sheehy, *Pontificia Hibernica,i,* (Dublin, Gill and Sons, 1962), 15-16; Curtis and McDowell, *Irish Historical Documents, 1172-1922* (London: Methuen, 1943), 17.

[41] Watt, *The Church in Medieval Ireland,* 236-237.

[42] Flanagan, *Irish Society, Anglo-Norman Settlers,* 8-9.

[43] Robin Frame, *Colonial Ireland,* 11-13.

[44] J.F. O'Doherty, "The Anglo-Norman Invasion, 1167-71," *Irish Historical Studies* 1 (1938-9): 154-157; "Rome and the Anglo-Norman Invasion of Ireland," *Irish Ecclesiastical Record* 42 (1933): 131-45.

[45] D. Bethell, "English Monks and Irish Reform in the Eleventh and Twelfth Centuries." *Historical Studies 8.* (1971): 111-135.

[46] Watt, *The Church in Medieval Ireland,* 237.

[47] Flanagan, *Irish Society, Anglo-Norman Settlers,* 8.

[48] Flanagan, *Irish Society, Anglo-Norman Settlers,* 7n1.

[49] Watt, *The Church in Medieval Ireland,* 237; Watt, *The Church and the Two Nations,* 7.

[50] Robert of Torigny, 186. The value of Robert's account has been challenged by some (most notably H.L. Warren, *Henry II* (London, 1973)); nevertheless, it seems relevant to point out that Robert gave precise and correct dates in his work while discussing this period. See Flanagan, *Irish Society, Anglo-Norman Settlers,* 39n90.

[51] Flanagan, *Irish Society, Anglo-Norman Settlers,* 40-41.

[52] Lanfranc, *Letters,* 50-1; Bede, *Ecclesiastical History,* i.27.

[53] *Robert of Torigny,* 166.

[54] *The Historia Pontificalis of John of Salisbury,* 71-2.

[55] *Metalogicon,* ed. C.C.J.Webb (London, 1929), 217-218.

[56] Watt, *The Church and the Two Nations,* 35.

[57] Flanagan, *Irish Society, Anglo-Norman Settlers,* 53.

[58] Frame, *Colonial Ireland,* 11; Watt, *The Church in Medieval Ireland,* 237.

[59] Sheehy, *Pontificia Hibernica,* i, 21-2.

[60] Watt, *The Church and the Two Nations,* 36-37.

[61] Watt, *The Church in Medieval Ireland,* 34.

[62] Giraldus Cambrensis. *Expugnatio Hibernica.* Book

1, Chapter xxxiv. Howden, *Gesta Henrici II.* I.26-28. Howden, *Chronicon.* 2: 30-32. Ralphy of Diceto, *Ymagines Historia* I.350-51. For a translation of the passage noted in Giraldus, see Curtis and McDowell, *Irish Historical Documents,* 18-19.

[63] *Chartularies of St. Mary's Abbey, Dublin: with The Register of Its House at Dunbrody and Annals of Ireland,* Vol. II. ed. John Gilbert (London: Rolls Series, 1884), 272-273. Watt takes the eighth canon that is included in Giraldus as more of a summation of all the canons in that the over-riding emphasis of the synod was to bring the Irish church into line with the English church. See Watt, *The Church in Medieval Ireland,* 35.

[64] Curtis and McDowell, *Irish Historical Documents, 18.*

[65] Curtis and McDowell, *Irish Historical Documents,* 18.

[66] *Annals of St. Mary's Abbey,* 272; Curtis and McDowell, *Irish Historical Documents,* 18.

[67] Curtis and McDowell, *Irish Historical Sources,* 19

[68] *Annals of St. Mary's Abbey,* 272.

[69] Watt, *The Church and the Two Nations* , 38n2(d).

[70] Roger of Howden, *Gesta,* 28

[71] Curtis and McDowell, *Irish Historical Documents, 20.*

[72] Sheehy, *Pontificia Hibernica,* i, 20.

[73] Sheehy, *Pontificia Hibernica,* i, 23.

[74] Sheehy, *Pontificia Hibernica,* i, 21-22.

[75] See James Brundage, *Law, Sex and Christian Society in Medieval Europe* (Chicago: University of Chicago Press, 1987).

[76] The *Remonstrance* was a document composed by several Irish kings that was sent to Rome to justify their support of the invasion of Edward Bruce. According to the document, the Kings of England had not supported religion in Ireland, which was one of the major justifications for England's intervention in Ireland as laid out in *Laudabiliter.*

[77] The role of ethnic bias in the monasteries and friaries in this period will be examined later in this chapter.

[78] Chapters were groups of men who held posts such as dean or precentor and who held the responsibility for electing new bishops and archbishops. The English system of election was adopted by the church in Ireland at the Second Synod of Cashel, and most of the cathedrals in Ireland also adopted the use of chapters to elect bishops. The ethnic background of each chapter usually corresponded with the ethnic background of the neighboring locality. This usually meant, of course, that the bishop elected was also of the same ethnic background. See Gwynn and Hadcock, *Medieval Religious Houses, Ireland,* 47-57.

[79] Watt, *The Church and the Two Nations,* 73.

[80] Sheehy, *Pontificia Hibernica, i,* 108.

[81] *Calendar of Documents Relating to Ireland, 1171-1251,* no. 736.

[82] Sheehy, *Pontificia Hibernica, i,* 140, 158.

[83] Gwynn, "Henry of London, Archbishop of Dublin." *Studies.* XXXVI (1949): 302.

[84] Otway-Ruthven, *History of Medieval Ireland, 131.*

[85] Watt, *The Church in Medieval Ireland,* 102.

[86] Orpen, *Ireland Under the Normans,* iii, 29-31.

[87] *Theiner,* 6.

[88] Otway-Ruthven, *History of Medieval Ireland,* 130-1.

[89] Watt, *The Church in Medieval Ireland,* 102.

[90] Watt, *The Church in Medieval Ireland,* 102.

[91] Frame, *Colonial Ireland,* 39-40.

[92] Watt, *Church in Medieval Ireland,* 102.

[93] MacNeill, *Phases of Irish History,* 325.

[94] James Lydon, "A Land of War," in *New History of*

Ireland, ii, Medieval Ireland, 1169-1534, ed. Art Cosgrove (Clarendon Press, Oxford, 1987), 241.

[95] Otway-Ruthven, *History of Medieval Ireland*, 195.

[96] Otway-Ruthven, *History of Medieval Ireland*, 195.

[97] G.J. Hand, *English Law in Ireland, 1290-1324* (Cambridge: Cambridge University Press, 1967), 199.

[98] Hand, *English Law in Ireland*, 201.

[99] Hand, *English Law in Ireland*, 202.

[100] *Calendar of Documents Relating to Ireland, 1252-84*, no. 1400.

[101] A.J. Otwary-Ruthven, "The Request by the Irish for English Law, 1277-80," *Irish Historical Studies* VI (Sept. 1949): 267, 268-9.

[102] Otway-Ruthven, "The Request by the Irish for English Law," 261.

[103] Otway-Ruthven, "The Request by the Irish for English Law," 269.

[104] Watt, *The Church in Medieval Ireland*, 114-5.

[105] Otwary-Ruthven, *History of Medieval Ireland*, 137.

[106] Hand, *A History of Irish Catholicism*, ii.3., 39.

[107] Otway-Ruthven, *History of Medieval Ireland*, 189.

[108] Otway-Ruthven, "The Request for the Irish of English Law," 262; Watt, *The Church in Medieval Ireland*, 115.

[109] H.G. Richardson and G.O. Sayles, "The Irish Parliaments of Edward I," *Proceedings of the Royal Irish Academy*. XXXVIII, Section C, No. 6 (1928): 142-3.

[110] *Statutes and Ordinances of Ireland*, 430-31.

[111] Swanson, *Church and Society in Late Medieval England*, 142-3.

[112] Cosgrove, *Late Medieval Ireland, 1370-1541*, 5.

[113] *Statutes and Ordinances of Ireland*, 272-3.

[114] John Clyn, *Annales Hibernie*, ed. R. Butler (Dublin: Irish Archaeological Society, 1849), 12; *Calendar of Close Rolls*, 1313-18, 307-8;

[115] Gwynn and Hadcock, *Medieval Religious Houses, Ireland*, 114-20.

[116] See in particular Barry O'Dwyer, *The Conspiracy of Mellifont, 1216-1231* (Dublin: The Dublin Historical Association, 1970), 8-13.

[117] Barry O'Dwyer, "The Impact of the Native Irish on the Cistercians in the Thirteenth Century," *Journal of Religious History*. 3 (1965): 238-245; "Gaelic Monasticism and the Irish Cistercians c.1228," *Irish Ecclesiastical Record*, CVIII (1967): 19-28; The Conspiracy of Mellifont; "The Crisis of the Cistercian Monasteries in Ireland in the Early Thirteenth Century," *Analecta Cisterciensia*, xxi-xxxii (1975-6): 267-304, 3-112.

[118] Stephen of Lexington, *Letters from Ireland*, 1228-1229, ed. Barry O'Dwyer (Kalamazoo: Cistercian Press, 1982).

[119] O'Dwyer, *The Conspiracy of Mellifont*, 13.

[120] O'Dwyer, *The Conspiracy of Mellifont*, 14.

[121] O'Dwyer, *The Conspiracy of Mellifont*, 14.

[122] Watt, *The Church in Medieval Ireland*, 53.

[123] Watt, *The Church in Medieval Ireland*, 53

[124] Watt, *The Church and the Two Nations*, 88.

[125] Watt, *Church in Medieval Ireland*, 52.

[126] R.A. Stalley, *The Cistercian Monasteries of Ireland*, (New Haven: Yale University Press, 1987), 16.

[127] Stalley, *The Cistercian Monasteries of Ireland*, 19.

[128] Stalley, *The Cistercian Monasteries of Ireland*, 16.

[129] See Watt, *The Church and the Two Nations*, 89n1, for the citation of the letter of Abbot Walter of Ochie from *Registrum Epistolarum Stephani de Lexington*, ed. B. Griesser. Analecta s.o. Cisterciensis. 2 (1946), I.12-13.

[130] The collection of the letters survives because the book was lost when a boat on which Stephen was travelling was attacked by Pisan ships in alliance with Frederick II. Stephen escaped the attack, while several other abbots, including the abbot of Clairvaux, were captured. In the fray, the book was lost, but later turned up in Turin, where it is National Library, Turin MS D. VI.25. See O'Dwyer's introduction in *Letters from Ireland*, 12-13.

[131] In addition to the comment by Stephen of Lexington, Giraldus Cambrensis, in his *Topographia Hiberniae*, describes the bestial offspring of a man and a cow and a woman who had fallen in love with a goat, elaborating that bestiality is a particular vice of the Irish. *Topographia*, 74.

[132] Watt, *The Church and the Two Nations*, 105.

[133] *Registrum*, 52.

[134] Mooney, *The Church in Gaelic Ireland*, 53-4.

[135] Watt, *The Church in Medieval Ireland*, 70.

[136] Gwynn and Hadcock, *Medieval Religious Houses, Ireland*, 246, 249.

[137] Fitzmaurice and Little, *The Franciscan Province of Ireland*, 130-3.

[138] Fitzmaurice and Little, *The Franciscan Province of Ireland*, 133-4.

[139] *Calendar of Documents Relating to Ireland, Vol. III,* 10.

[140] Fitzmaurice and Little, *The Franciscan Province in Ireland,* 52-53.

[141] Annales de Prioratus de Wigornia, *Annales Monastici, Vol. 4*, ed. Henry Luard, Rerum Britannicarum Medii Aevi Scriptores (London, 1869), 505-6; also cited in Fitzmaurice, and Little, The Franciscan Province in Ireland, 64.

[142] *Bartholomaei de Cotton Monachi Norwicensis Historia Anglicana*, ed. Henry Luard, Rerum Britannicarum Medii Aevi Scriptores (London, 1859), 431; also cited in *Fitzmaurice and Little, Materials for the History of the Franciscan Province in Ireland*, 63-4.

[143] Otway-Ruthven, *History of Medieval Ireland*, 138; Lydon, *A New History of Ireland, ii*, 240-74; Watt, *The Church and the Two Nations*, 182-83; Watt, *The Church in Medieval Ireland*, 78-9; Cosgrove, "The Medieval Period," in *Irish Church History Today*. ed. Réamonn O Muirí (Monaghan: Cummann Seanchais Ard Mhacha, 1990), 17.

[144] Thomas Clabby, *The Franciscans in Ireland, 1400-1534* (unpublished doctoral dissertation, National University of Ireland, Galway: 1998), 10-11.

[145] *Annales Wigornia*, 504, 513-14.

[146] Fitzmaurice, E.B., and Little, A.G. *Materials for the History of the Franciscan Province in Ireland*, 64.

[147] Lydon, J.F. "The Bruce Invasion of Ireland." *Historical Studies, IV* (London: Bowes and Bowes, 1963); Lydon, J.F. "The Impact of the Bruce Invasion, 1315-27." *A New History of Ireland, ii, the Middle Ages* (Oxford: Clarendon Press, 1981), 275-302; Frame, Robin. "The Bruces in Ireland, 1315-18." *Irish Historical Studies XIX* (March, 1974): 3-37; Duncan, A.A.M. "The Scots Invasion of Ireland, 1315." *The British Isles 1100-1500*. ed. R.R. Davis. (Edinburgh: Edinburgh University Press, 1988), 100-117.

[148] Lydon, "The Bruce Invasion of Ireland," 114; P.R.O., E. 372/152 (Pipe roll I Edward II), m. 35d.

[149] Fitzmaurice and Little, *Materials for the History of the Franciscan Province in Ireland*, 95 ff.

[150] *Calendar of Close Rolls, 1313-18*, 561.

[151] *Annals of Ireland by Friar John Clyn and Thady Dowling*, ed. R. Butler (Dublin, Irish Archaeological Society, 1849), 68.

[152] *Annals of Ireland by Friar John Clyn and Thady Dowling*, 12.

[153] J.A. Watt, "Negotiations Between Edward II and John XXII Concerning Ireland," *Irish Historical Studies* X (1952): 1-20.

[154] Thomas Rymer, *Foedera*, 3.620-2.

[155] Mooney, *The Church in Gaelic Ireland*, 9.

[156] Otway-Ruthven, *History of Medieval Ireland*, 189.

Chapter Five:
Legal Systems and Medieval Ireland

The ways in which societies collectively decide to organize and rule themselves are expressions of identity, since those ways of organizing the group reveal specific ideals espoused by the group, and are not arbitrary. In one sense, legal and political structures result from the group's effort to define its society. The acceptance of these structures enables the individual to gain a social identity.

It is not surprising that the inhabitants of medieval Ireland sometimes employed several systems of law. The Irish practiced Brehon law (the Irish system of law), while the Anglo-Normans could use either English law or Brehon law as the situation or financial prophet dictated.[1] In the fourteenth century, parliamentary statutes forbade all English courts within Ireland from collecting fines as restitution for felonies. However, some Anglo-Norman magistrates continued the practice into the sixteenth century. Ultimately, the acceptance of a particular legal system and administrative organization conveyed an expression of national identity because it was often based upon both an ethnic differentiation (English or Irish) and a geographic perception (the land of peace or the land of war).

The Use of Legal Systems as a Form of Identity

A "postivistic" orientation characterizes nearly all modern analyses of medieval law in Ireland, in that most scholars base their research solely and literally upon legal sources and disregard social and intellectual influences upon legal systems.[2] In other words, historians consider the legal systems at face value and refuse to offer critique or speculation by way of explanation for the material.[3] One might even consider that this method of studying medieval Irish legal history is actually a type of "value-free" history that Bradshaw attacked; yet, little movement from this method has taken place.[4] Sean Duffy's recent article, however, is important in this regard because he considers degeneracy[5] as an ideological concept in medieval Ireland that shaped the law. This mental concept

preceded parliamentary legislation of 1297 which dealt with degeneracy.[6] The proscription forbidding colonists from adopting Irish cultural traits reveals the ambiguity which resulted from Anglo-Normans living in a frontier. The statutes reveal that as distinctions between Anglo-Norman and Irish blurred, the Anglo-Normans established a framework to end the ambiguity and clearly differentiate between Irish and those of English extraction.

Law itself encompasses both prescriptive norm and descriptive fact.[7] It incorporates prescriptive norm in that a system of laws contains a tacit understanding of the ideal society. Yet, at the same time, it is a descriptive fact such that law refers to social conditions that actually already exist. For instance, a law against murder reveals that the society views murder as a socially disruptive act; the very existence of the law reveals that murder actually occurs in that society. Phrased differently, laws reveal the norms of society, but these norms reveal societal experiences and cognitive structures. For the Irish, value-free historian, further analysis is unneccessary because the law in and of itself mirrors the society for which it was created.

Recent legal theorists, however, increasingly draw attention to the relationship between the ideology and legal structures within society, as opposed to simply taking the law as reflective of society.[8] Laws become a cultural symbol for society and reveal an ideology which suppresses social inequalities. Within this understanding of ideology, society maintains certain values and ideas as givens and immutable truths. Specific pre-existing ideas and beliefs condition the experience of the individual; the experience, in turn, reinforces those pre-existing beliefs. Alternate views and evidence which contradict pre-existing beliefs are judged as anomalies and are disregarded. In other words, ideology includes an assumed perception of reality and rejects beliefs which contradict that perception.

Class and power conflict can also lead to the acceptance

of legal structures within society. Legal systems serve the interests of society's powerful individuals by facilitating the maintenance of that power; those in power tend to view the law as perfectly acceptable and appropriate. Law becomes an agent of class and power conflicts. These conflicts protect and preserve the common and shared interests not of society, but of the dominant members of society.[9] For those members who do not occupy positions of power and whose experience of law consists only of condemnation and imprisonment, the law is unacceptable. While tenable, this dichotomy requies that certain ideological constructs be in place before it can exist. Those in power may oppose the legal system if it appears to contradict their maintained values. Those without power may support the legal system if they accept their social condition as a given or if they view oppression as the price of social order.[10]

Some legal anthropologists use a similar approach in the study of law. Pierre Bourdieu, for instance, showed that the codification of law is based upon certain linguistic features, such as the use of the indicative mood when pronouncing norms.[11] Further, the codification of laws equates to a symbolic ordering process associated with state bureaucracies. Legal codification of the law fixes the beliefs of both the state and the people, even if the laws do not accord with reality.[12] Cross-cultural analyses show that the codification process usually indicates the appearance of a new social order in which a new authority exerts its dominance over society. The ruling segments explain the codification as a social good and portray their law as a logical and rational system of order. As a consequence of this codification of laws by the dominant political power in society, traditional laws not included in the legal code are usually abolished.

Rouland's argument deserves mention. He implies that the imported law (a textual, codified legal system) replaces the indigenous law (usually an orally codified legal system). He cites African examples which could prove instructive in the study of legal interaction in medieval Ireland. However, Rouland concerns himself more with the interaction between the legal system of a state (imposed from without by a colonial power) and the legal system of an indigenous, often tribal, society. The native law-colonial law dichotomy certainly applies to medieval Ireland. However, the fact that Irish society already possessed a three century old codified system of laws should limit the comparison those medieval interactions with similar modern colonial interactions.

The traditional approach of studying medieval Irish law draws distinctions within the practice of English law (such as who may or may not utilize English law)[13] and distinctions between the practice of English law and non-English law (march law and Irish Brehon law).[14] The recent approaches to the social and anthropological analysis of law discussed above are relevant to this study because the ideology of the nation shaped the application of law in medieval Ireland both from the perspective of the Anglo-Normans and from the perspective of the native Irish. From the Irish perspective, this ideology of the nation was based upon the dual concept of a perceived common past and a tie with a geographical entity called Ireland (see Chapter 2). In the literature of the native Irish, the division between native and foreigner enhanced this ideology. The early literature of the Anglo-Normans reflects this division as well, except that the distinction between 'civilized' and 'barbaric' informed the division.[15] Anglo-Norman society viewed its culture as superior because it was perceived as 'civilized.' Concerning the law, though, certain inequalities were deemed acceptable by both Anglo-Norman and Gael. For the Anglo-Norman, English law represented a contact with civility and order, while the Irish law represented barbarism and conflict. For the Irish, English law could only be used through intermediaries, either by asking an Anglo-Norman lord to plead at court or by seeking a grant of English law. Irish law was part of the learned tradition of Ireland that connected that past with the present. In both cases, the use of English law and Irish law became expressions of national ideology.

Aspects of the Application of English Law

The great fire in the Four Courts Building during the Irish Civil War in 1922 destroyed most of the legal and administrative records of medieval Ireland. Although the loss of those documents has severely hampered the study of Ireland's legal history in the middle ages, many of those documents had been catalogued at the end of the nineteenth century. Duplicates of the manuscripts were also sometimes sent to London at the time that the documents were created. The existence of those catalogues and copies enables scholars to create a general understanding of the application of English law in Ireland.

However, the lack of local legal and administrative records limits any attempt to understand the way in which customary law was practiced in manorial courts, especially during the early years of the colony. As in England, the local lords were left to apply law as long as they had been granted the privilege of administering common law. In Ireland, the records of manorial courts have not survived. The concept of law as practiced in England in the late twelfth century must have been brought with the earliest Anglo-Norman settlers in Ireland, but the lack of source material prevents further analysis of the process.[16]

From the earliest stages of Anglo-Norman settlement in Ireland, the Anglo-Norman lords met to discuss issues concerning the security and well being of the colony. These councils adopted an increasingly formal setting throughout the thirteenth century, and by the end of that century, the gathering of nobles approximated the structure of parliament. The statutes of these parliaments remain vital sources for the legal history of medieval Ireland for two reasons. First, the statutes are often the only source of data that describe the condition of the whole colony. The lords who gathered at parliament enacted these statutes because they recognized the needs and problems of the colony and attempted to legislate solutions. Second, the parliament in Ireland was less concerned with the application of English law in Ireland than the security of the colony. Thus, while unable to contradict the laws of England sent from London, the parliament in Ireland nevertheless exercised great freedom to deal with issues exclusive to Ireland. Statutes enacted by the parliaments in medieval Ireland, then, represent a local understanding of local problems and local solutions to deal with those problems within the overall context of English law.

The Introduction of English Law to Ireland

English law was brought to Ireland at a time when it was still under development in England.[17] Hand rightly assumes that the earliest settlers brought a system of customary law to Ireland and that they had probably set up seignorial courts from the outset. However, no record survives from that early period. In fact, the only existing sources concerning the application of English law in thirteenth century Ireland are the statutes and ordinances either sent to Ireland from England or from statutes and ordinances established by councils and parliaments within Ireland.[18] By the late thirteenth century, the situation improves somewhat in that several rolls of the justiciar's court[19] exist from the reign of Edward I.[20] Essentially, though, conclusions concerning the actual practice or the scope of English law at the local level remain elusive due to the limited nature of surviving documents.

The law of England became the law of Ireland after King John united the lordship of Ireland (given to him by his father, Henry II) with the English crown. To bring a legal proceeding in the justiciar's court, the plaintiff had to purchase a writ which was a formulaic text based upon a previous legal precedent.[21] In 1204, John authorized the issue of five original writs by his justiciar in Ireland: right, *mort d'ancestor*, *novel disseisin*, *de fugitivis et nativis*, and *de divisis faciendis*.[22] The writ of right allowed a plaintiff to claim land as his 'right.'[23] The writs of *mort d'ancestor* and *novel disseisin* were used by plaintiffs to reacquire lands which were wrongfully siezed. *De fugitivis et nativis*, probably the same writ as the English *de nativo habendo*, allowed a lord to bring action to recover a runaway villein.[24] The final writ of *de divisis faciendis* apparently refers to the writ of *de rationabilibus divisis* which allowed the reasonable division of land between heirs.[25] Three years after these original writs were issued, the king decreed that robbers in Ireland should be driven from the land and that they and those who receive them should be dealt with according to the law of England.[26]

In 1216, the Great Charter was extended to Ireland during the first year of the reign of Henry III.[27] After a report to the king's council in 1222, the council ordered the justiciar, Archbishop Henry of London, to enforce pleas of bounds in Ireland as they were in England. Furthermore, the counsel reminded the justiciar that the law of England was to be followed in Ireland.[28] In June of 1226, the justiciar was again reminded to keep and cause to be kept the laws and customs of England.[29] The following year, Ireland received a register of writs from England which meant that the writs used for creating precedent in Ireland would henceforth be recorded as they had been in England.[30] The justiciar Richard de Burgh was ordered to observe English law in Ireland again in 1228.[31]

Within thirty years, the Crown established a firm parallel between the law of England and the law of Ireland; in other words, it assured that laws that applied to England were applicable to Ireland.[32] However, while that point was officially re-iterated numerous times in the early thirteenth century, in practice the application of that law by the administration in Ireland was rarely comprehensive.

Although over half of Ireland was settled by the Anglo-Normans by the end of the thirteenth century, certain areas within that settlement maintained liberty status throughout the thirteenth century. In these areas, the pleas of the crown (evidently the four pleas of rape, arson, treasure trove and forestall), jurisdiction in error, and the legal status of church lands within the liberty were reserved to the king.[33] This situation in Ireland existed in stark contrast to the situation in the Marches of Wales where the royal writ of error did not run. According to Otway-Ruthven, "...the lord of an Irish liberty was thus an agent of the royal government, though [he enjoyed] a position of great power and prestige and privileged to receive those dues which would otherwise have gone to the king."[34] Within these great liberties, including Meath, Ulster and Leinster, the lord's peace prevailed over the king's. The lord of the liberty created an administrative system that mirrored that of the king. Unless the lord failed to exercise a royal writ, the king's officials were barred from the liberty.[35] Throughout the fourteenth century, these lords consistently defended their independent legal rights, but often those rights were only acknowledged by the king after the good service of the lord.[36] Thus, while the lords of the liberties exercised a fair degree of independence, they were ultimately bound by English law.[37]

Statutes of Parliaments and Councils in Ireland

Ireland's earliest extant justiciary rolls date from the very late thirteenth and early fourteenth centuries.[38] These rolls offer a glimpse at the types of proceedings that took place in the early fourteenth century in Ireland and, hence, give us a view crimes perpetrated at that time. However, records also exist from the parliamentary gatherings of the Anglo-Norman lords in Ireland from this period. Enactments passed at these parliaments and councils expose the perceived state of the colony since at these gatherings the nobility raised particular issues that the colony faced and created pertinent legislation to deal with those issues.

Like the introduction of English law in Ireland, the origins of parliament in Ireland are obscure. Two councils met at Castledermot in June and December of 1264; it was at the December council that the justiciar, Richard de la Rochelle, became a prisoner of Marice fitz Gerald and Maurice fitz Maurice. In 1265, an assembly was called in Dublin to discuss the matter, and it was decided that after gaining the peace, provisions should be made to restore estates to their rightful owners as before the conflict of the previous year. Richardson and Sayles stated that the gathering in 1264 resembled a parliament more than the assembly in 1265, since the 1265 assembly was essentially the work of Geoffrey de Joinville and not a commonalty of the magnates of Ireland.[39] Nevertheless, the gatherings do

reflect the magnates' growing awareness of responsibility for the governance of Ireland.

By the end of the thirteenth century, though, the gatherings of lords of Ireland clearly began to take on a more formal hue since they tended to increasingly represent various aspects of the colony. In the 1297 parliament, two knights were called from each of the ten counties and five liberties. Sheriffs of counties and stewards of liberties were also called.[40]   Representatives of towns and boroughs were required to attend the 1300 parliament although representatives from cities and boroughs visited by foreign merchants attended the 1299 parliament.[41] Distinctions between "Lords" and "Commons" did not occur until the later fourteenth century when popular representation was apparently marked as separate from the gatherings of the nobility.[42] However, because the evidence is lacking, it may be the case that representatives of towns and boroughs met with the nobility to discuss colonial matters.[43]

The parliaments in medieval Ireland had three basic functions: judicial, administrative, and legislative.[44] Parliament could hear pleas to the court of the justiciar, primarily because all parties (the justiciar, the plaintiff and the defendant) likely attended.[45] Administrative issues of the colony that reveal the concerns of the magnates often arose at parliament . The security of the colony was of primary importance; references to making war against the enemies of the king[46] and garrisoning castles[47] are common. The king's legislation in the English parliaments also held in Ireland, but not vice versa; therefore, the legislation enacted in Ireland only concerned Irish matters.[48]   In several cases in the late thirteenth century, the English parliament and the king issued legislation particular to Ireland. Issues such as the status of Irish people at English law and the cultural state of the colony were constant issues in the Irish parliaments of the late thirteenth and early fourteenth centuries.[49]

The Irish Parliament of 1297 received a great deal of attention in a collection of essays to mark the anniversary of the parliament in 1997.[50] The monograph's essays were not as concerned with the actual parliament itself than with the social conditions in Ireland during the late thirteenth century. These social conditions, according to the authors, may explain the parliament's foundation.

The enactments of the 1297 parliament primarily addressed the lack of social stability in the colony.[51] Much of the blame for colonial instability was placed on magnates who held lands in the marches but who did not adequately administer those lands.[52] Irish felons used these lands as passages to commit crimes on the English in the lands of peace, and those English in the lands of peace who were victims of the disturbances failed to defend the lands and failed to raise hue and cry.[53] The cost of magnates' independent armies created a considerable burden on the people of the colony, particularly in those march areas subject to hostilities.[54]

The parliamentary topic which has gained the most attention is that of cultural interaction and degeneracy.[55] The eleventh enactment of the parliament states that some English (*Anglici*), as if degenerate, wear Irish clothing and shave their heads in an Irish style known as a *culan*.[56] This seemingly innocuous reference to hairstyle had wider implications because it was difficult to differentiate between English and Irish felons. Englishmen mistaken as Irish were frequently slain giving rise to hostility and bloodshed. In addition, Irish felons, when captured, were to be punished differently than English felons.[57] Presumably, the two different ways refers to the different punishments enacted if an Englishman were to kill an Englishman (for which he could be hanged) or an Irishman (for which he could be fined).[58]

The parliament of 1297 indicates the colony's advanced dilapidation by the century's end, although the Anglo-Norman settlement experienced instability throughout the thirteenth century. Irish raids into the settled portions of Leinster continued on a regular basis from the higher elevations of the Wicklow Mountains and from Connacht.[59] The Irish, though never really fielding a trully united front, mounted several failed attempts to oust the Anglo-Normans.[60] Concurrently, English kings increasingly drained revenues from the colony in Ireland to support other ventures in Scotland, Wales and France.[61] The 1297 parliament was novel in that the Anglo-Normans blamed themselves for the state of the colony. More precisely, they blamed those Anglo-Normans who deviated from Norman cultural standards to become neither Irish nor English; in the *Remonstrance* of Domnall Ó Néill to Pope John 22 in 1310, Ó Néill writes that the English of the "middle nation" are different in character from the English of England.[62] No doubt these people of the "middle nation" are those referred to by the 1297 parliament as having adopted Gaelic culture and customs.

Also indicative of the cultural dichotomy existing

within Ireland were certain assumptions underlying the pronouncements of the 1297 parliament. The highest levels of authority within Ireland distinguished the Irish as "barbaric, war-like, undependable, and uncivilized," and the Anglo-Normans as "cultured, peaceful unless provoked, law abiding, and civilized."[63] The Anglo-Norman nobility viewed their world through this political frame; however, in reality members of that Anglo-Norman nobility living in close proximity to and forced to regularly deal with the Irish found themselves in a precarious position between two cultures.[64]

The parliament at Kilkenny in 1310 again raised the subject of the defense of the colony.[65] The usual complaints were leveled regarding the status of the defense of the colony, but this time the subject of coign and livery held primary importance.[66] Certain lords had maintained armed retainers at their tenants' expense, in effect populating the countryside with armed mercenaries.[67] According to Empey and Simms, the systematic practice of billeting mercenary soldiers originated with the Vikings, but the practice was frequently adopted by the Irish during the twelfth century.[68] By the early thirteenth century, some Irish kings employed Anglo-Normans, and by the late thirteenth century Anglo-Norman lords billeted mercenary troops on their tenants' lands. The 1297 parliament also condemned the practice of coign,[69] but numerous examples of the practice by Irish and Anglo-Norman lords occurred during the early fourteenth century. Scottish galloglas troops were granted the ability to exact fees from the tenants of the Irish kings of Ulster while the first Earl of Desmond made an agreement with his kern such that they could levy food, drink, and wages, both inside and outside his lordship.[70]

The parliament was noteworthy because of the unusually large attendance. More than 100 men, earls, barons and others attended, along with two knights from every county and two citizens or burgesses from every city or borough.[71] The justiciar and council submitted a program of legislation to the assembly which then gave assent to the ordinances in final form.[72]

Under provisions passed by the parliament of 1310, native Irish prelates were prvented from living in religious houses located within English districts. Those that gathered at the parliament thought that these Irish clerics acted as subversives within English districts. Considering that five years later clerics in the west supported the Bruce invasion this may not have been such an outrageous concern.[73]

In July 1349, while the plague spread through Ireland, Thomas de Rokeby was appointed justiciar. De Rokeby arrived in Ireland in late 1349 and immediately toured the south of Ireland to survey the extent two which English law was practiced. After his show of force to the Irish of the Wicklow Mountains, they swore to keep the peace towards the king and his people.[74]

Based upon his surveys and what was reported to him in council at Kilkenny in June 1350, de Rokeby received instructions from England directing him to review the entire system of government in Ireland, including the exchequer accounts and the system of courts.[75] Further, he was instructed to investigate the customs practiced in Ireland by the Anglo-Norman lords that removed them from the king's fealty, and the disestablishment of peace in the realm.[76] The result of this general request for reform from England resulted in the list of ordinances issued at a great council at Kilkenny in November 1351.

The main point of the ordinances, like those enactments from previous councils and parliaments, called for the securing of peace in the realm. In this sense, defense issues occupied primary importance since landlords were ordered to provide for the defense of their lands, or submit the revenue of those lands for defense.[77] Determining the type of law practiced by Anglo-Normans held equal import. Anglo-Normans settled disputes with each other not with English law, but with the law of the march and with Irish law. As well, Anglo-Norman lords made private agreements with known rebels (both English and Irish) and entered into alliances by marriage, fosterage and otherwise with the king's enemies, again both English and Irish.[78]

Otway-Ruthven's statement on the matter is no doubt correct: "It is difficult to see why the Statutes of Kilkenny have been taken by modern writers as marking a watershed in the history of the English colony in Ireland, for in fact there is very little in them that is new..."[79] The Statutes themselves reiterate common problems of cultural and social degradation noticed since well before the 1297 parliament.[80] The enactments of the Kilkenny parliament forbade any sort of interaction between the Irish and Anglo-Normans and prohibited Anglo-Normans from adopting Gaelic cultural traits, just as the parliament of 1297 had.

The preamble of the Statutes made evident the particular problems in the colony.[81] The English, who previously used the English language, dress, and law, now used the language, dress, and law of the Irish. The parliament of 1297 stated that the Anglo-Normans wore Irish clothes and cut their hair in an Irish fashion. The ordinances issued in 1351 by de Rokeby forbid alliances with the Irish and the use of Irish law. No parliament or ordinances before 1366 refer to the use of the Irish language by the Anglo-Normans.[82] In fact, what we can see from this brief discussion of the statutes and ordinances of Ireland from 1297 to 1366 are the signs of a colony already in decline by the late thirteenth century and the continuation of that decline through the calamities of the early fourteenth century, such as the famine, Bruce invasion, and mid century plague. Counsels and parliaments, in attempts to address the decline, created more laws and legislation to prevent what was already happening. Of course, these lords failed to recognize that the law's application itself contributed significantly to the colony's descent.

The Status of the Irish in English Law

Four decades ago, several scholars examined the topic of the status of the native Irish in English law, but recently the issue has not received any attention or new appraisals.[83] Murphy and others recognized that the interpretation of the status of the Irish in English law was hindered by the use of various vocabulary to describe the common Irish of servile status.[84] *Hiberbicus* could be used for an Irish person in general or for a villein, while the Irish term *bíatach* was transformed from an Irish meaning of "commoner" to a term that was used by the Anglo-Normans meaning villein.[85] The Anglo-Normans grouped the Irish (both free and unfree) into the category of *bíatach* without consideration of the use of the term within Irish land tenure.[86] The general use of the term by the Anglo-Normans implies a binding of the betagh (the English term for *bíatach*) to the land, in a similar sense to the villein in English law.[87] *Nativus* was another technical term used by the Anglo-Normans to describe the Irish.[88]

Regardless of the particular vocabulary used in Anglo-Norman legal material to describe the Irish, the fact remains that the Irish were generally quite limited in their ability to use English law. First, like the villein in England, an Irish tenant relied upon his lord to bring legal action for him.[89] Second, if an Irish person were killed and the accused could prove that they were English, upon conviction the guilty party could simply pay a fine for the offense. The lord of the murdered Irishman collected the fine, and if the Irish person had no lord, the guilty party could escape with impunity. Third, in civil proceedings, an action could be easily defeated by simply alleging that the person bringing the action was in fact Irish.[90] An Irish defendant in a civil case apparently did not suffer any impediment in court.[91]

These three limitations for the Irish assume that in regions unconquered by the Anglo-Normans the Irish were left to use their own law. Those Irish who lived in regions that had been conquered were denied access to English law unless they had been granted the right to use English law or the action was brought by their lord. Modern research has generally considered this situation as similar to that of the villein in England,[92] and that the Irish, while dependent upon their lord, suffered no great hardship under English law. Otway-Ruthven stated that "The position [of the Irish] had clearly many practical inconveniences…"[93] Hand follows Otway-Ruthven and states that the actions of the courts and the demands of everyday life "…served in different ways to make matters more tolerable for the native Irish…"[94] However, Hand continues, by suggesting that the legal disabilities of the Irish "…could be bitterly felt, and…must have remained a constant invitation to malice and greed."[95] Elsewhere, Hand argued that the comparison of the disabilities of the Irish with those of villeins in England is attractive because of the similarity in the forms of exceptions for both and because the lord could possibly of a lord enfranchising Irish or villein.[96]

However, Murphy contradicts this view, stating that "…so far as the servile population in Ireland are concerned, they suffered disabilities from which the villein in England was at that time free."[97] For instance, while the Irish betagh could not bring action against anyone in an English court, the villein could sue in English courts against any person other than his own lord.[98] Both Hand and Otway-Ruthven bear categorization as proponents of the supposedly "value-free" school of history described by Brendan Bradshaw;[99] hence, their analysis, centered around Anglo-Norman evidence, might be more severely skewed than originally realized.

The view of law as both proscriptive and descriptive[100] indicates that the inability to use English law means that the Irish should not use English law, and reveals the ethnic division within the colony. Further, the relationship between those who could and those who could not indicates a power relationship that Hand and Otway-Ruthven missed. Anglo-Normans possessed the right to use English law because of a perceived cultural

superiority. In contrast, the power relationship between lord and villein in medieval England was predicated solely upon a perceived social structure rather than an ethnic distinction.

Clear indications exist showing that the Irish perceived this distinction. In fragmented societies where one segment of society controls the law, the perceived inequality is not necessarily understood by the part of society that does not control the law. The part of society without legal control could perceive the inequality as a social fact of nature;[101] however, in the case of the Irish in medieval Ireland, this inequality was perceived as an injustice.

This perception of legal inequality is best found in the *Remonstrance* of Domnall Ó Néill and other Irish kings to Pope John 22 in 1317.[102] The *Remonstrance* was a list of grievances composed by several Gaelic lords who were supportive of the Bruce brothers during the Bruce invasion of Ireland. In it the Gaelic lords argue that because the Anglo-Normans failed to fulfill their obligations as set out in *Laudabiliter*,[103] Gaelic lords need not support the king or his nobles, and could therefore support an alternate king, Edward Bruce. Henry II and his successors should have extended the bounds of the Irish church and brought the people of Ireland under the rule of law but the *Remonstrance* argued that they did not. In form, the Remonstrance bears similarities to the Scottish *Declaration of Arbroath*; a comparison of the two reveals a possible Scottish influence for the complaints, especially considering that an Irish ally of the Bruce brothers wrote the *Remonstrance*.[104]

Hand did consider the four legal grievances raised in the *Remonstrance*.[105] Otway-Ruthven, while accepting that many of the grievances listed in the *Remonstrance* were accurate, felt that "…the statement of the Irish case was a little disingenuous."[106] She states that Ó Néill's claim to represent an Irish coalition was suspect given both his personal conflict with his de Burgh overlord and his repeated depositions in the late thirteenth century. She also states that the unanimous support of the Irish kings for Edward Bruce was grossly exaggerated. Ultimately, she concedes that the claims in the *Remonstrance* were justified but gives the matter little further attention. While Frame considers the text a meaningful piece of propaganda and that the claims listed in the *Remonstrance* as very real disabilities for the Irish, he too does not further elaborate on the matter.[107]

The first complaint in the *Remonstrance* charges that Irishmen may be brought into the King's court in Ireland without restriction; on the other hand, all Irishmen, lay or cleric, are refused recourse to the law by the fact of being Irish.[108] As mentioned earlier, an action brought to court could be defeated with the allegation that the plaintiff was Irish. The Irish person would normally bring an action to court through his own lord, just as the villein would in England.[109] However, there is a great difference between a villein in England not being able to bring an action independently and an Irish person's inability to bring an action. In the case of a villein, the inability stems from a social class distinction that reveals the dependency of the peasant to the lord. For an Irish person, the reason that they could not bring an action was because of their ethnicity and not necessarily their social standing. Indeed, the lower social standing of the Irish was predicated upon their inferiority as perceived by the Anglo-Normans.

The second point that the *Remonstrance* addressed concerned the belief that an Englishman could kill an Irishman and not expect any punishment.[110] If a coroner's jury found that a deceased person had been murdered and was Irish, the accused could easily be acquitted. Hand suggests that the reason for this lies in the Irish law of paying fines for murder to the deceased family members' kin. As Hand elaborates, it was possible for an Anglo-Norman to escape without a fine if the murdered Irish person had no Anglo-Norman lord to sue for compensation. It is also true that early in the fourteenth century murder of an Anglo-Norman by another Anglo-Norman could also be punishable by fine.[111] Nevertheless, the claim made in the *Remonstrance* proves valid because when the issue concerned inter-cultural criminal proceedings, clear differences existed in the way that English or Irish were punished. These differences existed as a result of the perceived inferiority of both Irish law and Irish ethnicity.

The third claim made in the *Remonstrance* concerns the inability of Irish women to receive any sort of dower if they had married an Anglo-Norman.[112] Hand dismisses the issue as of "...lesser scope and importance..."[113] and thereby misses the claim's relevance. The inability of an Irish widow to bring an action to receive dower was no doubt due to the exception discussed above; that is, if a person proved to be Irish the action would be halted. Hand ignores the substance of this injustice; if an Irish woman could not receive dower because she was in fact Irish, even if the reason for that inability was due to another aspect of the law (that Irish could not bring action on their own),

how is it not to be considered anything other than a policy of ethnic exclusion?[114]

The final point made in the *Remonstrance* concerns the testamentary incapacity of the Irish.[115] This complaint, that the Irish were unable to dispose of their property by their last wishes or to make a last will and testament was raised previously by the archbishop of Tuam in 1255.[116] While Hand correctly states that the "...lack of adequate surviving records of the medieval Irish ecclesiastical jurisdictions makes it impossible to say much more...,"[117] the fact that the same complaint was raised sixty years before the *Remonstrance* suggests the issue's importance. Indeed, it is similar to the passage concerning dower; a lord might seize chattels of Irish because, as Irish, they were unfree. The implication, then, points to this unfree Irish status based more upon the Anglo-Norman view of Irish ethnic inferiority than upon a class distinction.

Besides discussing law in Ireland, the *Remonstrance* described Anglo-Norman banquets to which were invited Gaelic lords. After dining, the hosts murdered then beheaded their Gaelic guests and sold the heads to Gaelic rivals.[118] The *Remonstrance* includeds the example of Piers de Bermingham, who invited his Ó Conchobhair neighbors to a banquet at which they were murdered.[119] In another case from 1277, Thomas de Clare, brother of the earl of Gloucester, invited Briain, the Red Prince of Thomond and de Clare's own godson, to his house to further their bonds. As a mark of unity they shared the same communion host, but then de Clare turned on Briain, had him dragged behind a horse and beheaded.[120] The deeds went unpunished, and certain members of the clergy supported such acts, stating that it was no sin to kill an Irishman.[121] If the *Remonstrance* was the only source to consider, the validity of the claims may be questioned considering the propagandistic nature of the text itself. But Turville-Petre showed that other sources substantiate the *Remonstrance*.[122] A poem that praises the ambush of the Gaelic lords by de Bermingham in British Library MS Harley 913 reveals that the Irish were plotting against de Bermingham and that the English lords had made a pact to destroy them. Though the other Anglo-Norman lords did not honor the pact, de Bermingham was praised for not failing and for murdering the Ó Conchobhair who came to feast with him. The poet portrayed the act not as an outrage, but as an example of nobility similar to hunting hares.[123]

The most simple manner for an Irish person to use

English law was to have their lord bring the action to court. A person of Irish blood could also pay an English lord small sums to be under their protection, as was the practice in Wales.[124] Several royal families known as the "five bloods," the Ó Néill of Ulster, Ó Maíl Shechnaill of Meath, Ó Conchobhuir of Connacht, Ó Briain of Munster, and Mac Murchadha of Leinster, could freely use English law.[125] From the sources it is unclear whether a Gaelic lord from one of these royal families could bring an action to English law for one of their subjects.

Also unclear was the ability of Irish prelates and bishops to take advantage of English law. However, given that at various times in the thirteenth and fourteenth century Irish clerics were legally forbidden to receive benefices in Anglo-Norman areas, the fact that they were Irish may have negated their status as clerics.[126]

Another method by which a person of Irish exraction might use English law was through a royal grant. Technically this grant could only be issued by the king, but there is evidence that individual lords issued the grant themselves.[127] Charters of English law granted to Irish were enrolled on the Patent Rolls; Murphy has tabulated the evidence beginning in the reign of Edward II.[128] Grants given in the reign of Edward II numbered ten, in the reign of Edward III eighteen, and in the reign of Richard II sixteen.

At some point between 1277 and 1280, Irish clerics attempted to purchase English law for all the Irish.[129] The main force behind the attempt, David MacCarwell, the archbishop of Cashel, was seemingly guided by a desire to improve his standing as archbishop of Cashel (which was a matter of dispute) and the standing of the Church in Ireland (see Chapter Four). The amount of money offered for this grant was a huge sum between seven and ten thousand marks. Ultimately Edward I seemed amenable to the idea since he considered the laws of the Irish detestable, and not even laws. However, he left the final decision to the local magnates in Ireland. These local lords aparently disapproved of the idea, since the grant never occurred.[130] The matter might have been discussed in a parliament in 1280, but since so few of the lords were in Ireland to attend, no decision was reached. Either the lords rejected the idea, or they simply put off the decision.[131] In either case the attempt to grant English law to the Irish failed.

Aspects of the Irish System of Law

While the field of early Irish law has received considerable attention in recent decades, its relationship to Irish law practiced in post-Norman Ireland is still not well understood.[132] The outline of the early Irish legal system, dating from the seventh and eighth centuries, was compiled in legal tracts which generally were not altered over time; glosses which were later added explained legal terms in light of contemporary practice. The legal tracts themselves, though, remained static throughout the middle ages, even if contemporary legal scholars could not fully understand the meaning of the tracts.[133] Irish law, like history and literature, was considered one of the major branches of Irish learning, and hence legal scholars of the middle ages tended to be conservative in outlook when considering actual legal texts.

The glosses and commentaries form the basis of what is known about legal practice in the later middle ages. However, it is very difficult to define clearly which glosses result from the post-Norman period and which are earlier.[134] Several fourteenth century legal handbooks exist that show how scholars were taught the law in schools of law;[135] these handbooks have been used to great effect by modern scholars to show a higher incidence of interaction between the legal systems of England and Ireland than previously thought.[136]

The early Irish law tracts themselves had become less relevant to the practice of Irish law before the thirteenth century.[137] The law tracts served as a source of maxims and general rules used in pleadings and decisions, but had little relevance to their original context.[138] Irish judges and lawyers, like other learned classes in medieval Ireland, were products of hereditary families, including the Mac Egan, the Mac Clancy, and the Mac Cawell.[139] Parties seeking legal recourse employed these legal families as judges, pleaders and advocates. In actual cases, the judge gave decisions at public assemblies located on hilltops.[140] The decision itself, a form of arbitration to which the parties must submit, required adherance; fines were levied against an individual failing to abide by the decision of the judge. The judge received a payment, *oiledhéag*, which was equal to an eleventh of the demanded sum or awarded damages.[141]

In contrast to the system of criminal law developed within English law in the middle ages, Irish law resolved theft and murder through the payment of fees for damages to the injured party, or, in the case of the murder of the individual, to his or her lord and family. Irish law enforced no punishment comparable to the death penalty in English law for conviction of the same acts. The fine that was levied, or *eric*, varied based upon the status of the wronged individual. For the accidental death of a man of learning in 1400, the *eric* levied amounted to 126 cows (the value of which equivalled 126 ounces of silver).[142] In addition to the fee paid to the individual wronged or the family of the individual wronged, the individual's lord could also claim a portion of the *eric*. For crimes of theft, the wronged individual would receive payment of several times the value of the item stolen.

The guilty party was not exclusively responsible for payment of *eric*. Just as the family and lord of a wronged individual could claim a portion of *eric*, the guilty party's family was also responsible for the payment of the *eric* after a family member had been convicted.[143] If the individual failed in the payment of *eric*, the family of the individual would be held responsible. If the immediate family failed to pay, the fee could be extended to a wider family group.[144]

The English described the Irish system of land tenure using the same term *gavelkind,* a term applied to the custom of inheritance that had prevailed in Kent and Wales in which lands were divided between sons as opposed to a system of primogeniture.[145] In Ireland, the system was predicated upon the view of the the family rather than the individual as the land-holding entity. This meant that land could not be alienated from the family by an individual through marriage, and the land could not be passed to a daughter because if the daughter married, the land would be considered part of the husband's family's holdings.[146] It also meant that land could easily be redistributed within the family. If the kin group had grown to such a degree that the family land could not support all the members of the kin, the senior member of the family, *sinnsear*, would re-divide the land based upon the senior members of the family.[147] Nicholls and O Conor have suggested that this process of land redistribution could explain the lack of permanent settlement in Gaelic Ireland throughout the middle ages.[148]

The Use of Irish Law by Anglo-Normans

Proscriptions against usage of Irish law did not begin with the Anglo-Normans. The Irish reformers of the twelfth century church recognized certain problems with Irish law, most notably those concerning marriage, divorce and concubinage.[149] However, church condemnations of these practices seem to have focused on the practices within the church itself, and not on society in general.[150] According to Simms, early Irish legal scholars were proficient in both secular and ecclesiastical law.[151] After the reforms of the twelfth century, the reformist members of the church hierarchy in Ireland attempted to align the laws of the Irish church with those of the rest of Europe.

The arrival of the Anglo-Normans at the end of the twelfth century complicated Irish law's status within Ireland. From the outset the Anglo-Norman settlers seem to have practiced the same legal procedures as in England, although earliest references to the imposition of a legal system that mirrored the law of England only date to the reign of King John.[152] However, the Anglo-Norman legal sources notably do not mention Irish law during the early period.

The arrival of the Anglo-Normans in Ireland coincided with the establishment of Common Law in England, and at first glance, it would seem that Wales appears to provide a useful comparison to the application of English law to Ireland. However, the differences outweigh the similarities.[153] The Anglo-Norman liberties more closely resembled the liberties in England than the Marcher lordships of Wales.[154] While the Statute of Wales legitimized aspects of Welsh law in 1284, by the middle of the thirteenth century litigants in an Irish case brought to the King's Bench declared that "the land of Ireland ought to be ruled by the laws and customs used in England."[155] This statement apparently refers to the impossibility of an Anglo-Norman using Irish law, although this and other references to identical laws practiced in Ireland and England do not explicitly refer to Irish law.

Thomas de Rokeby's ordinances of 1351 comdemned the practice of both march law and Irish law, and fifteen years later the condemnation was reiterated in the Statutes of Kilkenny.[156] The Dublin government grew increasingly unable to enforce English law in the marginal areas of the colony and left the application of English law to the lords themselves. Anglo-Normans on the frontier had to interact with Gaelic lords, meaning that they were likely to use Irish law as much as English law depending upon the circumstances.[157] In England, large areas of legal practice were left undefined and freely conceded to local practice and custom. In Ireland, on the other hand, the Anglo-Normans may have relied on local courts as well, but the difference in Ireland was that the local custom (ie., Irish Brehon law) often involved elements that contradicted English law. The meager sources for local courts in Ireland only lead to speculation.[158]

The version of English law practiced in Ireland did incorporate certain aspects of Irish law. For instance, the parliament of 1278 introduced Irish kin liability (*cin comfhocuis*) into English law in Ireland as *kynkonges*.[159] The introduction of this legal principal initially only applied to those Irish who lived at peace with the Anglo-Normans. For the Anglo-Normans in the same territories English law still applied.[160] Generally, the customs of the land of Ireland were usually older or local variations of English custom that had been brought by the early settlers and not local adaptations of English law.[161]

Mac Niocaill explored the benefits enjoyed by Anglo-Norman using Irish law.[162] In terms of homicide, Irish law possessed the great advantage of requiring a cash or kind payment to the kin of the murdered person rather than the English custom of hanging. In the same year as the Statutes of Kilkenny issue (1366), the Earl of Ormond and the Ó Ceinnéidigh of Ormond contracted a relationship showing this use of Irish law. If any of the Earl's men were murdered by treachery, whether they be English or Irish, the guilty party or, if he cannot be found, the guilty party's lord or his kin, had to pay a fine to the dead person's lord and double the fine to the dead person's immediate kin.[163] In 1358, another agreement between the Earl of Ormond and an Ó Ceinnéidigh established fines for trespass, a practice legislated against by de Rokeby in his ordinances of 1351.[164]

The Ormond lords adopted Irish legal principles even after such principles were outlawed in 1351 and 1366. Thus the use of Irish law by the Anglo-Norman lords seems fairly widespread. Of course, the sources are notoriously limited, but they nevertheless indicate that the adoption of Irish legal principles predates the parliament of 1297 since only a widespread application of these principles would receive comment at parliament.

The Anglo-Norman lords, and the Ormonds in particular, used Irish criminal law to their distinct advantage. In practice, the selection of one legal system over another was simply a matter of pragmatic profiteering.[165] Anglo-

Norman lords were "legally ambidextrous," using both English law and Irish law as the occasion and their own profit dictated.[166] An Anglo-Norman lord could use English land tenure law to his advantage; he could also use Irish law to his benefit in a criminal case. In another sense, the use of Irish law or of a modified form of English law by Anglo-Normans living on the periphery of the colony reveals the incomplete conquest of the island and the growing relevance of the Gaelic lords in the unconquered and unsettled regions of Ireland.

Conclusions

Societies usually view law as a device with which to maintain order and provide stability for their members. Yet, as this study has shown, though, the law meant to instill order and stability in society can sometimes cause instability and chaos. In thirteenth and fourteenth century Ireland, two related facets of legal practice simultaneously contributed to the overall decline of the colony and the expansion of Gaelic power.

First, during this time, the overarching legal framework in Ireland barred a large segment of the population from using English law. In a general sense, this first point is not unique within the context of medieval European history; due to their social standing as peasants or villeins many large segments of populations in medieval Europe were hindered or prevented from using law. The significant difference in post-Anglo-Norman Ireland, though, was that the group barred from using the dominant legal system was an entire ethnic group identified by the colonizers, not merely a social class within the population of the geographic region governed by the law. This created a system of dominance that was resented by the Irish, and this resentment was made manifest in the early fourteenth century Remonstrance.

Secondly, the Anglo-Normans never fully conquered Ireland; hence, large areas of the island were controlled by Gaelic lords who continued to practice Irish law. The marches between the Gaelic lordships and the Anglo-Norman lordships were expansive and fluid. Anglo-Norman lordships were located in close proximity to each other, and, as the fortunes of the Dublin administration declined in the late thirteenth century, Anglo-Norman lordships located in close proximity to each other became susceptible to cultural interaction with the Gaelic lordships. The Anglo-Norman lords in these frontier areas were as likely to use Irish or march law as English law because of desperate frontier conditions. Irish law proved far more pragmatic, since their neighbors used it and it enabledd them to collect much needed income in a troubling economic atmosphere.

Finally, other Anglo-Norman lords in Ireland realized the situation's gravity, and so created more laws that attempted to prohibit further cultural degeneracy. However, they failed to realize that the law itself created part of the problem. They created more laws to prevent cultural degeneracy, and merely cemented and enhanced divisions within Ireland that were an aspect of the colony from the outset. As mentioned in previous chapters of this study, though, the process began much earlier than the fourteenth century. Indeed, the sources cited as evidence of the colonies decline in the fourteenth century are actually after the fact responses to events that occurred throughout the thirteenth century as the colony expanded into the regions of Ireland more strongly controlled by Gaelic lordships.

In this way, Ireland's difference from the other realms of the English kings in the thirteenth and fourteenth centuries lay in the facts that the native law practiced by the Irish was never formally recognized, and was, in fact, a mark of barbarism and incivility, and that the benefits of English law never replaced what Anglo-Norman colonists and church leaders perceived to be an inferior system of laws.

[1] Frame, *Colonial Ireland*, 133-4.

[2] For example, consider Geoffrey Hand, *English Law in Ireland, 1290-1324* (Cambridge: Cambridge University Press, 1967); Otway-Ruthven, *A History of Medieval Ireland*; H.G. Richardson and G. O. Sayles, *The Irish Parliament in the Middle Ages* (Philadelphia: University of Pennsylvania Press, 1952).

[3] By positivistic I simply mean that the approach generally used by scholars concerned with medieval law in Ireland has lacked any sort of metaphysical interpretive quality, and not that approach in legal studies known as legal postivism. One reason for this gap in the field may be that throughout the twentieth century most scholars (Otway-Ruthven, for example) were pioneers in the interpretation of recently published legal material. The only synthesis on the topic of law in medieval Ireland is still Hand, *English Law in Ireland*, but it is over thirty years old.

[4] Brendan Bradshaw, "Nationalism and Historical Scholarship in Modern Ireland," 336.

[5] In the statutes of the parliament of 1297 some English were acting "as if degenerate" ("*quasi degeneres*") because they had adopted the Irish manners of dress and hair-style.

[6] Sean Duffy, "The Problem of Degeneracy," in *Law and Disorder in Thirteenth-Century Ireland: The Dublin Parliament of 1297*, ed. James Lydon (Dublin: Four Courts Press, 1997), 87-106.

[7] Roger Cotterrell, *The Sociology of Law: An Introduction* (London: Butterworths, 1992), 8, 12.

[8] Cotterrell, *Sociology of Law*, 114-117;

[9] Alan Hunt, "Marxism and the Analysis of Law," in *Sociological Approaches to Law*, ed. Adam Podgorecki and Christopher J. Whelan (London: Billing and Sons Limited, 1981), 95.

[10] Cotterrell, *Sociology of Law*, 174.

[11] Pierre Bourdieu, "La Force du Droit. Elements pour une sociologie du champ juridique," *Actes de la Recherche en Sciences Sociales*, 64 (September 1986): 3-19.

[12] Norbert Rouland, *Legal Anthropology*, trans. Philippe G. Planel (London: The Athlone Press, 1994), 309.

[13] Geoffrey Hand, "English Law in Ireland, 1172-1351," *Northern Ireland Legal Quarterly*, xxiii, 4 (winter, 1972): 393-422; A.J. Otway-Ruthven, "The Native Irish and English Law in Medieval Ireland," *Irish Historical Studies*, vii (1950-51): 1-16.

[14] J.F.M. Lydon, "The Middle Nation," in *The English in Medieval Ireland*, ed. J.F.M. Lydon (Dublin: Royal Irish Academy, 1984), 1-26.

[15] Scott and Martin, *Expugnatio Hibernica*, 135, 249; J. O'Meara, *The Topography of Ireland by Giraldus Cambrensis*, 84, 85.

[16] Hand, *English Law in Ireland*, 1.

[17] Hand, *English Law in Ireland*, 1-20.

[18] Hand, *English Law in Ireland*, 1-4, 262-63.

[19] "Justiciar' was the title given to the chief governor of the colony in Ireland through the thirteenth and fourteenth centuries. He was the king's representative in Ireland, and dispensed justice in his own court in Ireland. As well, the justiciar had the power to raise armies for the defense of the colony, to raise taxes for the support of the colony, and to proclaim royal service. See Otway-Ruthven, *History of Medieval Ireland*, 145-8; idem, "The Chief Governors of Mediaeval Ireland," *Journal of the Royal Society of Antiquaries of Ireland*, XCV (1965): 660-2.

[20] *Calendar of Justiciar Rolls, 1295-1303; Calendar of Justiciar Rolls, 1304-1307; Calendar of Justiciar Rolls, 1308-1314.*

[21] J.H. Baker, *An Introduction to English Legal History* (London: Buttersworths, 1990), 65.

[22] *Rotuli Litterarum Patentium*, 47; *Statutes and Ordinances of Ireland*, 3.

[23] Baker, *English Legal History*, 68.

[24] Hand, *English Law in Ireland*, 2n1; Baker, *English Legal History*, 534-5.

[25] Hand, *English Law in Ireland,* 2n1.

[26] *Statutes and Ordinances of Ireland,,* 4.

[27] *Calendar of Patent Rolls, 1216-25,* 31; *Statutes and Ordinances of Ireland,* 5.

[28] *Statutes and Ordinances of Ireland,* 20.

[29] *Statutes and Ordinances of Ireland,* 21; *Calendar of Patent Rolls, 1225-1232,* 48.

[30] F.W. Maitland, "The Introduction of English Law into Ireland," *English Historical Review,* iv (1889): 516-17.

[31] *Statutes and Ordinances of Ireland,* 23.

[32] Hand, *English Law in Ireland,* 3-4.

[33] Otway-Ruthven, *History of Medieval Ireland,* 182.

[34] Otway-Ruthven, *History of Medieval Ireland,* 184.

[35] Otway-Ruthven, *History of Medieval Ireland,* 185-7.

[36] Hand, *English Law in Ireland,* 113-34.

[37] Frame, *Colonial Ireland,* 100.

[38] *Calendar of Justiciary Rolls, 1295-1307; Calendar of Justiciary Rolls, 1308-14.*

[39] Richardson and Sayles, *The Irish Parliament in the Middle Ages,* 59.

[40] *Statutes and Ordinances of Ireland,* 194-6.

[41] *Statutes and Ordinances of Ireland,* 212, 228-30.

[42] Richardson and Sayles, The Irish Parliament in the Middle Ages, 76-7.

[43] Richardson and Sayles, The Irish Parliament in the Middle Ages, 78.

[44] Richardson and Sayles, The Irish Parliament in the Middle Ages, 63-9.

[45] Calendar of Justiciary Rolls, 1295-1303, 74; Richardson and Sayles, Irish Parliament in the Middle Ages, 63-4.

[46] *Calendar of Justiciary Rolls, 1295-1303,* 73.

[47] *Calendar of Justiciary Rolls, 1305-1307,* 353, 355.

[48] Richardson and Sayles, *Parliament in Medieval Ireland,* 68.

[49] *Statutes and Ordinances of Ireland,* 194-212.

[50] James Lydon, ed., *Law and Disorder in Thirteenth-Century Ireland: The Dublin Parliament of 1297* (Dublin: Four Courts Press, 1997).

[51] A superior edition of the enactments was published by Philomena Connolly, "The Enactments of the 1297 Parliament," in Lydon, *Law and Disorder,* 148-61; previous versions of the enactments are found in *Statutes and Ordinances of Ireland,* 194-213, and an adequate translation is found in Curtis and McDowell, ed., *Irish Historical Documents, 1172-1922.*

[52] Connolly, "The Enactments of the 1297 Parliament," 150-51.

[53] Connolly, "The Enactments of the 1297 Parliament," 150-53.

[54] Connolly, "The Enactments of the 1297 Parliament," 154-55.

[55] Duffy, "The Problem of Degeneracy;" Lydon, "The Middle Nation."

[56] Connolly, "The Enactments of the 1297 Parliament," 158-59.

[57] Connolly, "The Enactments of the 1297 Parliament," 158-9.

[58] Hand, *English Law in Ireland,* 202-3.

[59] Otway-Ruthven, *History of Medieval Ireland,* 201.

[60] The most notable example is the raising, with support from Áed O'Connor and Teig O Brien, of Brian Uí Neill

as king. The confederation was defeated at the Battle of Down in 1260. *Annals of Connacht*, s.a. 1259, 1260; Otway-Ruthven, *History of Medieval Ireland*, 194-5; J.A. Watt, "Gaelic Polity and Cultural Identity," *A New History of Ireland, ii, Medieval Ireland*, ed. Art Cosgrove (Oxford: Clarendon Press, 1987), 348.

[61] James Lydon, "The Years of Crisis," *A New History of Ireland, ii, Medieval Ireland, 1169-1534*, ed. Art Cosgrove (Oxford: Clarendon Press, 1987), 432.

[62] James Lydon, "The Middle Nation," 1.

[63] Scott and Martin, *Expugnatio Hibernica*, 135, 249; J. O'Meara, *The Topography of Ireland by Giraldus Cambrensis*, 84, 85.

[64] Lydon, "The Middle Nation," 3.

[65] *Statutes and Ordinances of Ireland*, 264-76.

[66] Richardson and Sayles, *The Irish Parliament in the Middle Ages*, 95.

[67] C.A. Empey and Katharine Simms, "The Ordinances of the While Earl and the Problem of Coign in the Later Middle Ages," *Proceedings of the Royal Irish Academy*, 75C (1975): 180-1.

[68] Empey and Simms, "Ordinances of the White Earl," 179.

[69] Connolly, "The Enactments of the 1297 Parliament," 154-55.

[70] Empey and Simms, "Ordinances of the White Earl," 180-1.

[71] Richardson and Sayles, *The Irish Parliament in the Middle Ages*, 96.

[72] *Statutes and Ordinances of Ireland*, 262.

[73] James Lydon, "The Impact of the Bruce Invasion, 1315-27," *A New History of Ireland, ii, Medieval Ireland, 1169-1534*, ed. Art Cosgrove (Oxford: Clarendon Press, 1987). 293.

[74] Otway-Ruthven, *History of Medieval Ireland*, 277.

[75] *Calendar of Close Rolls, 1349-54*, 195.

[76] *Calendar of Patent Rolls, 1348-50*, 590, 592.

[77] *Statutes and Ordinances of Ireland*, 374-96.

[78] Otway-Ruthven, *History of Medieval Ireland*, 278-9.

[79] Otway-Ruthven, *History of Medieval Ireland*, 291.

[80] *Statutes and Ordinances of Ireland*, 430-68.

[81] *Statutes and Ordinances of Ireland*, 430-1.

[82] Otway-Ruthven, *History of Medieval Ireland*, 292.

[83] J. Otway-Ruthven, "The Request for English Law,"261-70; J. Otway-Ruthven, "The Native Irish and English Law in Medieval Ireland," *Irish Historical Studies*, vii (1950): 1-16; Aubrey Gwynn, "Edward I and the Proposed Purchase of English Law for the Irish, c. 1276-80," *Royal Historical Society Transactions, 5th series*, x, (1960): 111-27; G.J. Hand, "The Status of the Native Irish in the Lordship of Ireland, 1272-1331," *Irish Jurist, new series, i* (1966): 93-115; Hand, *English Law in Ireland*, 187-213; Bryan Murphy, "The Status of the Native Irish after 1331," *The Irish Jurist, new series*, ii (1967): 116-38.

[84] Murphy, "The Status of the Native Irish," 117.

[85] Gerard MacNiocaill, "The Origins of the Betagh," *The Irish Jurist, new series, i* (1966): 297.

[86] MacNiocaill, "The Origins of the Betagh," 298.

[87] Hand, *English Law in Ireland*, 195.

[88] Hand, *English Law in Ireland*, 196.

[89] Otway-Ruthven, *Medieval Ireland*, 188.

[90] Hand, *English Law in Ireland*, 199-200.

[91] Otway-Ruthven, *Medieval Ireland*, 188; Hand, *English Law in Ireland*, 201.

92 Hand, *English Law in Ireland*, 199.

93 Otway-Ruthven, *Medieval Ireland*, 188.

94 Hand, *English Law in Ireland*, 213.

95 Hand, *English Law in Ireland*, 213.

96 Hand, "Aspects of Alien Status in Medieval English Law, with Special Reference to Ireland," *Legal History Studies, 1972: Papers Presented to the Legal History Conference at Aberystwyth, 18-21 July 1972*, ed. Dafydd Jenkins (Cardiff: University of Wales Press, 1975), 132.

97 Murphy, "The Status of the Native Irish," 118.

98 Murphy, "The Status of the Irish," 118.

99 Bradshaw, "Nationalism and Historical Scholarship," 336.

100 Cotterrell, *The Sociology of Law*, 8.

101 Cotterrell, *The Sociology of Law*, 174.

102 The text of the Remonstrance is found in Fordun's *Scotichronicon*, and has been edited several times: Thomas Hearne, ed., *Fordun's Scotichronicon, vol. III*, (Oxford, 1722), 908-26; W. Goodall, ed., *Fordun's Scotichronicon, vol.II* (Edinburgh, 1759), 259-67. It is also found with translation in *Scotichronicon, by Walter Bower*, ed. D.E.R. Watt, et al. (Aberdeen: Aberdeen University Press, 1991), 384-403. Other English translations of the text appear in R. King, *Primer of the Church History of Ireland, vol. II, 3rd ed.* (Dublin, 1845-51), 1119-35; and Curtis and McDowell, ed., *Irish Historical Documents*, 38-46.

103 Watt, "Gaelic Polity and Cultural Identity," 349.

104 R.G. Nicholson, "Magna Carta and the Declaration of Arbroath," *University of Edinburgh Journal*, (Autumn, 1965): 143.

105 Hand, *English Law in Ireland*, 198-210.

106 Otway-Ruthven, *History of Medieval Ireland*, 236.

107 Frame, *Colonial Ireland*, 109.

108 The Latin passage is cited by Hand, *English Law in Ireland*, 198, while a translation is in Curtis and McDowell, *Irish Historical Documents*, 41, and *Scotichronicon, Book XII, §28*.

109 Hand, *English Law in Ireland*, 199; *Scotichronicon, Book XII*, 28.25.

110 Hand, *English Law in Ireland*, 201; Curtis and McDowell, *Irish Historical Documents*, 41; *Scotichronicon, Book XII*, 28.37

111 *Calendar of Judiciary Rolls, 1295-1303*, 95.

112 Hand, *English Law in Ireland*, 204-5; Curtis and McDowell, *Irish Historical Documents*, 41; *Scotichronicon, Book XII*, 28.48.

113 Hand, *English Law in Ireland*, 204.

114 Hand, *English Law in Ireland*, 204.

115 Hand, *English Law in Ireland*, 205; *Irish Historical Documents*, 41; *Scotichronicon, Book XII*, 28.53.

116 Hand, *English Law in Ireland*, 205; Sheehy, *Pontificia Hibernica, ii*, no. 417; *Calendar of Close Rolls, 1254-6*, 214.

117 Hand, *English Law in Ireland*, 205.

118 *Scotichronicon, Book XII*, 28.20-28.49

119 *Scotichronicon, Book XII*, 28.29-28.40.

120 *Scotichronicon, Book XII*, 28.41-49.

121 *Scotichronicon, Book XII*, 30.25.

122 Thorlac Turville-Petre, *England the Nation: Language, Literature, and National Identity, 1290-1340* (Oxford: Clarendon Press, 1996), 156-7.

123 Turville-Petre, *England the Nation*, 157-8.

124 *Red Book of Ormond*, 40-1; Hand, *English Law in Ireland*, 197.

[125] Hand, *English Law in Ireland*, 206; Otway-Ruthven, "The Native Irish," 6.

[126] The most notable examples of these exclusions were the 1217 mandate against Irish clerics and the statue from the 1366 parliament at Kilkenny.

[127] *Calendar of Justiciary Rolls, 1295-1303*, 271.

[128] Murphy, "Status of the Irish," 123.

[129] Otway-Ruthven, "The Request of the Irish for English Law, 1277-80," *Irish Historical Studies, vi* (1948-9): 261-70; A. Gwynn, "Edward I and the Proposed Purchase English Law for the Irish, c. 1276-80," *Royal Historical Society Transactions, 5th series* (1960): 111-27; Watt, *The Church in Medieval Ireland*, 115.

[130] Otway-Ruthven, "The Request for the Irish of English Law," 262; Watt, *The Church in Medieval Ireland*, 115.

[131] H.G. Richardson and G.O. Sayles. "The Irish Parliaments of Edward I." Proceedings of the Royal Irish Academy. XXXVIII, Section C, No. 6: 142-3.

[132] Gearóid Mac Niocaill, "The Contact of Irish and Common Law," *Northern Ireland Legal Quarterly*, 23:1 (1972): 16.

[133] Nicholls, "Gaelic Society and Economy," 429.

[134] Kelly, *Early Irish Law*, 251.

[135] Kelly, *Early Irish Law*, 251.

[136] Gearóid Mac Niocaill, "The Interaction of Laws," in *The English in Medieval Ireland, ed. James Lydon* (Dublin: Royal Irish Academy, 1984), 105-17.

[137] Nicholls, "Gaelic Society and Economy," 429.

[138] Daniel Binchy, "Ancient Irish Law," *Irish Jurist, new series,* I (1966): 84-91; Kenneth Nicholls, *Gaelic and Gaelicised Ireland in the Middle Ages* (Dublin: Gill and MacMillan, 1972), 44; Nicholls, "Gaelic Society and Economy," 429.

[139] Nicholls, *Gaelic and Gaelicised Ireland*, 46; Kelly, *Early Irish Law*, 252-4.

[140] Nicholls, "Gaelic Society and Economy," 429.

[141] Nicholls, *Gaelic and Gaelicised Ireland*, 50-52.

[142] Nicholls, *Gaelic and Gaelicised Ireland*, 54; Kelly, Guide to Early Irish Law, xxiii.

[143] Nicholls, *Gaelic and Gaelicised Ireland*, 56.

[144] Kelly, *Early Irish Law*, 13.

[145] Nicholls, "Gaelic Society and Economy," 432.

[146] Nicholls, "Gaelic Society and Economy," 433.

[147] Nicholls, *Gaelic and Gaelicised Ireland*, 59-62; Nicholls, "Gaelic Society and Economy," 432.

[148] Nicholls, "Gaelic Society and Economy," 432; Kieran O Conor, *Settlement and Society in Medieval Gaelic Ireland*, 97-99..

[149] Cosgrove, "The Medieval Period," 22-23.

[150] Katharine Simms, "The Brehons of Later Medieval Ireland," *Brehons, Serjeants and Attorneys: Studies in the History of the Irish Legal Professions*, ed. Daire Hogan and W.N. Osborough (Dublin: Irish Academic Press, 1990), 53.

[151] Simms, "The Brehons of Later Medieval Ireland," 51.

[152] *Rotuli Litterarum Patentium*, 47; *Statutes and Ordinances of Ireland*, 3.

[153] Rees Davies, "Frontier Arrangements in Fragmented Societies: Ireland and Wales," in *Medieval Frontier Societies,* ed. Robert Bartlett and Angus MacKay (Oxford: Clarendon Press, 1989), 77-100.

[154] J. Otway-Ruthven, "The Constitutional Position of the Great Lordships of South Wales," *Royal Historical Society Transactions, 5th series, vii* (1958): 1-20; Hand, English Law in Ireland, 113.

[155] *Calendar of Documents, 1252-84*, no. 1450; Hand,

"English Law in Ireland," 398.

[156] Statutes and Ordinances of Ireland, 388-91, 434-6.

[157] James Lydon, The Making of Ireland (London: Routledge Press, 1998), 85-6.

[158] Otway-Ruthven, *History of Medieval Ireland,* 160.

[159] Hand, *English Law in Ireland,* 203; Kelly, *Guide to Early Irish Law*, 13.

[160] MacNiocaill, "The Interaction of Laws," 110.

[161] Hand, *English Law in Ireland,* 177.

[162] MacNiocaill, "Irish and Common Law," 20-22.

[163] MacNiocaill, "Irish and Common Law," 21; Curtis, *Calendar of Ormond Deeds I* (1932): no. 682.

[164] *Calendar of Ormond Deeds, II*, no. 46; *Statutes and Ordinances of Ireland,* 388-91.

[165] MacNiocaill, "The Interaction of Laws," 112.

[166] MacNiocaill, "The Interaction of Laws," 112.

Conclusion

In Irish historiography, the emergence of the nation has been equated with the formation of the modern Irish state, and this has significantly hindered historians in their attempts to define the society that existed in Gaelic Ireland in the thirteenth and fourteenth centuries. As discussed in Chapter One, the debate concerning the existence of a nation in medieval Ireland has been dominated by the questions of whether the medieval nation, if it in fact existed, has some relationship to a modern Irish state (the position of the nationalist historian), or whether the modern idea of a nation has been read into the past (the position of the revisionist historian).

This study, though, has shown that a nation did exist in medieval Gaelic Ireland and that there were particular causes and manifestations of that nation. This issue is not merely a question of semantics and definition. Regardless of what modern definition we use to define a nation, we are still left with the underlying fact that the inhabitants of medieval Ireland used the term nation to describe themselves in certain circumstances, particularly when they encountered a foreign "other" such as the Scandinavians in the eight and ninth centuries or the Anglo-Normans in the twelfth and thirteenth centuries. From the modern observer's perspective, the most important indicators of a nation should not be political unification or the establishment of government bureaucracy. Instead, the historian must consider the nation as essentially the social acceptance of an idea of common ethnic ancestry and an idea of geographic origins. Whether that idea took tangible form in unified and institutionalized structures of governmental power is immaterial based upon the definition of a nation used in this study. In Chapter One, the term nation was defined as a form of ideology in which individuals identified themselves and their group as having common ethnic descent and a relationship with a definable geographic area. Using this definition, this study has shown that a nation did exist in medieval Ireland.

The clearest example of the manifestation of the idea of a Gaelic nation in the middle ages results from the examination of bardic poetry that was created in the thirteenth and fourteenth centuries. No studies have comprehensively analyzed the complete corpus of surviving bardic poetry in this period, and hence this study offers a new understanding of the Gaelic mind in medieval Ireland. The nation of Ireland in the middle ages was never a unified bureaucratic entity; if a nation is defined as an inherently political structure, then we would not be able to say that there was a nation in medieval Ireland. Indeed, this fact has led to some of the most bitter aspects of the debate about the nation in Irish history. Certainly the modern Irish state can be construed as a nation. But this nation is a modern construct and was related only to the past insofar as the modern proponents of the Irish nation claimed a connection with the medieval nation. The nation in medieval Ireland was primarily a way in which Gaelic people in Ireland viewed themselves and their world. It was a way of defining themselves ethnically, as well as a way of defining their geographic space. Gaelic lords and poets in Ireland used this idea of a nation to support their own political power which was understood in national language.

Geographically this study has shown that from the outset of the thirteenth century several dynamic features characterized settlement in the thirteenth and fourteenth centuries. A divide certainly existed between the Gaelic and Anglo-Norman lordships, as was noticed by Orpen and MacNeill in the early twentieth century. But the divide was much more fluid and complicated than they could appreciate, and this study has shown, by using complex and intricate spatial models that the frontier was in a state of flux. In the early thirteenth century, Anglo-Norman settlement was centered in the southeast lowland regions or Ireland. Towards the end of the thirteenth century, the settlers, instead of expanding the borders of the colony, tended to consolidate their holdings. What has not been explored is the fact that in the late thirteenth century a significantly higher number of raids were staged by Gaelic lords across the frontiers into the Anglo-Norman colony and that it is after these raids that new settlement in the colony abated. In other words, the response of the Gaelic kings to encroachments upon their territory at least partially explains the lack of growth in the colony before the great social calamities of the fourteenth century, such as the famine and Bruce invasion.

The divide in the colony based upon ethnic identity and geographic division extended into the church of medieval Ireland. Many of the conflicts within the church have been described as national;[1] this statement is substantively true, but requires modification. First, the divisions in the church were often the result of disputes over land (as in the origins of the 1217 mandate against Irish clerics) and ecclesiastical authority (as in the Conspiracy of Mellifont). These disputes were consequences of divisions of national feeling, not the causes of national conflict; these conflicts were more symptomatic of a national division within society.

Law in medieval Ireland was another aspect of society in which the ethnic gulf within the colony was made manifest. First, a clear divide existed because a significant percentage of the population was unable to use English law. The law was administered in Ireland as it was administered in England; however, local authority in Ireland maintained the right to dictate unique and local legislation for the preservation and safety of the colony. As shown in Chapter Five, law in medieval Ireland was both descriptive and prescriptive. For instance, parliaments in Ireland issued statutes that attempted to dictate the behavior of Anglo-Norman lords who had adopted Gaelic ethnic traits. These statutes indicate an assumption that those Gaelic traits were inferior, and that the practice of adopting those traits was worthy of attention at parliament. Local authority in Ireland issued particular statutes based upon the declining condition of the colony, and those statutes reflected a national divide. These laws, like the conflicts described above concerning the church in medieval Ireland, were not the causes of enhanced national divisions but were rather arenas in which already existing divisions were magnified.

This study has primarily focussed on the question of whether the idea of a Gaelic nation existed in medieval Ireland and has answered in the affirmative. Originally, the scope of this project included the Celtic fringes of the Anglo-Norman world in the thirteenth and fourteenth centuries, but such a work would have been unwieldy to complete as a short monograph. It would no doubt be profitable to apply the same definition of nation to Wales and Scotland. For example, the lords of medieval Wales, as pointed out in Chapter Two, also employed poets to sing their praise, and these poets used similar motifs such as the prophesied king and marriage with the land. Robin Frame, for instance, has investigated the intertwined relationship between the Anglo-Norman aristocracies of the British Isles and to some extent the nature of aristocracies in Ireland, Wales and Scotland.[2] However, his work is primarily concerned with the workings of government and lordship and therefore does not discuss the ideological aspects of society that may in fact reveal more than one nation in the British Isles. More research may reveal a multiplicity of nations in the British Isles.

Another area that is in need of further research is the analysis of the Anglo-Norman lords of Ireland in the thirteenth and fourteenth century. Lydon has already pointed out that in the middle ages they were termed *media natio*; but, to what extent does that term mean that they had formed some sort of nation in terms of the definition applied in this study?[3] What Lydon's study reveals is that the distinction of a nation is also a relative term. To the English in England, these Anglo-Normans seemed Irish, while to the Irish they seemed English. Certainly such ambiguous descriptions do not enhance our understanding of their identity. The question that should be asked is whether these Anglo-Norman lords, who occupied a particular and definable geographic space, really developed a unique literature with an imbedded mythology that would reveal a common cause or identity.[4]

[1] See Watt, *The Church and the Two Nations*.

[2] Robin Frame, *The Political Development of the British Isles, 1100-1400* (Oxford: Clarendon Press, 1990).

[3] James Lydon, "The Middle Nation," 26.

[4] Alan Bliss, "Language and Literature," in *The English in Medieval Ireland*, ed. James Lydon (Dublin: Royal Irish Academy, 1984), 27-45.

Bibliography

Primary Sources

"*Beg nár bháith Áodh oighidh cuinn.*" RIA MS A/iv/3.

Berry, H.F., ed. *Statutes and Ordinances and Acts of Parliament of Ireland, King John to Henry V.* Dublin, 1907.

Butler, R., ed. *The Annals of Ireland by Friar John Clyn and Thady Dowling.* Dublin: Irish Archaeological Society, 1849.

"*Connuimh rom taighidh a Aodh.*" RIA MS 490, p. 162.

Curtis, E., ed. *Calendar of Ormond Deeds, 1172-1603.* (6 volumes). Dublin, 1932-43.

Dictionary of the Irish Language, Based Mainly on Old and Middle Irish Materials, Compact Edition. Dublin: Royal Irish Academy, 1990.

Freeman, A. Martin, ed. *The Annals of Connacht.* Dublin: Dublin Institute for Advanced Studies, 1944.

Gilbert, John, ed. *Chartularies of St. Mary's Abbey, Dublin: with The Register of Its House at Dunroby and Annals of Ireland, Vol. II.* London: Rolls Series, 1884.

Hennessey, W.M., ed. *The Annals of Loch Ce.* (2 volumes). Dublin, 1871.

Hennessey, W.M., and B. McCarthy, ed. *The Annals of Ulster.* (4 volumes). Dublin, 1887-1901.

MacAirt, S., ed. *The Annals of Inisfallen.* Dublin: Dublin Institute for Advanced Studies, 1951.

Mac Mathúna, Séamus, ed., "An Inaugural Ode to Hugh O'Connor?" *Zeitschrift für Celtische Philologie.* 49-50 (1997): 548-75.

McKenna, Lambert, ed. "*Do togbhadh meirge Murchaidh.*" *Irish Monthly.* 47: 102.

McKenna, Lambert, ed. *Aithdioghluim Dana: A Miscellany of Irish Bardic Poetry, Historical and Religious, including the Historical Poems of the*

Duanaire in the Yellow Book of Lecan. London: Irish Texts Society, 1939-40.

McKenna, Lambert, ed. *The Book of Magauran: Leabhar Méig Shamhradháin.* Dublin: Dublin Institute for Advanced Studies, 1947.

McKenna, Lambert, ed. "A Poem by Gofraidh Fionn Ó Dálaigh." *Eriu* 16 (1954):132-9.

Mills, J., and M.C. Griffith, ed. *Calendar of Justiciary Rolls, Ireland.* (3 volumes). Dublin, 1905-14.

Murphy, D., ed. *The Annals of Clonmacnoise.* Dublin, 1896.

O Cuiv, Brian. "Poem in Praise of Raghnall, King of Man." *Eigse.* 8 (1956-7): 283-301.

O'Donovan, J., ed. *The Annals of the Kingdom of Ireland by the Four Masters* (7 volumes). Dublin, 1848-51.

O'Grady, Standish Hayes, ed. *Caithreim Thoirdhealbhaigh.* (2 volumes). London: Irish Texts Society, 1929.

O'Meara, J.J., ed. *Topographia Hibernica: The History and Topography of Ireland by Gerald of Wales.* London: Harmondsworth, 1982.

Quiggin, E.C. "A Poem by Gilbride MacNamee in Praise of Cathal O Conor." In *Miscellany Presented to Kuno Meyer.* Dublin, 1912.

Quiggin, E.C. "O'Conor's House at Cloonfree." In *Essays and Studies Presented to William Ridgeway,* ed. E.C. Quiggin. Cambridge: Cambridge University Press, 1913: 333-52.

Scott, A.B., and F.X. Martin, ed. *Expugnatio Hibernica: The Conquest of Ireland by Giraldus Cambrensis.* Dublin: Royal Irish Academy, 1978.

Sheehy, Maurice, ed. *Pontificia Hibernica.* (2 volumes). Dublin: Gill and Sons, 1962.

Sweetman, H.S., ed. *Calendar of Documents Relating to Ireland, 1171-1307.* (5 volumes). London, 1875-86.

Watt, D.E.R., et al., ed. *Scotichronicon, by Walter Bower.* Aberdeen: University of Aberdeen Press, 1991.

Webb, C.C., ed. *Metalogicon.* London, 1929.

Williams, N.J., ed. *The Poems of Giolla Brighde Mac Con Midhe.* London: Irish Texts Society, 1980.

Secondary Sources

Anderson, A.O. "The Prophecy of Bearchán." *Zeitschrift Fur Celtische Philologie* XVIII (1930): 1-54.

Baker, J.H. *An Introduction to English Legal History.* London: Buttersworth, 1990.

Barry, Terry. *The Archaeology of Medieval Ireland.* London: Routledge, 1987.

Barry, Terry. "Late Medieval Ireland: the Debate on Social and Economic Decline, 1350-1550." In *An Historical Geography of Ireland*, edited by B.J. Graham and L.J. Proudfoot. London: Academic Press, 1993.

Barry, Terry. *The Medieval Moated Sites of South-East Ireland: Counties Carlow, Kilkenny, Tipperary, and Wexford.* Vol. 35, *British Archaeological Reports.* Oxford: BAR, 1977.

Bartlett, R. *The Making of Europe: Conquest, Colonization, and Cultural Change, 950-1350.* London: Penguin, 1993.

Bartlett, R., and A. Mackay, eds. *Medieval Frontier Societies.* Oxford: Clarendon Press, 1989.

Bergin, Osborn. *Irish Bardic Poetry.* Edited by David Greene and Fergus Kelly. Dublin: Dublin Institute for Advanced Studies, 1984.

Bergin, Osborn. "*Irish Grammatical Tracts, I.*" *Eriu* 8 (1916).

Bergin, Osborn. "*Irish Grammatical Tracts, II, §1-11.*" *Eriu* 8 (1916).

Bergin, Osborn. "*Irish Grammatical Tracts, II, §12-87.*" *Eriu* 9 (1921-23).

Bergin, Osborn. "*Irish Grammatical Tracts, II, §88-207.*" *Eriu* 10 (1926-28).

Bergin, Osborn. "*Irish Grammatical Tracts, III, IV.*" *Eriu* 14 (1946).

Bergin, Osborn. "*Irish Grammatical Tracts, V.*" *Eriu* 17 (1955).

Bethel, D. "English Monks and Irish Reform in the Eleventh and Twelfth Centuries." In *Historical Studies*, 111-135, 1971.

Bieler, Ludwig, ed. *The Patrician Texts in the Book of Armagh.* Vol. 10, *Scriptores Latini Hiberniae.* Dublin: Dublin Institute for Advanced Studies, 1979.

Binchy, Daniel. "Ancient Irish Law." *Irish Jurist, new series* I (1966): 84-91.

Bourdieu, Pierre. "La Force du Droit. Elements pour une sociologie du champ juridique." *Actes de la Recherche en Sciences Sociales* 64, no. September (1986): 3-19.

Boyce, D. George. *Nationalism in Ireland.* 3rd ed. New York: Routledge Press, 1995.

Bradshaw, Brendan. "Nationalism and Historical Scholarship in Modern Ireland." *Irish Historical Studies* XXVI, no. 104 (1989): 329-351.

Bradshaw, Brendan. "Native Reaction to the Westward Enterprise: A Case Study in Gaelic Ideology." In *The Westward Enterprise: English Activities in Ireland, the Atlantic, and America, 1480-1650*, edited by K.R. Andrews, Nicholas Canny and P.E.H. Hair. Liverpool, 1978.

Brooks, E. *Knight's Fees in Counties Wexford, Carlow, and Kilkenny.* Dublin: Irish Manuscripts Commission, 1950.

Brundage, James. *Law, Sex and Christian Society in Medieval Europe.* Chicago: University of Chicago Press, 1987.

Burrough, P.A. *Principles of Geographical Information Systems for Land Resource Assesment.* Oxford: Clarendon Press, 1990.

Byrne, F.J. *Irish Kings and High-Kings.* London: B.T. Batsford, 1973.

Caball, Marc. "The Gaelic Mind and the Collapse of the Gaelic World: An Appraisal." *Cambridge Medieval Celtic Studies* 25, no. Summer (1993).

Cairns, C.T. *Irish Tower Houses: A Tipperary Case Study.* Vol. 2, *Irish Settlement Studies.* Dublin:

Group for the Study of Irish Historic Settlement, 1987.

Carney, J. "Literature in Irish." In *A New History of Ireland, ii*, edited by A. Cosgrove. Oxford: Oxford University Press, 1987.

Carr, A.D. *Medieval Wales*. London: St. Martin's Press, 1995.

Chibnall, M., ed. *The Historia Pontificalis of John of Salisbury*. Oxford: Clarendon Press, 1956.

Clabby, Thomas. "The Franciscans in Ireland, 1400-1534." Unpublished PhD. Dissertation, Department of History, National University of Ireland, 1998.

Clark, P.J., and F.C. Evans. "Distance to Nearest Neighbour as a Measure of Spatial Relationships in Populations." *Ecology* 35 (1954): 445-53.

Connolly, Philomena. "The Enactments of the 1297 Parliament." In *Law and Disorder in Thirteenth Century Ireland: The Dublin Parliament of 1297*, edited by James Lydon, 148-61. Dublin: Four Courts Press, 1997.

Cosgrove, Art. *Late Medieval Ireland, 1370-1541*. Dublin: Helicon, 1981.

Cosgrove, Art. "Marriage in Medieval Ireland." In *Marriage in Ireland*, edited by Art Cosgrove, 25-50. Dublin: Academic Press, 1987.

Cosgrove, Art. *New History of Ireland, ii, Medieval Ireland, 1169-1534*. Oxford: Oxford University Press, 1987.

Cosgrove, Art. "The Medieval Period." In *Irish Church History Today*, edited by Ó Muirí, 13-26. Armagh: Cumann Seanchais Ard Mhacha, 1990.

Cotterrell, Roger. *The Sociology of Law: An Introduction*. London: Butterworths, 1992.

Cubitt, Geoffrey. "Introduction." In *Imagining Nations*, edited by Geoffrey Cubitt, 1-16. Manchester: Manchester University Press, 1998.

Cuiv, Brian O. "A Poem for Cathal Croibhdhearg O Conchubhair." *Eriu* XXXIV (1983): 161-71.

Cuiv, Brian O. "A Poem of Prophecy on Ua Conchobair Kings of Connacht." *Celtica* 19 (1987): 31-54.

Curtis, Edmund. *A History of Medieval Ireland*. Dublin: Maunsel and Roberts, 1923.

Curtis, E., and R.B. McDowell. *Irish Historical Documents, 1172-1922*. London: Methuen, 1943.

Dalton, G.F. "The Tradition of the Blood-Sacrifice to the Goddess Éire." *Studies* 63 (1974): 343-54.

Davies, R.R. "Frontier Arrangements in Fragmented Societies: Ireland and Wales." In *Medieval Frontier Societies*, edited by R. Bartlett and A. MacKay, 77-100. Oxford: Oxford University Press, 1989.

Davies, R.R. *The Revolt of Owain Glyndwy*. Oxford: Oxford University Press, 1995.

Dice, L.R. "Measures of the Amount of Ecological Associations Between Species." *Ecology* 26 (1945): 297-302.

Duffy, Sean. *Ireland in the Middle Ages*. Dublin: Gill and MacMillan, 1997.

Duffy, Sean. *The MacMillan Atlas of Irish History*. New York: MacMillan Press, 1997.

Duffy, Sean. "The Problem of Degeneracy." In *Law and Disorder in Thirteenth Century Ireland: The Dublin Parliament of 1297*, edited by James Lydon, 87-106. Dublin: Four Courts Press, 1997.

Duncan, A.A.M. "The Scot's Invasion of Ireland." In *The British Isles, 1100-1500*, edited by R.R. Davies. Edinburgh: John Donald Publishers, 1988.

Dunne, T.J. "The Gaelic Response to Conquest and Colonisation: The Evidence of the Poetry." *Studia Hibernica* XX (1980): 7-30.

Eco, Umberto. "Interpretation and History." In *Interpretation and Overinterpretation*, edited by Stefan Collini, 23-44. Cambridge: Cambridge University Press, 1992.

Edwards, O. Dudley, and B. Ransome, eds. *James Connolly: Selected Political Writings*. London, 1973.

Ellis, Steven. "Historiographical Debate: Representations of the Past in Ireland: Whose Past and Whose Present?" *Irish Historical Studies* XXVII, no. 108 (1991): 289-308.

Ellis, Steven. *Ireland in the Age of the Tudors*. London: Longman Press, 1998.

Ellis, Steven. "Nationalist Historiography and the English and Gaelic Worlds in the Late Middle Ages."

Irish Historical Studies XXV, no. 97 (1986): 1-18.

Empey, C.A., and Katharine Simms. "The Ordinances of the White Earl and the Problem of Coign in the later Middle Ages." *Proceedings of the Royal Irish Academy* 75C (1975): PAGES.

Etchingham, Colman. "Episcopal Hierarchy in Connacht and Tairdelbach Ua Conchobair." *Journal of the Galway Archaeological and Historical Society* 52 (2000): 13-29.

Finan, Tom, and Kieran O Conor. "The Moated Site of Cloonfree." Journal of the Galway Archaeological and Historical Society 54 (2002): 72-87.

Fitzmaurice, E.B., and A.G. Little. *Materials for the History of the Franciscan Province of Ireland.* Manchester: University Press, 1920.

Flanagan, Marie-Therese. *Irish Society, Anglo-Norman Settlers, Angevin Kingship: Interactions in Ireland in the Late Twelfth Century.* Oxford: Clarendon Press, 1989.

Foote, Kenneth, and David Huebner. *The Geographer's Craft Project.* Austin: Department of Geography, University of Texas at Austin, 1995.

Frame, Robin. "The Bruces in Ireland." *Irish Historical Studies* XIX, no. March (1974): 3-37.

Frame, Robin. *Colonial Ireland, 1169-1369.* Dublin: Helicon, 1981.

Geertz, Clifford. *The Interpretation of Cultures.* New York: Harper Books, 1973.

Gellner, E. *Nations and Nationalism.* Oxford: Oxford University Press, 1983.

Getis, A. "Temporal Land Use Pattern Analysis with the Use of Nearest Neighbor and Quadrat Methods." *Annals of the Association of American Geographers* 54 (1964): 391-9.

Glasscock, R.E. "Moated Sites and Deserted Boroughs and Villages: Two Neglected Aspects of Anglo-Norman Settlement in Ireland." In *Irish Geographical Studies*, edited by N. Stephens and R.E. Glasscock, 162-77. Belfast, 1970.

Graham, B.J. "The Towns of Medieval Ireland." In *The Development of the Irish Town*, 28-60. New Jersey: Rowman and Littlefield, 1977.

Gwynn, Aubrey. "Edward I and the Proposed Purchase of English Law for the Irish, c. 1276-80." *Royal Historical Society Transactions, 5th Series* x (1960): 111-27.

Gwynn, Aubrey. "The First Synod of Cashel, 1101." In *The Irish Church in the Eleventh and Twelfth Centuries*, edited by Gerard O'Brien, 158-65. Dublin: Four Courts Press, 1992.

Gwynn, Aubrey. "Henry of London, Archbishop of Dublin." *Studies* XXXVI (1949): 297-306, 389-402.

Gwynn, Aubrey. *The Twelfth Century Reform.* Edited by Corish. Vol. II, fasc. 1, *A History of Irish Catholicism.* Dublin: Gill, 1968.

Gwynn, Aubrey, and R. N. Hadcock. *Medieval Religious Houses, Ireland.* Dublin: Irish Academic Press, 1970.

Habermas, Jurgen. "The Hermeneutic Claim to Universality." In *The Hermeneutic Tradition*, edited by G.L. Ormiston and A.D. Schrift. Albany: State University of New York Press, 1990.

Hand, Geoffrey. "English Law in Ireland, 1172-1351." *Northern Ireland Legal Quarterly* xxiii, no. 4 (1972): 393-422.

Hand, G.J. "Aspects of Alien Status in Medieval English Law, with Special Reference to Ireland." In *Legal History Studies, 1972: Papers Presented to the Legal History Conference, Aberystwyth, 18-21 July 1972*, edited by Dafydd Jenkins. Cardiff, 1975.

Hand, G.J. *The Church in the English Lordship.* Edited by Corrish. Vol. II, fasc. 3, *History of Irish Catholicism.* Dublin: Gill, 1968.

Hand, G.J. *English Law in Ireland, 1290-1324.* Cambridge: Cambridge University Press, 1967.

Hand, G. J. "The Status of the Native Irish in the Lordship of Ireland, 1272-1331." *Irish Jurist* 1 (New Series) (1966): 93-115.

Harrison, Stephen. "Re-Fighting the Battle of Down: Orpen, MacNeill and the Irish Nation State." *The Medieval World and the Modern Mind.* Dublin: Four Courts Press, 2000.

Henken, Elissa. *National Redeemer: Owain Glyndwr in Welsh Tradition.* Cardiff: University of Wales Press, 1996.

Hodder, Ian, and Clive Orton. *Spatial Analysis in Archaeology*. Cambridge: Cambridge University Press, 1976.

Hoffman, Richard. "Outsiders by Birth and Blood: Racist Ideologies and Realities around the Periphery of Medieval European Culture." In *Studies in Medieval and Renaissance History, IV*, edited by J.A.S. Evans and R.W. Unger: University of British Columbia Press, 1983.

Hudson, Benjamin. *The Prophecy of Berchán: Irish and Scottish High-Kingship in the Early Middle Ages*. London: Greenwood Press, 1996.

Hunt, Alan. "Marxism and the Analysis of Law." In *Sociological Approaches to Law*, edited by Adam Podgorecki and Christopher J. Whelan. London: Billing and Sons Ltd., 1981.

Keating, Geoffrey. *Foras Feasa ar Éirinn, III*. Edited by Fr. Patrick Dineen. London: Irish Texts Society, 1908.

Kelly, Fergus. *A Guide to Early Irish Law*. Dublin: Dublin Institute for Advanced Studies, 1988.

Kiberd, Declan. "Literature in Ireland." In *The Oxford Illustrated History of Ireland*, edited by R.F. Foster. Oxford: Oxford University Press, 1987.

Knott, Eleanor. *Irish Syllabic Poetry*. 2nd ed. Dublin: Dublin Institute for Advanced Studies, 1994.

Knott, Elenor, ed. *The Poems of Tadhg Dall O Huiginn, 1550-1591*. London: Irish Texts Society, 1922.

Lanfranc. *The Letters of Lanfranc, Archbishop of Canterbury*. Edited by H. Clover and M. Gibson. Oxford: Clarendon Press, 1979.

Laurd, Henry, ed. *Annales de Prioratus de Wigornia, Annales Monastici, Vol. 4*. London: Rerum Britannicarum Medii Aevi Scriptores, 1869.

Laurd, Henry, ed. *Bartholomaei de Cotton Monachi Norwicensis Historia Anglicana*. London: Rerum Britannicarum Medii Aevi Scriptores, 1859.

Leask, H.G. *Irish Castles and Castellated Houses, 3rd Edition*. Dundalk: Dundealgan Press, 1977.

Leersen, Joep. *Mere Irish and Fíor Ghael: Studies in the Idea of Irish Nationality, Its Development and Literary Expression Prior to the Nineteenth Century*. Cork: Cork University Press, 1996.

Lewis, Bernard. *History: Remembered, Recovered, Invented*.

Lexington, Stephen of. *Letters from Ireland, 1228-1229*. Edited by Barry O'Dwyer. Kalamazoo: Cistercian Press, 1982.

Lydon, James. "A Land of War." In *New History of Ireland, ii, Medieval Ireland, 1169-1534*, edited by Art Cosgrove, 240-74. Oxford: Clarendon Press, 1987.

Lydon, James, ed. *Law and Disorder in Thirteenth Century Ireland: The Dublin Parliament of 1297*. Dublin: Four Courts Press, 1997.

Lydon, James. *The Making of Ireland*. London: Routledge Press, 1998.

Lydon, James. "The Middle Nation." In *The English in Medieval Ireland*, edited by James Lydon. Dublin: Royal Irish Academy, 1984.

Lydon, James. "Nation and Race in Medieval Ireland." In *Concepts of National Identity in the Middle Ages*, edited by Simon Forde, Lesley Johnson and Alan V. Murray. Leeds: Leeds University Press, 1995.

Lydon, James. "The Problem of the Frontier in Medieval Ireland." *Topic: A Journal of the Liberal Arts* 13 (1967): 5-22.

Lydon, James. "The Years of Crisis." In *New History of Ireland, ii, Medieval Ireland, 1169-1534*, edited by Art Cosgrove, PAGE. Oxford: Oxford University Press, 1987.

Lydon, J.F. "The Bruce Invasion of Ireland." In *Historical Studies, IV*. London: Bowes and Bowes, 1963.

Lydon, J.F. "The Impact of the Bruce Invasion of Ireland, 1315-27." In *New History of Ireland, ii, Medieval Ireland*, edited by Art Cosgrove, 275-302. Oxford: Oxford University Press, 1987.

MacCana, Proinsias. "Early Irish Ideology and the Concept of Unity." In *The Irish Mind: Exploring Intellectual Traditions*, edited by R. Kearney. Dublin: Wolfhound Press, 1985.

MacManus, Damian. "Classical Modern Irish." In *Progress in Medieval Irish Studies*, edited by Kim McCone and Katharine Simms. Maynooth: Department of Old Irish, St. Patrick's College, 1996.

MacMathúna, Séamus. "An Inaugural Ode to Hugh

O'Connor?" *Zeitschrift fur Celtische Philologie* 49-50 (1997): 548-75.

MacNeill, Eoin. *Phases of Irish History*. Dublin, 1919.

MacNiocaill, G. "The Contact of Irish and Common Law." *Northern Ireland Legal Quarterly* xxiii (1972): 16-23.

MacNiocaill, G. "The Interaction of Laws." In *The English in Medieval Ireland*, edited by J.L. Lydon, 105-117. Dublin: Royal Irish Academy, 1984.

MacNiocaill, Gearoid. *The Medieval Irish Annals*. Dublin: Dublin Historical Association Medieval Irish History Series, 1975.

MacNiocaill, G. "The Origins of the *Betagh*." *The Irish Jurist* new series i (1966): 292-.

Maguire, David. *Computers in Geography*. New York: Longman Scientific and Technical Press, 1989.

Mahaffy, J.P. "Two Early Tours of Ireland." *Hermathena* XVIII, no. 40 (1914): 3-9.

Maitland, F. W. "The Introduction of English Law to Ireland." *English Historical Review* iv (1889): 516-7.

McKenna, Lambert. *A Ghearóid déana mo dháil*, 1919.

McKenna, Lambert. *Irish Bardic Syntactical Tracts*. Dublin: Dublin Institute for Advanced Studies, 1944.

McNeill, Tom. *Castles in Ireland*. New York: Routledge, 1997.

Meyer, Kuno. "Das ende von Baile in Scáil." *Zeitschrift fur Celtische Philologie* XII (1918): 232-38.

Meyer, Kuno. "Mitteilungen aus Irischen Handschriften." *Zeitschrift fur Celtische Philologie* iii (1918).

Monmonier, Mark. *How to Lie With Maps*. Chicago: University of Chicago Press, 1996.

Monmonier, Mark. *Mapping It Out: Expository Cartography for the Humanities and the Social Sciences*. Chicago: University of Chicago Press, 1993.

Mooney, Canice. *The Church in Gaelic Ireland: Thirteenth to Fifteenth Centuries*. Edited by Corish. Vol. II, fasc. 5, *History of Irish Catholicism*. Dublin: Gill, 1969.

Murphy, Bryan. "The Status of the Native Irish after 1331." *Irish Jurist, new series* ii (1967): 116-38.

Nicholls, Kenneth. *Gaelic and Gaelicised Ireland in the Middle Ages*. Dublin: Gill and MacMillan, 1972.

Nichols, Kenneth. "Gaelic Society and Economy in the High Middle Ages." In *New History of Ireland, ii, Medieval Ireland, 1169-1534*, edited by Art Cosgrove, 397-438. Oxford: Oxford University Press, 1987.

Nicholson, R.G. "Magna Carta and the Declaration of Arbroath." *University of Edinburgh Journal* Autumn (1965): PAGE.

NíMhaonaigh, Máire. "*Cogadh Gáedel re Gallaib:* Some Dating Considerations." *Peritia* 9 (1995).

Nitze, William A. "The Fisher King in the Grail Romances." *Publications of the Modern Language Association of America* 24 (1909): 365-418.

O Buachalla, Breandan. "Aodh Eangach and the Irish Hero-King." In *Sages, Saints and Storytellers: Celtic Studies in Honour of Professor James Carney*, edited by Donnchadh Ó Corráin, Liam Breatnach and Kim McCone. Maynooth: St. Patrick's College, 1989.

O Dwyer, Barry W. *The Conspiracy of Mellifont*. Dublin, 1970.

O Dwyer, B.W. "The Crisis in the Cistercian Monasteries in Ireland in the Early Thirteenth Century." *Analecta Cisterciensis* XXXI, XXXII (1975): 267-304, 3-112.

O Dwyer, B.W. "Gaelic Monasticism and the Irish Cistercians, c.1228." CVIII, no. December (1967): 19-29.

O Dwyer, B.W. "The Impact of the Irish on the Cistercians in the Thirteenth Century." *Journal of Religious History* IV (1967): 287-301.

O Riordan, Michelle. *The Gaelic Mind and the Collapse of the Gaelic World*. Cork: Cork University Press, 1990.

O'Conor, Kieran. "Irish Earthwork Castles." *Fortress* 12 (1992): 1-12.

O'Conor, Kieran. "The Later Construction and Use of Motte and Bailey Castles in Ireland." *Journal of the Kildare Archaeological Society* 17 (1987-91): 13-29.

O'Conor, Kieran. *Settlement and Society in Medieval Gaelic Ireland*. Dublin: Discovery Program Monographs, 1998.

O'Corrain, Donnchadh. "Nationality and Kingship in Pre-Norman Ireland." In *Nationality and the Pursuit of National Independence*, edited by T.W. Moody, 99-111. Cork: Cork University Press, 1990.

O'Cuív, Brian. *The Irish Bardic Duanair or "Poem Book"*. Dublin: National Library of Ireland, 1973.

O'Cuív, Brian. "Literary Creation and Irish Historical Tradition." *Proceedings of the British Academy* xlix (1963): 233-62.

O'Cuív, Brian. "A Poem in Praise of Raghnall, King of Man." *Eigse* 8 (1956-7): 283-301.

O'Curry, Eugene. *Lectures on the Manuscript Materials of Ancient Irish History*. Dublin: 1995 Four Courts Reprint, 1861.

O'Doherty, J.F. "The Anglo-Norman Invasion, 1167-71." *Irish Historical Studies* 1 (1938-9).

O'Doherty, J.F. "Rome and the Anglo-Norman Invasion of Ireland." *Irish Ecclesiastical Record* 42 (1933): 131-45.

O'Grady, S. H., ed. *Caithréim Thoirdhealbhaig*. Vol. XXVI. London: Irish Texts Society, 1927.

O'Grady, Standish Hayes. *Catalogue of Irish Manuscripts in the British Library*. Vol. 1. Dublin: Dublin Institute for Advanced Studies, 1926.

O'Rahilly, T.F. "On the Origins of the Name Érainn and Ériu." *Eriu* 14 (1943-8): 14-21.

Orpen, G.H. *Ireland Under the Normans*. Vol. 1-4. Oxford: Clarendon Press, 1911-20.

Otway-Ruthven, A.J. "The Chief Governors of Medieaeval Ireland." *Journal of the Royal Society of Antiquaries of Ireland* XCV (1965): 227-36.

Otway-Ruthven, A.J. "The Constitutional Position of the Great Lorships of South Wales." *Royal Historical Society Transactions, 5th series* vii (1958): 1-20.

Otway-Ruthven, A.J. *A History of Medieval Ireland*. London: Ernest Benn, 1968.

Otway-Ruthven, A.J.. "The Character of Norman Settlement in Ireland." In *Historical Studies V*, edited by J. L. McCracken, 1965.

Otway-Ruthven, A. J. "Knight Service in Ireland." *Journal of the Royal Society of Antiquaries of Ireland* LXXXIX (1959): 1-15.

Otway-Ruthven, A.J. "The Request by the Irish for English Law, 1277-80." *Irish Historical Studies* VI (1949): 261-70.

Otway-Ruthven, A.J.. "The Medieval County of Kildare." XI, no. March (1959): 181-199.

Otway-Ruthven, Jocelyn. "The Native Irish and English Law in Medieval Ireland." VII, no. March (1950): 1-16.

Phillips, J.R.S. "Edward II and the Prophets." In *England and the Fourteenth Century: Proceedings of the 1985 Harlaxton Symposium*, edited by W.M. Ormond, 189-201. London, 1986.

Pounds, N.J.G. *The Medieval Castle in England and Wales*. Cambridge: Cambridge University Press, 1994.

Quiggin, E.C. "A Poem by Gilbride MacNamee in Praise of Cathal O Conor." In *Miscellany Presented to Kuno Meyer*. Dublin, 1912.

Richardson, H.G., and G.O. Sayles. *The Irish Parliament in the Middle Ages*. Philadelphia: University of Pennsylvania Press, 1952.

Richardson, H.G., and G.O. Sayles. "The Irish Parliaments of Edward I." *Proceedings of the Irish Academy* XXXVIII, C (1928): 128-47.

Ricoure, Paul. *Interpretation Theory: Discourse and the Surplus of Meaning*. Fort Worth: Texas Christian Press, 1976.

Rouland, Norbert. *Legal Anthropology*. Translated by Philippe G. Planel. London: The Athlone Press, 1994.

Ryan, John, S.J. *Toirdelbach O Conchubair (1088-1156): King of Connacht, King of Ireland Co Fresabra, O'Donnell Lecture Series*. Dublin: University College Dublin, 1966.

Scowcroft, R. Mark. "*Leabhar Gabhála*, Part II: the Growth of the Tradition." *Ériu* XXXIX (1988).

Simms, Katharine. "Bardic Poetry as a Historical Source." In *The Writer as Witness*, edited by T.

Dunne. Cork, 1987.

Simms, Katharine. "The Brehons of Later Medieval Ireland." In *Brehons, Serjeants and Attorneys: Studies in the History of the Irish Legal Professions*, edited by Daire Hogan and W.N. Osborough, PAGE. Dublin: Irish Academic Press, 1990.

Simms, Katharine. *From Kings to Warlords*. Woodbridge, 1987.

Simms, Katharine. "Literacy and the Irish Bards." In *Literacy in Medieval Celtic Soceties*, edited by Huw Pryce. Cambridge: Cambridge University Press, 1998.

Smith, Anthony D. "National Identities: Modern or Medieval?" In *Concepts of Nationality in the Middle Ages*, edited by Simon Forde, Lesley Johnson and Alan V. Murray, 21-46. Leeds: Leeds University Press, 1995.

Smith, Anthony D. *National Identity*. London: Harmondsworth, 1991.

Stalley, R.A. *The Cistercian Monasteries of Ireland*. New Haven: Yale University Press, 1987.

Stokes, Whitley. "The Irish Abridgement of the *Expugnatio Hibernica*." *English Historical Review* XX (1905): 77-115.

Stout, Matthew. *The Irish Ringfort*. Dublin: Four Courts Press, 1996.

Swanson, R.N. *Church and Society in Late Medieval England*. London: Blackwell Publishers, 1989.

Sweetman, David. *The Irish Castle*. Dublin: Office of Public Works, Ireland, 1999.

Thompson, J. *Critical Hermeneutics: A Study in the Thought of Paul Ricoeur and Jurgen Habermas*. Cambridge: Cambridge University Press, 1981.

Todd, J.H., ed. *Cogadh Gaedhel re Gallaibh, The War of the Gaedhil with the Gaell*. Vol. 48, *Rolls Series*. London: Her Majesty's Press, 1867.

Turville-Petre, Thorlac. *England the Nation: Language, Literature, and National Identity, 1290-1340*. Oxford: Clarendon Press, 1996.

Watt, J. "*Ecclesia inter Anglicos et inter Hibernicos*: Confrontation and Coexistance in the Medieval Diocese and Province of Armagh." In *The English in Medieval Ireland: Proceedings of the First Joint Meeting of the Royal Irish Academy and the British Academy*, edited by J.L. Lydon, 46-64. Dublin: Royal Irish Academy, 1984.

Watt, J.A. *The Church and the Two Nations in Medieval Ireland, Cambridge Studies in Medieval Life and Thought*. Cambridge: Cambridge University Press, 1970.

Watt, J.A. *The Church in Medieval Ireland*. Vol. V, *The Gill History of Ireland*. Dublin, 1972.

Watt, J.A. "Gaelic Polity and Cultural Identity." In *New History of Ireland, ii, Medieval Ireland, 1169-1534*, edited by Art Cosgrove, 314-56. Oxford: Oxford University Press, 1987.

Watt, J.A. "Negotiations between Edward II and John XXIII Concerning Ireland." *Irish Historical Studies* X (1956): 1-20.

www.ingramcontent.com/pod-product-compliance
Lightning Source LLC
Chambersburg PA
CBHW061000030426
42334CB00033B/3307

9 781841 716008